Gods Vs Mortals

Gods Vs Mortals

Paul Keane

Irish Sports Publishing

Published by Irish Sports Publishing (ISP)
Ballybeg, Kells, Co Meath

First published 2010

A CIP record for this book is available from the British Library

ISBN 978-0-9563598-4-1

Printed in Ireland with Print Procedure Ltd
Typesetting and Layout: Paul McElheron & Associates
Cover Design: Jessica Maile
Front Cover Photograph: Sportsfile
Inside Photographs: Sportsfile, Inpho Sports Agency Ltd, and personal collections.

To Liam Whelan, the victims of the Munich Air Disaster,
George Best, Laurie Cunningham, 'Juanito', Barry Kehoe,
Bobby McGregor, Jackie Jameson, Dr Tony O'Neill,
Ollie Byrne and all the great football men who are forever missed.

ACKNOWLEDGEMENTS and SOURCES

As kids, my big brother, Martin, and I came to a solemn conclusion; true friends are those who will jump in behind you when the going gets tough on the football field and then lend you a pound at the shop on the cycle home. Those same values of support and selflessness, in a strange kind of way, still hold good for me and neatly sum up the multitude that helped out with this book. To Mam, Dad, Martin, Adrian and, particularly, my new wife, Lorna, who immediately backed this project and put up with my months of moodiness, late-night interviews and typing that went on even later into the night, I am eternally grateful. To all of those who contributed directly to the book by lending an interview, a picture or a mere memory, I am equally indebted.

The following were interviewed; Eamon Dunphy, Liam Tuohy, Ronnie Nolan, Damien Richardson, Tommy Hamilton, Jimmy 'Maxie' McCann, Shamie Coad, Jimmy McGeough, Johnny Matthews, Alfie Hale, John O'Neill, Peter Thomas, Paddy Crerand, Cyril Barnicle, Paul Martin, Eugene Davis, Pauric Nicholson, Mick O'Brien, John Minnock, Eoin Hand, Kevin Fitzpatrick, Dave Mahedy, Des Kennedy, Karl Spain, Tony Ward, Gerry Duggan, Mick Fairclough, Dermot Keely, Jim McLaughlin, Tommy McConville, Tony Galvin, Dave Connell, Paul Doolin, Dermot O'Neill, Ian Redford, David O'Brien, Ricky O'Flaherty, Martin Moran, Sean Kelly, Paul McGee, Paul Mason, Sean Og de Paor, Ian Doherty, Tim Dalton, Liam Coyle, Jonas Thern, Pat Morley, Pat Fenlon, Pat Scully, Mark Rutherford, Liam Kelly, Finbarr Flood, Stuart Byrne, Glen Fitzpatrick, Jason Byrne, Owen Heary and Graham Hunter. Their lucid memories and patience made my task infinitely easier.

To Pat Nolan, a sounding-board throughout this project, your help was always appreciated. The encouraging words and direction of Sam Robinson, Jim Murphy, Ian Doherty and Damian Lawlor at various points were warmly welcomed, too.

Thanks to Neil O'Riordan, Michael Scully, Paul O'Hehir, James Rogers and Aidan Fitzmaurice for helping me out with numbers and contact details. In this regard, I am also thankful for the help of Eoghan Rice, Peter Sweeney, Matt Keane, Frank Nicholson, Aidan Corr and Gerry Kelly.

For all their assistance with pictures, I owe a pint or three to Liam Kelly, Arthur

Duffy, Shamie Coad, Mike McCartney, Frank Nicholson, Aidan Corr, Jim Smyth, David Nail and Paul McGee. Thanks to Ronan O Coisdealbha at TG4, *The Waterford News & Star*, *The Athlone Voice*, *The Argus*, the *Derry Journal* and the clubs whose match programme images are reproduced.

The principle sources for this book were, of course, the players themselves and those involved in and around the games. The archives of *The Irish Times* and the *Irish Independent*, along with uefa.com and rsssf.com also proved invaluable research resources.

Thanks to the *Irish Daily Star* newspaper for the Gino Lawless quote regarding his goal for Bohemians against Rangers, and to Bohs TV for the John Reynor quote in the same chapter. In the Galway v Groningen chapter, I sourced Bernie O'Connell's quote in *The Irish Sun* newspaper while the comments by Peter Houtman, Henk Hagenauw and Aidan Gallagher are taken from TG4's documentary 'UEFA Sa Ghaeltacht'.

I borrowed, a little and a lot, from 'A Strange Kind of Glory – Sir Matt Busby and Manchester United' by Eamon Dunphy, 'We Are Rovers – An Oral history of Shamrock Rovers' by Eoghan Rice, 'The Lost Babes – Manchester United and the Forgotten Victims of Munich' by Jeff Connor, 'George Best – Blessed, The Autobiography', 'The End Of An Era – A History of Limerick Senior Soccer at the Market's Field 1937/1984' by Aidan Corr and Bernard Spain, 'The History of Dundalk FC – The First 100 Years' by Jim Murphy, 'We All Live In A Perry Groves World, My Story' by Perry Groves with John McShane, 'Ireland's Greatest – 60 Years of Football Heroes' by Dean Hayes, 'Ireland On Three Million Pounds A Day' by Declan Lynch, 'Eddie Mahon's Derry City' by Eddie Mahon, 'The Four-in-a-Row Story' by Robert Goggins, 'Paolo Di Canio, The Autobiography' by Paolo di Canio with Gabriele Marcotti.

Thanks to Liam Hayes and Kevin MacDermot at Irish Sports Publishing for their leap of faith, in both myself and this book. Finally, thanks to Jenna Dowds and Paul McElheron for their hard work and dedication.

CONTENTS

CHAPTER 1

SHAMROCK ROVERS VS MANCHESTER UNITED
September 25 and October 2, 1957

"The 'Busby Babes' were huge to me and looked awesome in the flesh at Dalymount Park. They had this style and elegance about them. The way they played that night was phenomenal. The power and the elegance and the skill, it was awesome. It was very, very inspiring. Of course, when the Munich air crash happened a few months later, all of us who'd been at Dalymount – well, everyone in the world – mourned them, but it was particularly poignant for those of us who'd seen them that night."
EAMON DUNPHY

Liam Tuohy's early football education consisted of Sunday afternoons at Tolka Park watching the wing play of Leo Ward. Trekking across from the family home in East Wall to follow his beloved Drumcondra was a pleasure Tuohy indulged in as often as he could, the sight of his hero, Ward, enough to light up the drabbest of winter afternoons. Ward was a player apart, apparently fated for greatness when signing for Manchester City in 1939 only to arrive back home four months later with the outbreak of World War II. Six years of hostilities stole what would have been the best years of his career in England. Despite invitations to return to City when the war ended in 1945, he declined. He'd laid down successful business roots in Ireland in the meantime and the IR£8 a week he was receiving for playing for Drumcondra, double the League average at the time, supplemented his income nicely. City's loss proved Drumcondra's gain and, in time, he'd leave a rich legacy to the entire League. It's not stretching the truth to say that Ward, unbeknownst to him, shaped the career of one of the greatest servants Irish football has known in Tuohy, a future international player, manager and Shamrock Rovers legend. It wasn't just by chance that Tuohy developed his own game as an outside left. As a schoolboy international he worked hard on improving the same attributes that had lifted Ward above the norm as a Drums winger – pace, passing, shooting and heading. Scouts around Dublin soon recognised the same qualities in Tuohy that had made Ward great. Rovers acted quickest and, in 1952, dispatched Paddy Murphy down to Tuohy's house to ask if he'd fancy signing up. It created a dilemma for Tuohy, however, as that would effectively mean sleeping with the enemy.

LIAM TUOHY: "I was a mad Drums fan, grew up a mad Drums fan. But, in East Wall, there was a fella called Paddy Murphy, 'Spud' Murphy we used to call him. He was scouting for Shamrock Rovers and he brought myself and Noel Peyton from East Wall out to Milltown. I wasn't too sure at the time if I was happy about going out because I was born and reared a Drumcondra supporter. But then, sure it was the best thing I ever did."

Tuohy took a leap of faith by signing for Rovers, making an investment in his career that would pay off handsomely in the coming years and decades. Inside forward, Peyton, virtually the same height, weight and age as Tuohy, joined him at Milltown. It wasn't by chance that their characteristics dovetailed. Two years after taking over as Rovers' player/manager following the death of Jimmy Dunne, Paddy Coad had a clear idea of the sort of player he wanted at Milltown – young and gifted. Tuohy and Peyton fitted the bill perfectly, and many more followed. Coad trawled through schoolboy and youth international team sheets and cherry-picked the very best rising talent. By 1952 he'd signed Mickey Burke, Gerry Mackey, Ronnie Nolan, Jim 'Maxie' McCann and Shay Keogh, all elite young players who, aside from Burke, would go on to win senior caps while at the club. Coad – now touching thirty but still the best passer and brightest football brain in the League with eleven International caps – was well established in the team alongside forward

Paddy Ambrose and wing half-back Liam Hennessy. The greatest League of Ireland side ever was now officially born – 'Coad's Colts'.

RONNIE NOLAN: "In those days, the League of Ireland fellas used to do five laps, twenty sprints, another five laps, and so on, for training. They'd never see a football. Paddy Coad was different. He would have about ten footballs for us and we'd be out practicing with them all the time. He was developing the best young talent at Milltown into a team. Some of them didn't make it but most of them did. We basically all started at eighteen years of age with Rovers."

Elaborate game plans and detailed team tactics, as we know them today, were unheard of in the 1950s. That wasn't just in Ireland but in the English League, the self-styled best league in the world. Even at Manchester United, Matt Busby's training regime consisted of weights and bodywork exercises for his players before sending them 'round the back' to the cinder strewn car park for a kick-about. Substitutions weren't permitted during games either, so the same eleven players would start and finish each match. It wasn't uncommon for a player with a torn hamstring or gashed knee to hobble through the last twenty minutes or so on the wing, just to keep up the numbers. Managers like Coad had to get their team selections spot on, as there was no chance of withdrawing an underperforming player. Thankfully for him, his 'Colts' clicked as a unit early on and, throughout the 1950s, he had the luxury of fielding a largely unchanged team who riveted the Irish soccer public. Even now, over fifty years later, those old enough to remember 'Coad's Colts' reel off their names in a flash, from goalkeeper Christy O'Callaghan – replaced later by Eamon 'Sheila' Darcy – all the way through to Nolan, Keogh and Hennessy to outside left Tuohy, the last man on the team sheet. In 1954, Rovers won their first League title in fifteen years. Two more league wins followed that decade as well as two FAI Cup successes. It's not exactly a stunning haul considering their slick, sophisticated passing style of play was credited with changing the face of domestic Irish soccer. But every match they won was a victory for pure football as

'Coad's Colts' played with an abandon not previously seen in the League. They were footballing pioneers. On soggy pitches with heavy, often rain-sodden footballs they still managed to make soccer an art form, bringing the beautiful game to life as never before.

LIAM TUOHY: "I wouldn't like to be critical of other teams but we were the best team in the League of Ireland at that stage. What I would say is that other teams probably didn't have as many good players as Rovers had in those days, and League of Ireland football was at a reasonably high standard. I think you could judge that by how many times League of Ireland players played on international teams in those days. Ronnie Nolan got lots of caps, and so on."

In November 1956, Ireland beat then World Cup champions West Germany 3-0 in an international friendly at Dalymount Park. Four Rovers players – Nolan, McCann, Peyton and Mackey – played. McCann scored the third goal in an extraordinary win. The following year Ireland came within seconds of beating England in front of a record 47,500 attendance at Dalymount, this time in a crucial World Cup qualifier. An injury time England goal dashed Ireland's ambitions of progression, but the fact that a Rovers player, the combative Nolan, played against the likes of English League stars Tom Finney and Johnny Haynes further strengthened Rovers' reputation as the leading Irish club. To a man, anyone who has commented on Rovers in the 1950s credits Coad with being the key influence as the player/manager who practised on the field of play what he preached off it.

LIAM TUOHY: "Paddy would tell you to concentrate on passing it. He didn't want too many long balls. He would say to me, 'If you're in trouble, I'm inside you, just pass it'. He got into your head that the game is about passing the ball. Some fellas, particularly when you're young, maybe eighteen or nineteen, want to do a bit too much with the ball. He used to say, 'Football is a passing game, let's pass it'. The fact that he was a great player himself and a great passer, which was probably his best asset, meant he led by example beside you."

Like Tuohy, future Irish international and Manchester United player Eamon Dunphy, who would collect an FAI Cup medal with Rovers at the tail end of his career in 1978, was a big Drumcondra fan in his formative years. Yet, he too, was spellbound by the magnificence of Coad at Rovers during the '50s.

EAMON DUNPHY: "Paddy Coad was a great player, a really great player by any standards of football. They were a wonderful team; 'Maxie' McCann, Coad, Liam Tuohy, Ronnie Nolan, Gerry Mackey. Liam Hennessy was in that team, too, another wonderful player. They were the best side that had ever been in the League of Ireland and were quite dominant."

Rovers didn't finish outside the top three in the League between 1952 and 1959. They won the title three times, claimed the runners-up spot twice and finished third three times in this period. They also competed in four FAI Cup finals in a row, between 1955 and 1958, winning two. Around Milltown they were loved by their supporters and, further afield, typically despised by their rivals. Whether you liked them or not, Rovers made for compulsive viewing and the crowds flocked to watch them.

RONNIE NOLAN: "Somewhere in the middle of that period we weren't doing so well. We were about fourth in the league, four or five points behind the leaders and the gates weren't big enough for the Cunningham family who owned the club. They wanted bigger crowds. They called us all in for an investigation, picking our minds as to what the problems were. We were something like fourth in the table, 'only' getting gates of about 14,000 people! They used to average 20,000 up in Milltown in the great days and we're all called in because they're only averaging around 14,000. They were looking for reasons as to how we can improve things. I'm looking at gates now and generally over the whole league you're lucky if you get a thousand at games."

Outside the Screen cinema in the city centre, fleets of 46A buses destined for Milltown would load up fans decked out in green and white. Others made their way by bicycle, which were left in piles three and four deep on the main routes approaching the ground. Traders made a mint selling oranges and sweets to the thousands that descended on the venue. Dazzled by the whole experience, a young Damien Richardson was instantly hooked on the Rovers drug. Eventually, he'd sign for the club and make history as a key member of the six-in-a-row cup winning team in the mid- to late-1960s.

DAMIEN RICHARDSON: "I followed Rovers as a boy. I lived off the South Circular Road. They were the local team. Myself and my dad had to walk up to games because all the buses going up would be packed every Sunday, or whenever they played at home. From about seven or eight years of age, I attended Shamrock Rovers games religiously until I started playing myself with Home Farm when I was fifteen or sixteen. Paddy Coad was the real brains behind it. He was a player/manager and the team was built around his ability. He was a magnificent player, a midfield player who could pass, one of those players who always seemed to have time no matter how frantic or frenetic the occasion was. He just always seemed to have time. His passing was impeccable. He could put the wingers in behind the full-backs. That was one of the great awakenings of my life, how he could pass the ball behind the full-back for the winger to run onto. The team was built in his style, with his philosophy. They set an example, a standard that players and spectators who followed on would compare against for a couple of generations afterwards. They weren't just a football team, they were the greatest sports club in the country. They received enormous adulation and also great rivalry wherever they went around the country because people who weren't Shamrock Rovers fans loved to see Shamrock Rovers getting beaten."

One match in particular secured iconic status for Rovers, the 1956 FAI Cup final. Trailing 2-0 to Cork Athletic with thirteen minutes left,

Tommy Hamilton – bought in '55 after a stint at Manchester United – pulled one back and Hennessy, the penalty king, equalised with a trademark spot kick. With time almost up, Coad belted in a Rovers corner, Nolan came thundering in at the back post and crashed a header to the net. Cork had thought the game was over at 2-0 and one of their directors went off to buy the champagne in a local pub. Outside the ground, he heard three huge cheers and didn't need any explanation about what was happening inside. Sportingly, he handed the champagne over to the celebrating Rovers players on his return. Rovers backed up the Cup win by claiming the League title the following season in 1957. For the first time, a league win now came with the carrot of a place in the new European Cup competition. It had begun in 1955 following the revival, by the French sports newspaper *L'Équipe*, of an idea that had been floating around for a number of decades. The first competition contained eighteen different teams, the champions of eighteen individual leagues across Europe. The entry list was expanded the following season to include an English team, Manchester United, for the first time. In 1957, three more new countries were invited to send their champions – The Republic of Ireland, Northern Ireland and East Germany. The first two competitions had been won by Real Madrid with Argentine Alfredo di Stefano the standout player scoring in both finals. However, the emergence of an exceptional young Manchester United team under Busby threatened to usurp Madrid's position at the head of European football. When the sides had met in the previous season's semi-final, Madrid scraped through 5-3 on aggregate. With the experience of a first European campaign under their belts, United's young guns were expected to push hard for the title in 1957/58. At the time, the European Cup draw was made on a regional basis so Rovers and United were placed in a pot with six other teams from 'West' Europe; Seville (Spain), Aarhus (Denmark), Glasgow Rangers (Scotland), Lisbon (Portugal), Glenavon (Northern Ireland) and St Étienne (France). Even if it had been a completely open draw, it seemed almost inevitable that two sides would be paired together – 'Coad's Colts' and 'Busby's Babes'. And so it was.

EAMON DUNPHY: "It was a fantastic draw. Liam Whelan from Dublin was playing for Manchester United and he was a star in that team. Manchester United were hugely popular in Dublin and the 'Busby Babes' were legends even at that stage. It was a match you said to yourself you had to see. It was a much more innocent time because we had no television and we had no real access to English football, except what we listened to on the radio or read in the newspapers. So, the prospect of actually seeing them was phenomenal. And Manchester United were champions of England as well. They'd had a good stab at the European Cup the year before. So, you knew it was going to be an incredible occasion. I'd say everyone that loved soccer made it their business to be there."

LIAM TUOHY: "United were a top team in England and you knew, obviously, of the great names that they had. You were aware that you were going to be playing above the standard that you were used to in League of Ireland football. They had great players and you knew all the names, because all of us who were playing football here – or just supporting the game – followed different clubs in England and were interested in the game, generally. I mean even if you take it on a bit, when George Best was at United, everybody here knew who he was and anyone that was interested in football wanted to see how he was doing. It was the same with the 'Busby Babes'."

In much the same way that Rovers revolutionised football in Ireland with a new attacking approach, Busby's team had developed their own style of fearless football. Players, like the powerful Duncan Edwards, the half-back who could play in any position, and striker Tommy Taylor, were young, bold and confident. They refused to be intimidated by any opposition and it showed in the way they knocked the ball around the field and ran at petrified English League defences.

EAMON DUNPHY: "Nobody had ever seen anything like them before. Duncan Edwards made his debut for United when he was just sixteen.

He played for England when he was eighteen."

Edwards became England's youngest post-war international when he was capped in 1955. In the World Cup qualifier against Ireland at Dalymount Park the following year, which ended 1-1, three 'Busby Babes' played; Edwards, Taylor and David Pegg. Club colleague Roger Byrne was also involved, though he was several years older. The amount of talented youth on United's books was frightening for their rivals. Bobby Charlton, who'd go on to win the World Cup with England in 1966, was still only twenty and being kept out of the team by twenty-two-year-old Irishman, Whelan. Prolific forward, Dennis Viollet, was just twenty-four, the same age as centre-half, Mark Jones. Winger Eddie Colman, the joker in the team who was nicknamed 'Snake Hips', was twenty-one, while Kenny Morgans, eighteen, was a highly rated outside right. Busby actually didn't like the moniker 'Busby's Babes'. He felt it hinted at a weakness in his team and gave a perception that his side would make the mistakes of exuberant youth. He preferred the tag 'Red Devils', which he felt indicated a harder core and a more uncompromising attitude towards winning games. He felt his team deserved to be feared as, even in their early years, they'd won back-to-back League titles and were seeking to emulate Herbert Chapman's three-in-a-row Arsenal team of the 1930s. They'd also played in the semi-final of the European Cup the season before.

EAMON DUNPHY: "The 'Busby Babes' tag was inevitable because, in those days, it was very rare for young players to be playing. Teenagers in the first team were unheard of, and he was the one that introduced it. Young players, in general, even in their early twenties, would be regarded as kids. Most of the teams in England would have had an average age of twenty-six, twenty-seven or twenty-eight even, experienced old pros. But these were brash, brilliant young kids who didn't give a fuck about anything. That was their attitude. They were called 'Teddy Boys', infamously, by Bob Lord who was the very reactionary Chairman of Burnley and President of the Football

League. He described them as 'Teddy Boys' which was the equivalent, I suppose, of being called a 'skinhead' later on. There was a brashness about them. They played their football that way, too."

Irish soccer fans felt their own unique connection to United as the club was home to exciting young Dubliner, Whelan, very much one of the 'Babes'. Busby snapped up the Cabra lad from Home Farm in 1953. By '57, still only twenty-two, he was a household name on both sides of the Irish Sea, an Irish international whose incredible twenty-six goals in thirty-nine appearances the previous season had been central to United's League success. Rovers' centre-forward Tommy Hamilton was close friends with Whelan having been at United himself between 1952 and 1955, before returning to play for the Hoops.

TOMMY HAMILTON: "Liam was still young and, for all he'd done in the game, we still hadn't seen the best of him. At international level, his first match for Ireland was against Holland in 1956. Ireland beat Holland 4-1 in Rotterdam and he was playing. But, at that stage, when we were playing them he'd only got two or three more caps, so we hadn't seen the best of him at all."

One would presume that Hamilton was relishing the opportunity of playing against United, to prove a point to his former club. But Hamilton's is not the typical story of an Irish lad being rejected by an English club and returning home soured by the experience. He was only back in Ireland playing for Rovers because he'd held his ground at United on an issue completely unrelated to football.

TOMMY HAMILTON: "Not many people know, but what happened with me was I was conscripted into the army. At the time there was conscription over there. They had told me that because I was coming home each summer for three months that I wouldn't be conscripted. Every year, all the Irish lads got papers to go and register for conscription, but all you'd do was hand them in to the secretary and you'd get word back that it had been deferred for another year. Anyway, I went back for my third year and we all got the forms, as usual, and handed them to the secretary, as normal. Everyone else was deferred for twelve months but I got word that I was to go and register for the British Army. I went to Busby, and he said, 'We'll look after that'. That was in July. It got to October '55 and he came back to me and said, 'Look, I've contacted Everton and I've contacted Arsenal where there are other Irish lads and there's nothing we can do, you'll have to go into the army'. I said, 'Well, I'm not going into the army'. He said 'I don't know what we're going to do so'. In the end he came back and said the directors had agreed that, 'If you go back home, whatever club you sign for, if they agree that if you're ever transferred back to England, United get 50 per cent of the transfer fee, then you can leave'. They were the conditions on which I could leave. I was delighted just to go."

When the Anglo-Irish European Cup tie finally came around, there was mass hysteria in Dublin at the arrival of the 'Babes'. Joe Cunningham, Rovers chairman, and his wife, May, met the United party at Dublin Airport and escorted them to the International Hotel in Bray where they stayed. The Cunninghams were good friends with the Busbys and would regularly host them. They also put Matt up at their house during his visits to Ireland to see United's Irish scout, Billy Behan. The night of the game itself was like nothing ever seen before in Phibsborough. A ticket to Dalymount to witness the first ever competitive European club fixture involving an Irish side was as rare as a hen's tooth. When the stiles eventually stopped clicking shortly before kick-off, 46,000 people had filed down the claustrophobic alleyways and narrow streets that led to the home of Irish soccer.

EAMON DUNPHY: "It was murder trying to get in. I was twelve, so I'd have been looking for a lift over the stile, which was the way we used to get in. I can't remember if I actually got the lift over or whether I managed to get the money to go. But it was a hot ticket. Getting in was a major operation, to be honest, SAS training required, but I got in anyway. There were matches when I didn't, but that was a must-see, so I got in somehow. When England played Ireland in the World Cup qualifier the same year, I didn't manage to get in. I had to listen to it on the radio. Thankfully, I got into the United game."

DAMIEN RICHARDSON: "The biggest attraction about Manchester United coming over was the fact that they were so packed full of English internationals; Roger Byrne, Tommy Taylor was the centre-forward, you had David Pegg, probably half a dozen English Internationals, in all, playing for them and, of course, Liam Whelan was playing which was a wonderful attraction for us. Their reputation as a team preceded them, not just because of the football they played, but because they had so many English internationals. At that time, the magazines would have espoused the fact that they were Manchester United and England. It was a wonderful thing for a youngster like me to see pictures of Colman, Taylor, Pegg, Roger Byrne, the great Duncan Edwards, Dennis Viollet and Bill Foulkes and then to see them in the flesh that night. Their reputations preceded every one of them."

The 'Busby Babes' lived up to their vast reputations, confirming at Dalymount every good word and salutation that had been uttered about them since they'd broken loose onto the English game. A young Dunphy watched from the School End of the ground, his eyes transfixed on the giants in the red jerseys with their fashionable haircuts and modern attire – they opted not to wear the dowdy baggy shorts that were common at the time – as they treated the crowd to an exhibition of football.

EAMON DUNPHY: "The glamour of the occasion was just extraordinary. It's indelibly in my memory bank. It was great to see. It was great to be there. There was a huge significance to a moment like that for those of us who loved soccer, because soccer was a pretty despised activity. It was the foreign game and all of that nonsense. I'd say there would have been a lot of Gaelic footballers, particularly the Dublin team of that era, who would have sneaked in that night and broken the ban (on GAA players attending soccer matches). They were so magnetic, the United guys, they were such big stars and, of course, even Busby was a star."

DAMIEN RICHARDSON: "I was very young at the time, only ten, but I can still picture moments from the game. I was down the other end of the ground, opposite the School End. I can still see things that happened in the game. I can still play them through my mind's eye, can still see them clearly, so many things that still live with me."

Before the game, writing in the *Irish Press*, Sean Piondar warned Rovers 'keeper, Eamonn 'Sheila' Darcy, that there will be, "no excuse for ball heading antics or bouts of temperamental showmanship". Darcy hardly needed reminding. With thirty-six minutes on the clock, he was beaten for the first time on the night. Tommy Taylor broke the Rovers' offside trap after a through ball from Viollet, and chipped the advancing Darcy beautifully. 1-0 to United. That's how things remained at half time. The game was still alive for both teams. Rovers were playing a containment game, and just about pulling it off. Nolan and Hennessy were holding their own in the wing-half slots. The 'Red Devils' were shifting the point of their attacks continually with long, cross-field passes, but without breaking through more than once, partly due to Darcy denying Whelan and Berry with point-blank saves. Things had looked much bleaker for Rovers against Cork Athletic in the Cup final a year earlier at the same venue, yet they'd fought back to win. They didn't possess a Duncan Edwards or a Tommy Taylor or a Liam Whelan, but they did have great talent, International talent. In all, nine of the eleven Rovers players who took on United would wear the green of Ireland as full Internationals. The only reason most of them hadn't crossed the water to play club football in England, was because it simply wasn't worth their while. The maximum wage rule, in force until 1961, meant a footballer couldn't earn more than Stg£20 a week in Britain. So, between playing for Rovers, collecting win bonuses and working in their day jobs, most players decided it was more profitable to stay at home, just like Leo Ward had done. Tuohy eventually transferred to Newcastle when he was twenty-seven, but that was purely out of a burning ambition to play at a higher level rather than chasing any money which simply wasn't there. Hamilton turned down interest from Birmingham City on one occasion while Ronnie Nolan rejected a move to Preston North End, a club very much in vogue at the time.

RONNIE NOLAN: "Preston North End, when they were in the First Division, offered Stg£8,000 for me in 1950-something. They had Tommy Docherty playing for them and transferred him to Arsenal so were looking for a replacement in the same position. Joe Cunningham called me in and he said, 'Preston have offered eight thousand for you, are you interested in going?' That was a lot of money in those days. I said, 'I'm interested in going if you give me two thousand out of that eight'. He said, 'Oh no, we can only give you a thousand'. I said a thousand wasn't good enough for me, I'd need another thousand with it. I had a house at the time and I could have bought a second house with the money. Young people mightn't understand, nowadays, buying a house for a thousand and five hundred pounds, a three bedroom semi-detached with a garage, but it was possible then. I wanted two grand to go away and I said, 'You'll get six grand, I'll get two. You should be happy with that'. But they wouldn't agree, so that was that. There were one or two other clubs that offered money, but there was only a Stg£20 maximum wage at the time, and Stg£15 in the summer. I was working away and between the work and the football, sure I was earning more than that."

Shamie Coad recalls how Everton pushed hard to sign his brother, Paddy, in the 1940s and early 1950s. They wanted him to link up with Irishmen Tommy Eglinton and Peter Farrell, but the maximum wage issue scuppered their plans too.

SHAMIE COAD: "There were enquiries for Paddy from all over the place, but especially from Everton. He could have gone there but he wouldn't go. He was making more between Shamrock Rovers and his job. He was a bookie's clerk at the time with the Cunninghams. He married into the Cunningham family and they were into the dog racing and the horse racing and had a few bookie shops. Paddy was into all that and happy. He had two great jobs; the bookies and the football. Why would he give up all that and go to England for less money and come back after seven or eight years with nothing?"

Aside from receiving decent money at Rovers, the players were treated like gods by the Cunninghams. It wasn't unusual for Coad and Co to travel to away games in Cork or Sligo by limousine. On arrival, they'd walk into their opponent's ground wearing their striking club suits, their shining boots with pressed gear waiting for them in the dressing room. Rival players heading into the game in their civvies couldn't believe what they were seeing – they had to carry their own boots under their arm in brown paper bags. At Dalymount, the Rovers players knew the next goal would probably decide their European battle with Manchester United. Score one and they were right back in the contest. Concede another and it was a long, long way back. Crucially, the next goal went United's way with Whelan, the local boy from Cabra, striking the decisive blow. Berry headed Viollet's fifty-first minute cross into Whelan's path and he slid the ball past Darcy to the net. Whelan underlined his class with his second six minutes later to make it 3-0. By full time, United had put six on the board, Taylor getting his second in the eighty-first minute before Berry and Pegg struck late on. Pegg's last goal was the pick of the bunch. Dunphy describes it as an, "exquisite (lob) ... perfection executed with impossible grace and assurance".

JIMMY 'MAXIE' McCANN: "I'll tell you what, that wasn't the Shamrock Rovers that played every week that went out that night. Man U were a fabulous team. They had one of the best footballers I had ever seen in Duncan Edwards. Roger Byrne was a great player, too, and, of course, our own Liam Whelan was the best of them on the evening. They had a fabulous team but we didn't give our best at all. You have to remember Rovers were a great team too. They didn't give away International caps willy nilly then. Rovers was full of Internationals and we felt we were good enough to play anybody. I just felt that we let the soccer public of Ireland down by playing the way we played in Dalymount Park."

Whatever about adopting defensive tactics that were alien to them, Rovers definitely suffered from inferior fitness levels to United. Apart from being back-to-back English champions and, in some people's eyes, the best team in Europe, United were full-time. Five of their six goals came from the fifty-first minute onwards. Three of the goals came in the last ten minutes.

DAMIEN RICHARDSON: "I remember my Dad talking to my Grandfather on the way home about this full-time thing, how they could play all the way through at a high tempo and how that was the essential difference between the teams."

EAMON DUNPHY: "I wasn't a Rovers supporter but they were magnificent players. The fact that they were wiped out by this great Manchester United team didn't in any way diminish Shamrock Rovers. Everyone knew how great Manchester United were and how young they were. This is the other thing, they were young, young men. They were just amazing. They'd won two English titles in a row, one by eleven points. They were very young and everyone thought they'd dominate the game in England and in Europe for a very long time. The average age of that United team was only about twenty-two."

As a statement of their European intentions United's dazzling second-half display at Dalymount was about as emphatic as it gets. With six goals in the bag, they were also effectively through to the second round before a ball was even kicked at Old Trafford. Rovers were now on odds of 100/1 to progress to round two. Even the Cunningham family, whose business was bookmaking, accepted that they weren't going to be paying out big money on a Rovers win. Driven by the sense that they had underperformed in the first leg, the Rovers players were eager to do themselves justice.

LIAM TUOHY: "I think we realised that we couldn't play a very open game over there. You have to consider that they weren't just full-time professionals we were playing, they were the cream of full-time professionals and all of us were part-time. They were used to playing football at a quicker pace than we would have been, and now they were playing at home also. Coming after a six-nothing hammering, I'm sure there were lots of worries about what kind of score it was going to be over there."

The cricket score many expected never materialised. In front of 33,000 at Old Trafford, Coad, then thirty-six, played the game of his life. He gave a master class in passing across midfield against a United side showing four changes from the team at Dalymount but in no way reduced in quality. Recovering from a defensive hammering when they conceded two goals in the first half hour, Rovers proved the equal of their opponents in skill and imagination thereafter. In the end, a narrow 3-2 defeat better reflected the standard of play which Rovers were capable of than the game at Dalymount. The fact that they scored in the tie was also hugely significant. 'Maxie' McCann's fifty-fifth minute goal, laid on by Peyton who'd dispossessed Viollet, was the first ever by a League of Ireland player in Europe.

JIMMY 'MAXIE' McCANN: "It was all just off the cuff. There were no plans worked out or anything. I was in the centre-forward position. The ball came in. I just hit it. Simple as that. Funnily enough, not many people remember the significance of the goal. It's not mentioned very much. The only one that would remind me of it would be the likes of Tuohy when he's having a go at me or having the craic, which is quite often! In fairness, we had the best man on the field that night, Paddy Coad. He was absolutely wonderful. He didn't want to play but a terrible 'flu bug was raging in Ireland and England and Coad had to play because Liam Hennessy went down with the 'flu. Coad came in at left-half and he was absolutely wonderful. That was the only reason he played. And such a game he played, you never saw anything like it."

LIAM TUOHY: *"They gave Paddy Coad a standing ovation that night. He was a great player. People used to say in those days, 'If you can do it at twenty, you can do it at forty'. I don't know about that, but it was true for Paddy. He was just a special player."*

Rovers' second goal was scored by Hamilton in the sixty-ninth minute. It wasn't going to alter the course of the tie, that was long over as a concern. Two goals from United hitman Viollet, and another from Pegg on the night, had seen to that. But, it was a proud moment for Hamilton to score at Old Trafford against his old team.

TOMMY HAMILTON: *"There was a bit of a mêlée in the goalmouth. It came to me and I hit it and it went into the corner. That was it. I'd love to say that I dribbled past ten of them and scored!"*

Appreciative United fans clapped the part-time visitors off the Old Trafford pitch. The Rovers players had redeemed themselves, not in front of the Irish public as they'd have liked, but in their hearts they'd proven a big point about their own individual abilities. What they couldn't possibly have suspected as they shook hands with the 'Busby Babes' coming off the field was that they'd be the second last European team to do so. Just four months later, five of the players who lined out against Rovers at Old Trafford – captain Roger Byrne, Eddie Colman, Mark Jones, Taylor and Pegg – were killed instantly in an air crash at Munich-Riem Airport. Whelan and Edwards, who hadn't featured in the second leg, also died. The physically powerful Edwards hung on to life for two weeks after the crash, a feat of bravery that stunned doctors, before finally passing away. An eighth player, reserve full-back Geoff Bent, was also cut down in his prime in the crash. In total, twenty-three of the forty-four passengers onboard the British European Airways Elizabethan plane attempting to complete the final leg of a round trip from Manchester to Belgrade following a European Cup quarter-final tie with Red Star Belgrade, died. After two failed attempts to take off because of 'boost surging' – an over-acceleration in the engines, apparently not uncommon with Elizabethan aircraft at airports above sea level such as Munich – a third attempt took place at 3.04pm. This time the 'boost surging' was controlled but, in treacherous snow and slush conditions, the plane failed to gain enough power and momentum to get airborne. With the point of no return passed on the runway and the plane unable to take off, it smashed through a fence and into both a house and a fuel hut, breaking into two pieces and shattering the snowy afternoon silence. Many of the passengers were killed instantly. Others were thrown clear to the relative safety of the freezing snow and lived to tell distressing tales. Harry Gregg, the Northern Irish goalkeeper who joined United shortly after the Rovers games, was hailed a hero for surviving the crash and pulling many from the wreckage, including team-mate Bobby Charlton who had taken Whelan's place in United's 5-4 aggregate win over Red Star Belgrade. Much has been written about events on the afternoon of February 6, 1958 in Munich, but little of it in the context of the Rovers players who'd developed a lasting bond with the 'Busby Babes' through the European Cup ties just eighteen weeks earlier. All of the Rovers players knew Whelan closely as he'd trained at Milltown with them when he was home from United. One of the many gruesome facts to emerge post-Munich was that, shortly before the final attempted take off, Johnny Berry had told Gregg, who was trying to lighten the mood, to stop being so jovial. Berry remarked that he thought, "We would all be killed". Whelan overheard the conversation and is said to have retorted, "Well if that's going to happen I'm ready for it".

JIMMY 'MAXIE' McCANN: *"We all sort of new him intimately and always had a great laugh with him. Tommy Hamilton and himself had been away in Manchester together for a few years. When the news broke, Tommy was in bits."*

TOMMY HAMILTON: *"Liam and a chap called Johnny Scott from Northern Ireland and myself were the best of pals when we were at United. We went everywhere together, played golf together and all sorts. I was working for an insurance company the day it happened. The chief clerk came up to me at around four o'clock and said, 'Did you hear the news? There's been a crash'. In fairness to him he said, 'You go away if you want to'. So, I went straight up to Liam Whelan's house, up to his mother. There was news coming through and bulletins about who was saved and who was this and who was that. It was late when we heard for certain. I'm not sure, but I think it was Billy Behan who came up and said Liam had been killed."*

Ronnie Nolan had played with Whelan for Ireland and, like Hamilton, developed a friendship with the easy-going devout church-goer.

RONNIE NOLAN: *"I used to work in the Irish Glass Bottle Company. Billy Behan, who was a chief scout for Manchester United, also worked there. When Liam was home from Manchester, a few weeks after we'd played them, he came out to the Irish Glass to have a chat with Billy Behan. It was the same year I got married and Liam was also getting married the same year. I was getting married in June. He was getting married in July, or shortly after me anyway. He said to me, 'Don't forget now to tell me what it's all about when you have your wedding'. But he never lived to see it. He was killed in the crash the next month."*

EAMON DUNPHY: *"I was in a barber shop in Millmount Avenue having my hair cut after school about half four or a quarter to five when I heard. Darkness was just falling. I can remember that day vividly. It was terrible. It just devastated everybody. There was no television or rolling news reports or anything like that. But people came out on the streets that night to talk to each other. It was like the assassination of John F. Kennedy. I remember where I was then and where I was after the Munich Air Crash. I think they're the two I remember vividly ... and Princess Diana's death, funnily enough. Liam Whelan and Liam's family were very well known. They were from Cabra which ... I was from Drumcondra and they were very much respected people. Liam was only twenty-two. It had a very deep impact in the city. There was always an Irish connection there with United, whether it was Billy Behan, John Giles, Liam or Harry Gregg. So there was, yeah, a great sense of shock over here. It was one of those occasions where people were traumatised even though they wouldn't necessarily have known very much about sport. It was just the idea of a young team like that dying."*

DAMIEN RICHARDSON: "I was ill at the time. I had a touch of pleurisy as a youngster and was due to go into Blanchardstown Hospital which at that time was out in the country, out in the fresh air. I was waiting to go out there and was at home having missed school for a couple of weeks because of the illness. I remember vividly sitting up in the bedroom before a fireplace, and my Dad came in with the newspaper. He was in a very agitated state explaining that there had been a crash. It's one of those moments, like John Kennedy passing or Elvis Presley. You always remember what you were doing when you first got the news."

On the day of Liam Whelan's death his sister, Alice, had been to a travel agency in Dublin's O'Connell Street to book his honeymoon for later in the year. He was due to marry his fiancée, Ruby, in the summer of 1958. The sense of a young life and a glorious talent thieved in its prime was palpable around Dublin for not just weeks and months but years. Whelan's funeral at Glasnevin Cemetery drew one of the biggest crowds ever to assemble there. The Rovers players swelled the numbers.

LIAM TUOHY: "People just referred to 'The Crash'. It was all 'Did you hear about the crash?' It went on and on. 'I heard about David Pegg and I heard about this' and so on. It was the biggest talking point for years and years, a huge tragedy. I can't remember who, exactly, but some League of Ireland follower from another club said something at a game against Rovers afterwards to the effect of, 'Sure our team couldn't have any luck after playing that gang Shamrock Rovers'. It was the bit of black humour, I suppose."

United were criticised by many for their handling of events after Munich, in particular how they dealt with the families and friends of the deceased. Johnny Berry survived but, like Jackie Blanchflower, was forced to retire from football. Berry's son, Neil, wrote a book entitled 'Johnny, the Forgotten Babe' which contains claims that, having played his last game for United, "The regime at the time did not want to know of his circumstances and preferred that he just vanished". In 2008, Rovers were asked to send a couple of representatives to Manchester for the fiftieth anniversary of the Munich disaster. It was recognition by United of the part Rovers played in the rise of the 'Busby Babes' before their untimely demise. Hennessy and 'Maxie' McCann went over on behalf of Rovers and bumped into Neil Berry.

JIMMY 'MAXIE' McCANN: "When we were over there a guy came to the table and sat down beside me. He said, 'You never knew my Dad. My Dad was Johnny Berry'. He'd written a book, 'The Forgotten Babe'. He gave me the book. He was a very angry young man, so he was. He hadn't got very nice things to say about Manchester United or Busby."

Busby, himself, sustained horrific injuries in Munich. Gregg found him clutching his chest in agony after the crash, his ribs fractured and his lung punctured. He had serious leg injuries and his foot was broken and contorted. While recovering in the local Rechts der Isar Hospital, the last rites were administered to him. A hospital statement even admitted, "We do not have much hope of saving him", though he pulled through.

In attempting to rebuild Manchester United from the ashes and the mangled ruins of Munich, Busby faced his greatest battle of all. "Manchester United will rise again", was the poignant declaration by chairman Harold Hardman in the match programme for the first game back. A decade later, another Irish team would bear testimony to the fact that United were as good as their word.

EUROPEAN CUP

First round, first leg
September 25, 1957
Dalymount Park, Dublin
Attendance: 46,000

Shamrock Rovers: 0

Manchester United: 6
(Taylor 36 and 81, Whelan 51 and 57, Berry 85, Pegg 86)

Shamrock Rovers: Darcy; Burke, Mackey; Nolan, Keogh, Hennessy; Peyton, Ambrose, Hamilton, Coad, Tuohy.

Manchester United: Wood; Foulkes, Byrne; Goodwin, Blanchflower, Edwards; Berry, Whelan, Taylor, Viollet, Pegg.

Referee: L. van Nuffel (Belgium).

First round, second leg
October 2, 1957
Old Trafford, Manchester
Attendance: 33,000

Manchester United 3
(Viollet 6 and 59, Pegg 22)

Shamrock Rovers 2
(McCann 55, Hamilton 68)

Manchester United: Wood; Foulkes, Byrne; Coleman, Jones, McGuinness; Berry, Webster, Taylor, Viollet, Pegg.

Shamrock Rovers: Darcy; Burke, Mackey; Nolan, Keogh, Coad; McCann, Peyton, Ambrose, Hamilton, Tuohy.

Referee: A. Alsteen (Belgium)

CHAPTER 2

WATERFORD VS MANCHESTER UNITED
September 18 and October 2, 1968

"I met Paddy Crerand again years after and said to him, 'Really Paddy, at the end of the day, I think we were a decent League of Ireland team'. He said, 'You weren't a decent bloody League of Ireland team, you were a decent bloody team, full stop'." ALFIE HALE

On the morning of June 14, 1965, a small article buried in the sports pages of the national newspapers commanded the attention of the Waterford sporting public. It was a report on the previous afternoon's meeting of the League of Ireland's Management Committee in Dublin. Waterford, having finished bottom of the League for the first time since 1939, had expected a few choice words to come their way from officialdom. Without the threat of relegation in a one-division League, it was common for the bottom team to receive a verbal dressing-down from League officials to highlight their shortcomings. Yet, nobody anticipated stumbling upon the news that, as a result of consistently poor performances over two seasons, Waterford's very existence in the League was under threat. Sam Prole, Chairman of both the League of Ireland and of champions Drumcondra, had laid it on the line in no uncertain terms; after consecutive finishes of second-bottom and bottom in the League it was time for Waterford to shape up, or ship out. Exactly twelve months earlier, Bohemians had received a similar warning after finishing last. But they escaped the ultimate punishment of not being re-elected to the League by explaining that, as they were "dedicated to amateur football", they would, on occasion, "find it extremely difficult to compete against professional players". Waterford offered no excuses when Prole publicly questioned their lack of achievement in the summer of 1965. Instead, they dedicated themselves to improvement and to never again suffering the ignominy of a public shaming in the national newspapers. Club secretary, Michael Bolger, responded to Prole at the meeting by stating, "It was no pleasure for us to finish up at the bottom of the table, but I can assure the meeting that it will be a different story next season". Little did Bolger, inside-forward Shamie Coad, or anyone else at Kilcohan Park realise that their vows to improve were to spark the most successful era the club has ever known.

SHAMIE COAD: "We'd been near the bottom for some time at that stage and were told that, unless we bucked ourselves up a bit, we could be out of the League. They were the famous words of Sam Prole: 'Pull up your socks or you'll be gone'. So we did."

Shamie Coad's brother, Paddy, had been manager of Waterford for only seven months at the time of the warning. The fact that the club was on its knees pained him, not because he'd been used to better as player/manager with the great Shamrock Rovers team of the 1950s, but because he was a Waterford man through and through. Blue blood bubbled in his veins as he considered Prole's public denouncement of the club. Aided by the chequebook of his old pal at Rovers, businessman Frank Davis who'd joined him as a director in Waterford, Coad set about the task of making his team great. His first act was to bring tough tackling, ex-Sheffield Wednesday half-back Jimmy McGeough down from Derry City where he'd just won the Irish League.

JIMMY McGEOUGH: "The first thing Paddy Coad reminded me of when I went there was that this was a family club. And it was. Everyone seemed to be someone's brother or pal. Shamie Coad was Paddy's brother, you had the Caseys, the Fitzgeralds, all the guys were local and seemed to know each other inside out. I found the spirit there to be tremendous."

McGeough proved a vital acquisition and quickly justified the substantial price tag of IR£3,000. He brought steel and balance to a team that liked to play football but leaked too many goals; forty-two in twenty-two games the previous season. For the 1965/66 season, his first full season as outright manager, Coad also brought in ex-International John O'Neill, a versatile player who'd won the league with Drumcondra, and outside-right Al Casey from Cork Celtic. Like his 'Colts' at Rovers in the '50s, Coad encouraged the Waterford players to attack and they quickly earned the reputation of being an exciting team to watch. Within months, Coad had turned things around to such an extent that Waterford were engaged in a thrilling battle with Shamrock Rovers for the title in early 1966. He made another astute signing to keep his club in pole position as the chequered flag loomed, that of English winger Johnny Matthews from Coventry City.

JOHNNY MATTHEWS: "Jimmy Hill was managing Coventry at the time. He called me in one Tuesday and said, 'Would you like to go to Waterford for six weeks?' I said, 'Where's fucking that?' The only club I had ever heard of in Ireland was Shamrock Rovers. Mick Lynch was at Waterford, a friend of Jimmy Hill's, and had rang up. They were looking for someone to score a few goals. It was only a loan deal. At the time Pat Saward, an Irish International, was coach at Coventry and said, 'You'll love it over there but people who cross the bridge in Waterford normally don't come back'. He was right!"

It's forty-four years now since Matthews first crossed the bridge into Waterford. He still hasn't left, the county at least, making his home in nearby Tramore close to goalkeeper Peter Thomas, who also joined from Coventry soon after him. Waterford duly held on to win the League by two points from Rovers in 1966, thanks to a record-breaking thirteen-match winning streak. It was the beginning of a golden era that would yield a sensational six League titles in eight seasons up to 1973. A 3-1 win over Drogheda at the Lourdes Stadium on April 17, 1966, officially clinched the Blues' first ever League crown. In just ten months, their fortunes had transformed beyond all recognition. There are differing opinions on how and why success followed on so quickly from near ruination. Some credit the introduction of McGeough as the decisive factor, others the tactical nous of Paddy Coad on the sideline, others again the spending power of Davis who dug deep into his pockets and regularly laid on win bonuses of IR£110 per game, a tenner a man. Davis stumped up the money to bring local hero, Alfie Hale, home from England before the defence of their League title. Hale had transferred to Aston Villa for Stg£4,500 in 1960. He picked up the first of fourteen International caps in attack for Ireland two years later, before rejoining Waterford for IR£3,000 from Newport County in August 1966.

ALFIE HALE: *"The year I came home they had won their first League Championship and that was the means of bringing me back. Michael Bolger was secretary of Waterford and had said, 'Don't come home until we have something here for you in terms of a foundation of a team'. When I first went to Aston Villa I didn't want to be there. I didn't want to be in England at all. But, because there was nothing to come home to, Michael Bolger said, 'When the time is right, we'll call you'. That all came together in 1966 with people like Frank Davis and Don Kennedy and some others who basically put that team together. I signed around the same time that Peter Thomas did. Peter Bryan came in as a back around that time too."*

Waterford didn't retain the League of Ireland title in 1967, finishing the season in a disappointing fifth position, but they were back on top the following year, winning the League in 1968 for the first of three consecutive seasons. The Waterford side virtually picked itself in these years due to the clear individual strengths of the players in the various positions around the field.

JOHNNY MATTHEWS: *"I still consider 'Thommo' the best goalkeeper I've seen in League of Ireland football. Alex Ludzic would have been another good 'keeper, Richie Blackmore was a good goalkeeper, too, and Mick Smyth of Shamrock Rovers. But 'Thommo' was probably the best reflex goalkeeper I played against, except Gordon Banks. I have to say that because I scored against Banks in an inter-league game! 'Thommo' was in goals as well then actually."*

JOHN O'NEILL: "For me, Shamie Coad was as good a player in his position as there was in the League of Ireland."

SHAMIE COAD: "We had a lot of great goal scorers in the team, everyone could score, I chipped in with a few myself, Jimmy scored a few, Johnny 'Matt', Alfie of course, everyone really was capable of putting them away. We really liked to go forward. At times we probably went forward too much and forgot to defend, but everyone wanted to see Waterford playing attacking football and we did that. People came from all over the country to see us playing. When we were doing well, fellas were writing postcards from different parts of the country looking for autographs. Waterford were a household name in how the game should be played."

After that fifth place League finish in 1967 Paddy Coad stood down as manager. "To bring the first title to my native Waterford leaves everything else in the shade," he said, reflecting on his legacy. Martin Ferguson, brother of current Manchester United manager Alex, had a short stint as player/manager before twenty-eight-year-old Vinny Maguire took over in the same capacity from February 1968. Regardless of the changes that occurred on the sideline, Coad's influence remained evident as Waterford continued to play some of the most attractive football in the League. The offensive, easy-on-the-eye and open approach meant that against superior opposition, which they'd face in their first European foray, they were liable to be exploited and potentially opened up. That's exactly what happened in August and September of 1966 when they played army side Vorwaerts of East Germany in the European Cup. Vorwaerts lived up their name – 'forwards' – by stuffing Waterford 12-1 over two legs and advancing with ease. Mick Lynch got the only Waterford goal at Dalymount Park. There were mitigating circumstances for Waterford's European embarrassment, quite aside from any swashbuckling approach they may have taken.

JOHN O'NEILL: "I left Dalymount after the Vorwaerts match and went to a hotel on Stephen's Green where a man from town here, a businessman, was staying and he drove me back to the paper mills in Waterford. I clocked in at four o'clock in the morning and went on to finish my shift. A lad helped me out by doing four hours for me; that was the only leeway you got. So, when you talk about 'preparation' for games and all that sort of stuff, it really didn't exist for a lot of us as you know it today."

Waterford won back the League title in 1968 with seven full-time players, roughly half the panel, and an increase of two on the previous year. Those who worked in day jobs generally performed manual roles which increased the burden on them as footballers. Full-back Noel Griffin, for instance, was a glass cutter, his defensive colleague Paul Morrissey a cabinet maker, Shamie Coad a machinist. Hale worked for Lyons Tea. When the draw for the 1968/69 European Cup was made, and sensationally pitted Waterford against holders Manchester United, the entire Waterford panel immediately assumed the same status regardless of who was full- or part-time. Compared to the squad that had been amassed by their opponents at Old Trafford they were all small fry. It was seven years since the maximum wage rule was abolished in England and while United were still notoriously low payers, their 'Holy Trinity' of George Best, Bobby Charlton and Denis Law could each have bought the entire Waterford club several times over. The day after the draw was made, two pictures appeared, side by side, in *The Daily Mirror* and signified the financial chasm between the champions of Ireland and England. One was of European Footballer of the Year, Best, the daringly talented Northern Irish forward, sitting on the bonnet of his new E-Type Jaguar. The other was of Matthews and Bryan smiling for the camera beside an old Austin Cambridge that they'd bought between them for IR£70. For all the new ground that Waterford were breaking in League of Ireland circles, with two titles in three seasons, it was a drop in the ocean compared to United who'd beaten Benfica 4-1 at Wembley on May 29 to become the first English winners of the European Cup.

SHAMIE COAD: "As soon as the draw was made, reporters and media people were coming from all over the place to talk to us. I remember we were all down in the pub at one stage getting our photographs taken. They were sending in papers and press from all sorts of places to cover the story because it was a big story. We just couldn't believe it. When we initially heard the draw it was, 'What? United?' It was a fantastic draw for us."

Irish football supporters maintained deep connections with United over the years through the influence of figures like Jackie Carey, Billy Behan, Johnny Giles and Tony Dunne at Old Trafford. Manager Matt Busby was close friends with the Cunninghams who owned Shamrock Rovers. Events at Munich-Riem Airport a decade earlier, in February, 1958, catapulted the club even further into the hearts and minds of the Irish. Dubliner Liam Whelan was one of seven 'Busby Babes' killed instantly when a plane carrying United players and officials crashed while attempting to take off from Munich Airport. An eighth player, Duncan Edwards, passed away weeks later. The significance of 'the crash' in an Irish context was highlighted again in the weeks before the Waterford game as Busby brought a full-strength team over to play a Drumcondra selection at Dalymount Park in a benefit game for John Whelan, Liam's brother. Young Liam Whelan and supremely talented team-mates like Edwards, David Pegg and Tommy Taylor, who passed away in Munich, had been expected to dominate the English game for the next decade. That Busby put together, arguably, an even better side and rebuilt a club utterly broken in body and spirit was the great football story of the 1960s, an era that also witnessed the rise of Bill Shankly's Liverpool,

Don Revie's Leeds United and Alf Ramsey's World Cup winners, England. Naturally, there were low days when Old Trafford seemed more a haven of nightmares than the 'Theatre of Dreams'. At times in the early '60s, it appeared Busby might not actually succeed in turning the club around. In the 1963/64 season, for example, young Irishman Eamon Dunphy, a future International, was selected as United's twelfth man for an away game against Nottingham Forest. Minding his own business on the team bus travelling east, a sheet of paper with a picture etched on it fell into his lap from the seat in front. He opened it up to discover a, "vicious caricature," of Busby, "drawn with great skill and care". The image was of Busby in typically stern repose but the cheeks were crudely replaced by testicles and the nose by a penis. It confirms that there was a possibility, however small, of Busby losing the United dressing room at certain stages in those transitional years. It's Dunphy's assertion that Busby, "never really recovered his health after (Munich) and I don't think he ever recovered his full vigour". Yet, in a relatively short time after the misery of Munich, Busby still achieved his dream of winning the European Cup with United, a feat that secured his place in sporting immortality.

EAMON DUNPHY: "Munich was never talked about at the club. But the whole club was transformed because of it. They had to go and buy players in the transfer market to replace the players who died. Some who had gone back after Munich, like Kenny Morgans and Albert Scanlon, were never the same again. From a club that had nurtured its own players and had a youth policy – the first one ever – they had to go into the transfer market. Then there was the friction between the players who were brought in and the players that were products of that earlier Busby era like Bobby Charlton. So, it wasn't a happy club in 1960 when I arrived. In fact, in 1963 when they won the next trophy, which was the FA Cup, they were nearly relegated. But then George Best came and Denis Law, and Bobby Charlton found his greatest form, and they built another great side, which won the League a couple of times and eventually won the European Cup in '68. So, the *club did recover but there was always the thing that Busby had never recovered emotionally. He was never the same man afterwards. People who knew him would say that, Johnny Giles, for example, who would have known him before the crash and afterwards."*

It was in March 1966, that Best's life truly changed forever. United beat Benfica 5-1 at the Stadium of Light in the quarter-finals of the European Cup and the teenage forward produced an exhilarating performance that yielded two goals. Afterwards, he was pictured jetting back into Manchester with a sombrero hat on. The papers christened him 'El Beatle'. George became 'Georgie'. He would later reflect that, from this moment, "life started to become crazy". The shy boy from Belfast, who was dismissed for being too quiet when Dunphy introduced him to a good-looking girl at a disco in 1961, would never be allowed to retreat into his own shell again. Best copper-fastened his reputation as the leading young talent in the world in 1968 by hitting the decisive first goal of extra-time in their eventual 4-1 European Cup final win over Benfica. A trio of Waterford players, Matthews, Hale and O'Neill, got a flavour for the life Best was leading when they guested for Drumcondra in the benefit match for John Whelan at Dalymount in August '68. Best was forced to position himself close to the sideline approaching the end of United's 2-1 win so he could make a quick and unimpeded beeline for the safety of the dressing room at the full-time whistle. The unprecedented box office appeal of Best, not to mention the pulling power of Law and Charlton, presented Waterford with the opportunity for a huge audience pay day. All three United players had been crowned European Player of the Year, between 1964 and 1968. In comparative terms, it equated to possessing Lionel Messi, Cristiano Ronaldo and Kaka in the one team and bringing them over here to play today. The only problem for Waterford was that United had been drawn out of the hat first, so the raging favourites would have home advantage for the opening leg. In practice, the Red Devils could easily put the tie to bed at Old Trafford and reduce the second leg in Ireland to a dull formality, severely affecting the attendance figure. The colour drained from

Waterford chairman Don Kennedy's face as he pondered that possibility. So, he picked up the phone, dialled Manchester United chairman Louis Edwards' number and chanced his arm with a request to play the first leg in Dublin to guarantee a bumper crowd. Edwards, presumably suspecting that United could beat Waterford anywhere of Kennedy's choosing, surprisingly agreed to the switch. Waterford's board now had another big call to make – where to play the game? There was no way compact Kilcohan Park, which only possessed seating for officials and the media, could deal with the frenzied public demand to see the biggest club fixture of the decade here. Dalymount Park was the obvious alternative, the ground where Shamrock Rovers had played the 'Busby Babes' in 1957 and where Ireland's home internationals were held. But Waterford officials were thinking even bigger and approached the IRFU about playing a one-off game at the home of Irish rugby, Lansdowne Road. The famous old ground possessed a greater seating and terracing capacity than Dalymount and could comfortably accommodate 50,000. While it was an innovative request, it risked getting Waterford offside with Irish soccer supporters in general. In latter years, Lansdowne Road became home to both International soccer and rugby fixtures but, before 1968, all major soccer games were held across the city at Dalymount. The Phibsborough venue was the undisputed home of soccer so, whatever about leaving Kilcohan Park for Dalymount, jettisoning home advantage in favour of a pay day at the home of Irish rugby could have been deemed heresy. Dissenters proved to be in the minority, however, and the sense of carnival and anticipation about the arrival of the greatest set of players in Europe dwarfed any ideological issues about the choice of venue.

ALFIE HALE: "The attitude was that we could have played them in Kilcohan Park with about 10,000 people attending. We could have went to Dalymount either. But we said, 'Look, this will be the first ever soccer match in Lansdowne Road', what a game to have there. Secondly, because Denis Law, George Best and Bobby Charlton had already been crowned European Players of the Year, getting to play

Manchester United was an incredible draw. So, Waterford opted to go to Lansdowne Road because they said, 'This is a national celebration as much as anything else'."

SHAMIE COAD: "When it was all sorted out it was something fantastic to be able to look forward to. You knew that, just to be on the same pitch, any pitch, as them was going to be the highlight of your life."

Waterford tried to treat the build-up to the game like any other. But it was impossible for everyone associated with the club not to keep one eye on United's form across the water in the preceding weeks. Optimists around Waterford suggested that United were suffering from a post-Europe hangover as Busby's side began the season with four losses, two draws and just three wins before arriving in Dublin. Waterford, admittedly competing against inferior opposition, blitzed the 1968/69 League of Ireland season from start to finish, beating Cork Hibs 5-0 on the opening day and going on to win sixteen of their twenty-two games, losing just twice. The managerial baton had been passed to player/manager Maguire, but Waterford still remained the market leaders in Irish football. Their style of play won them an army of admirers, inside and outside the county boundaries, as they finished the season with sixty-eight goals, twelve more than second placed Rovers and an average of over three a game.

PETER THOMAS: "We used to be a side that would have scored sixty or seventy goals a season, and probably let in ten or twenty. We would regularly give the other side a goal start before we'd start to play. The whole philosophy of it was that if we're going to score three, you'll have to score four to beat us. We were getting on average around 7,000, I'd say, at games, which they weren't getting in the second division in England at the time. With a small town of around 30,000, Kilcohan Park was the place where everyone wanted to go every second Sunday to watch Waterford. It was only in the latter years that the crowds started to dwindle. Regularly you'd drive up to the stadium and the car park and you'd have to be there an hour before the game to get a spot."

From the moment the European Cup draw was made on the morning of July 10 in Berne, Switzerland, a workload fell upon the club that no other League of Ireland side had experienced. That first afternoon, a request came in to Waterford from a foreign travel agency for two hundred stand tickets for the game. A mountain of letters built up with requests from individuals, clubs and groups in all thirty-two counties to purchase tickets. Enquiries arrived from Wales, Scotland, England, the United States and even Australia. In order to cope with the deluge, Waterford hired a team of experienced clerical staff who worked for eight weeks solid, dealing with ticket demands and tying up all sorts of loose ends associated with the fixture. Nobody was left in any doubt that hosting Manchester United was big business. United had a World Cup winning half-back in tough tackler Nobby Stiles. He was in the England team with Charlton when they beat West Germany at Wembley in 1966. Alongside Stiles were the likes of Best, Law and another World Cup winner, Charlton, but Irish soccer fans were keen to get a glimpse of United's Irish full-back Tony Dunne. He won the FAI Cup with Shelbourne in 1960 before moving to United for IR£5,000. Dunne was rated by Busby as the finest left full-back of his generation. He won the FA Cup with United in 1963 and claimed League medals in 1965 and 1967, but his greatest display in a red shirt was against Benfica in the European Cup final at Wembley. Scottish international half-back, Paddy Crerand, played alongside Dunne in United's defence during that famous win and rated his colleague highly.

PADDY CRERAND: "Tony was one of the best full-backs that ever played for Manchester United. He was tremendous. He, unfortunately, doesn't get the credit he deserves because when you've got George Best and Bobby Charlton and Denis Law in your team people don't realise how good you are, not that it bothered Tony. But he was a fantastic full-back. There weren't many better. If you picked a United team and had to include the very best full-backs in it, he'd be in it."

The cost of a ticket to watch Waterford entertain United's star troop at Lansdowne Road was initially set at five shillings. But that had to be reduced to four shillings, or twenty pence, at the behest of the FAI who claimed five shillings was too expensive. It was already going to be a costly occasion – both for individuals in Waterford who had to fork out fifteen shillings for the train to Dublin and for business owners who were stripped of much of their staff for the day. Lansdowne Road wasn't yet equipped with floodlights so the game had to be played at 5.45pm, meaning those leaving Waterford had to do so early in the day. On the evening of September 18, the occasion and the atmosphere was everything the 48,000 football fans lucky enough to get their hands on tickets hoped it would be. Outside Lansdowne Road, traders hawked giant posters of Best to infatuated young United fans. Match programmes were dispensed for a shilling each and became collectors' items in years to come. Nervous energy pulsed through the thronged streets. The carnival atmosphere outside the ground was completely at odds with a row that raged among the travelling Waterford players and officials over appearance money. Tension hung in the air as the stand-off continued during a police escort from their team base in Naas right up until shortly before the game in the dressing room.

PETER THOMAS: "What people don't know is that, forty-five minutes before kick-off, we weren't even stripped or changed. We were fighting over our bonus. They wanted to give us a hundred pounds for the two legs. We were looking for one hundred pounds for each leg. That is my very clear memory. We'd been negotiating that for two to three weeks prior to the game."

JOHN O'NEILL: "It was huge, huge money for us but to let it get to the stage it did was a disgrace to everybody involved. It should never, never have got to that stage in my opinion. It should have been sorted well before then. Fellas like Shamie Coad, Noel Griffin, myself, Paul Morrissey, Al Casey, we were never in it for the money. Now, we wouldn't have refused it if it came our way, but the whole thing became a sideshow which it never should have."

PETER THOMAS: *"Eventually one of the directors, Frank Davis, came in. He said, 'I'll cover that'. He was one of the few directors that was a players' man."*

JOHNNY MATTHEWS: *"We doubled our money! They wanted to give us fifty quid for each game, something like that, but we stuck 'em for a hundred for each game. We would have always gone out for the game, but we were sticking our necks out."*

It was hardly ideal preparation for what was the biggest match of most of the Waterford players' careers. Still, things weren't exactly ideal in the United dressing room approaching kick-off either.

PADDY CRERAND: *"I remember us having an awful job trying to get the gardai out of the dressing room before the game. You couldn't get them out. They were in there getting autographs. Matt wasn't bothered by it but we just couldn't get them out. I remember George even signing autographs on the side of the pitch just as the whistle was about to blow. I'm not sure if it was ball boys or police at that stage who were asking him, but he was signing away."*

On what was described in the following day's *The Irish Times* as a, "lush carpet of grass", United hit top gear almost immediately, shaking off their poor League form to stir the huge crowd swelled by the hundreds who'd scaled boundary walls to get in. After just eight minutes, Best shook off Maguire's challenge and played in Law who escaped Jackie Morley to bear down on goal. The inevitable duly materialised as Law struck to the net past Thomas who could only get a slight touch on the ball. Trailing so early in the game, there was the very real prospect of an embarrassing rout of Waterford in front of their fans. But, in one of the great performances turned in by the Blues in their glory era from 1966 to 1973, they managed to hold United to just two more goals. Before kick-off, McGeough had whispered in Law's ear, "You can score all the goals you like in England and Italy but you're getting nothing here tonight". Law, who'd signed from Torino for a then record Stg£115,000 in 1962, winked back, "Don't worry about me son, I'll be all right". And he was. Law scored all three of United's goals and walked away with the match ball. Not for the first time in a United shirt, however, it was Best who made the biggest mark with a piece of flair in the twenty-fourth minute that encapsulated his genius. Bobbing and weaving he kept close control of the ball outside the penalty area but the Waterford goal didn't appear in any grave danger.

ALFIE HALE: "Do I remember what happened? Will I ever forget it! I had a bird's eye view of it. I was positioned on the half-way line while they were attacking outside our box. Best took a ball on the outside of our penalty area. Myself and Nobby Stiles were up around midfield watching as he gets the ball, turns left, turns right, back again around more players but he still has his back to goal and about four players around him. Next thing, he just turns and bang! Peter Thomas is looking and going, 'Where's the ball?' It's behind him in the back of the net! It was incredible. It was disallowed because Denis Law was hovering for the rebound in the six-yard box and was offside. Under the rules as they apply today it would have been a perfect goal and would have stood. It would certainly have been one of the best goals ever seen."

JOHN O'NEILL: "He hit the ball from maybe twenty yards out and it just flew into the net. It was Denis Law, as far as I know, that was offside. But it was an absolute disgrace that they disallowed the goal because nobody saw the man offside. It just ended up in the net as far as we knew. No problem to Best. Bang!"

JOHNNY MATTHEWS: "After it was scored and it was ruled out for offside by Law, Best was coming back out and just said, 'Jesus Christ, that's about the fourth fucking time he's robbed me of a goal this season'."

PETER THOMAS: "To be perfectly honest I didn't see a bit of it going by me. He was over in the right wing position and he swivelled his hips and hit it at goal. It came back off the stanchion inside the goals and, only for Denis Law was standing in front of me, it would have stood. I never even seen the ball until it was coming back out."

PADDY CRERAND: "You know he did that so often that he probably didn't mind it being ruled out. Another one wasn't going to make a great deal of difference."

As it turned out, Best didn't score a legitimate goal over the two legs, a statistic goalkeeper Thomas still recalls with a grin to his team-mates whenever he meets them. But, that moment of inspiration was enough to convince anyone watching that he was the real deal, a world class finisher at the peak of his career. Law fitted into the same category and made it 2-0 for United when he headed home Brian Kidd's free-kick five minutes before the half-time whistle. In the fifty-third minute a steep hill became a mountain for Waterford to climb when Law claimed his third to put United into a commanding 3-0 lead. On this occasion, Maguire was dispossessed by Best, he played in Law who flicked a shot past Thomas. The three goal haul was no consolation for Law who'd heartbreakingly missed the European Cup final in May with a knee injury, but it served notice that his lethal instincts hadn't deserted him.

SHAMIE COAD: "You had the 'Holy Trinity' as they were called – Best, Charlton and Law. I always fancied Law in particular. He would have been my personal favourite down the years. Denis Law, a lovely, flashy, flamboyant fella and, boy, could he score. Law, to me, was great."

Shortly after Law's third goal, United were awarded a penalty. Best was Waterford's tormentor again as he drew the foul from full-back Peter Bryan in the box. Law stepped up to take it but, instead of making it four for the night, his shot hit the post and went wide. From the most perilous of situations Waterford drew renewed hope. Thomas had leaked three goals but couldn't be faulted for any of them and had pulled off several excellent stops from Law and Best. Morley, too, who'd transferred to Waterford after a long career with Cork Hibs – whom he'd captained for a lengthy spell – was generally holding the defence together well on a busy evening. Matthews, as he'd prove in subsequent European ties against Glasgow Celtic and Real Madrid, was capable of mixing it with the very best and, from time to time, emulating his idol at Benfica, Eusebio. In the sixty-fifth minute, winger Matthews conjured one of those magical moments to give the Waterford support what they'd travelled to Dublin for, a precious goal. Al Casey's initial shot was blocked, allowing Matthews to pick up possession on the edge of the box and strike a shot past Jimmy Rimmer, only just on as a replacement goalkeeper for Alex Stepney. Scoring against United meant everything to Matthews, the Coventry native whose father also played on the flanks for the local club. Johnny was eleven years old when the Munich Air Disaster occurred in February 1958 and, like most other football-mad school kids in England at the time, developed a deep fascination with the fortunes of the mortally wounded Lancashire club. He kept a scrapbook of the various clippings about the crash and could scarcely believe, ten years on, that he was playing against boyhood idols such as Charlton and Bill Foulkes, let alone scoring against them.

JOHNNY MATTHEWS: "I remember picking the ball up and, for one of the few times in the game, managing to elude Tony Dunne. I just cut inside and cracked the ball from the edge of the box. It flew into the top left-hand corner. It put a bit of pride back in the whole thing. The fans were well pleased. It was a great feeling."

The jubilant fans at Lansdowne threatened to overflow onto the pitch as Matthews wheeled away in delight and accepted the plaudits. Somehow, they were contained and the game restarted, leaving Waterford twenty-five minutes to capitalise on their momentum and reaffirm the European tie as an ongoing concern for United. Waterford had only managed three shots at United's goal in the first-half, and only one of them actually troubled Stepney. But they never gave up on their commitment to play exciting, attacking football, which had allowed them to eventually gain a foothold in the tie with Matthews' goal. The fact that many of the Waterford players were part-time compared to United's full-time regime should have been apparent in the last twenty minutes, but it wasn't, as the 'home' side pushed for a second. Six minutes from the full-time whistle, Hale hit the crossbar with a header when Rimmer was hopelessly beaten.

ALFIE HALE: "A few years ago I met Denis Law when he was over in Limerick for a function where he was the guest of honour. A few of us were together having a few drinks and I got talking to Denis. He started talking about the game at Lansdowne. I said, 'Sure you couldn't remember me'. He said, 'I do remember you. We were winning 3-1 and you put in a header with about ten minutes to go that hit the bar.' Honestly, I had forgotten about the chance. But he said, 'I remember it vividly because I was up the other end and it could have been 3-2. What might have happened in the last few minutes then anybody knows'. So, it certainly wasn't a stroll, from their point of view."

The score finished 3-1 to United. United were relatively happy with the result. Waterford felt they had given a good performance and hadn't let themselves down in the eyes of the nation, either.

ALFIE HALE: "We went into the game saying, 'Look, let's be honest, we're not going to go through to the second round of the European Cup on a two-legged affair with Manchester United'. So, we said we'd give it all we had. That wasn't to say that we'd just abandon all our defensive strategies, but we weren't going to close up shop and kill the game, either, in front of fifty-odd thousand. We took a kind of a strategy between having a right go at it and trying to defend well, too. I think the result of the match, 3-1, was a reflection of the game and of the amount of possession that both sides had."

Waterford had two weeks before the second leg at Old Trafford to come up with a plan to reel in United. In the meantime, United's attentions shifted to Argentina and specifically Buenos Aires where they were scheduled to take on South American champions Estudiantes in the first leg of the Intercontinental Cup final. It proved a venomous tie. The hosts' ire was fuelled by England manager, Alf Ramsey's, famous claim – made two years earlier following the spiteful 1966 World Cup quarter-final – that Argentina, beaten 1-0, had played like "animals". Crerand, and the rest of the United players in Buenos Aires, bore the brunt of Ramsey's comment as they were, "pinched, punched and kicked while head-butt victim, Nobby Stiles, was sent off for dissent" in a 1-0 loss. The second leg at Old Trafford was even nastier with the pitch, according to a TV commentator, resembling a "bear pit" at stages. Best, hacked down for the umpteenth time, was sent off for a retaliatory punch on Jose Medina, who also saw red. Estudiantes drew that second leg 1-1 with Juan Ramon Veron, father of the future United midfielder of the same name, netting what proved the winner overall. Against the background of those encounters, the prospect of facing Waterford in between was warmly welcomed by the United fans. They greatly appreciated the Irish champions' commitment to clean, attacking football. As a result, 42,000 paid in for the second leg, even though the tie was already over in many people's minds. The huge turnout meant that, over the two legs of their European adventure, Waterford played in front of an audience of 90,000.

ALFIE HALE: "I was dead chuffed in Manchester because Vinny Maguire was injured so he asked me to captain the side. Bobby

Charlton and myself led the teams out onto the pitch and we got a fantastic reception."

Waterford's trepidation about performing in the Theatre of Dreams wasn't misplaced. They were treated like royalty off the field by a club that prided itself on its hospitality but, on the field of play, were subjected to a merciless beating. The European champions flexed their muscle on their home turf and beat shell-shocked Waterford, 7-1. They did have to wait until the thirty-seventh minute before Stiles opened United's account with a rare goal. But, in the space of thirty, second-half minutes, Law knocked in four goals – one better than his Lansdowne Road hat-trick. The strikes ensured that Law finished three ahead of Johan Cruyff as top scorer in Europe with nine goals at the end of the campaign. Class may have trumped courage on the night but, in the sixty-eighth minute, trailing 9-1 on aggregate, Waterford's perseverance finally paid off when Casey netted to double their tally over the two legs. There was also consolation in the fact that Casey's deft chip from the edge of the box over Stepney's head was, perhaps, the goal of the night.

ALFIE HALE: "Al Casey was a shift worker in the local paper mills. He did stints of four to twelve and eight to four, those kinds of hours. He was also the sort of guy that wasn't easily impressed by anybody. Anyway, I think it was Paddy Crerand or Nobby, one of the boys, that got over to him after he scored. At this stage of the game we were all quite familiar with each other after the first game in Dublin and having got to know each other a bit. Al wouldn't get up after scoring, he was milking the applause, taking it all in. One of the United boys says, 'Look, Al, you've got your goal, brilliant goal, great, now let's get on with it'. Al says, 'Go and fuck off! You're playing golf in the morning. I'm on four to twelve in the paper mills'."

Charlton had the last word over the contest with an eighty-fourth minute goal to close out the scoring and seal a 10-2 aggregate win for United. Yet, for anyone familiar with Waterford in this era, it won't have surprised them to read a report stating, "One of the things which made this landslide defeat a little more palatable was Waterford's ability to play attractive football even while being heavily over-run." Waterford won many friends in defeat at Old Trafford and what followed at the final whistle will never be forgotten by the visiting players. All 42,000 supporters gave them an ovation off the field. The United players reacted to their fans' gesture by forming a guard of honour for Waterford as Hale led his team mates off the field. It wasn't meant as a patronising act and wasn't interpreted as one. Rather, it was a mark of appreciation from both the United supporters and their players for the efforts of a team that never deviated from a commitment to honest, attractive football. A defensive approach would have served Waterford better on the scoreboard but that would have meant denying their instincts to entertain.

ALFIE HALE: "You could say what they did was easy to do because they'd had a comfortable win over us but there was more to it than that. There was an identity association with the Irish for Manchester United. It was about Liam Whelan, all the guys who'd made connections between Ireland and Manchester United. It just went deeper than the match itself. It went deeper with the supporters."

SHAMIE COAD: "If you played the same teams tomorrow it would end up the same way because we would play the very same way. It was our own brand of football and wherever it took us, it took us."

As the two sets of players departed for their dressing rooms they chatted openly. Best asked Matthews if he and any of the Waterford lads fancied hitting the town afterwards. Matthews was up for it but had already arranged a meal with his parents. A few of the other Waterford players were in the same boat.

JOHNNY MATTHEWS: "Best said, 'Look, don't worry, I'll come back later on and collect you'. He came back in a red Jaguar, two-seater, and picked us all up. I think we got about five in it! This was before you had big bouncers on the doors. The little peep holes had just come in for them to monitor who was outside. Georgie just pulled up outside the first club, climbed out and up the steps to the club. The boys are looking through the peep hole, next thing the door opened, they all stood back and we trotted in behind Georgie, like Snow White and the Seven Dwarfs!"

PETER THOMAS: "He [Best] was a very sorry sight, actually. He was sat in the corner, tucked away in the corner out of the spotlight. Rodney Marsh came in and joined him."

PADDY CRERAND: "It's great to hear George treated the Waterford lads well. But you'd expect that from George. In fairness, he was probably the only one who would have known where to go on a Wednesday night as well. We were all married. We wouldn't have known where to go on a Wednesday night. George would have known all the places in the city. I didn't realise he took them all out. They must have been thrilled because, let me tell you, if George took you into town you were getting in for free. You didn't pay in anywhere or put your hand in your pocket when you were with George."

United didn't retain the European Cup after getting past Waterford. They were beaten 2-1 on aggregate by AC Milan in the semi-final and finished the League a dismal eleventh. The following year, Busby stepped down as manager though he returned for a brief period in 1970/71. United's poor League finish in 1969 was the beginning of an alarming fall from grace that shocked everyone in football. They finished the following seasons eighth, eighth, eighth, eighteenth and, in the 1973/74 season, second from bottom, suffering relegation for the first time ever. On the final day of that season Law, now playing for their neighbours and rivals Manchester City, scored against United with a typically cunning back flick. It was the one goal in his career he didn't celebrate. United's dramatic tail spin into Division 2 was heart wrenching for fans to witness, particularly on the back of their European climax just six years earlier. But nothing could compare with watching the descent of Best into a battle with alcoholism that finally claimed his life when he died from multiple organ failure in 2005. He enjoyed the most fruitful years of his career in his early-twenties and, at just twenty-eight, somehow found himself playing non-league football with Dunstable Town. During his short time there he played a friendly against Cork Celtic whom Hale was now playing for.

ALFIE HALE: "I met him in the corridor before the game and we looked at each other. He says, 'What are you doing here?' I just turned and said to him, 'What are you doing here? Whatever about me, I'm entitled to be here, it's Dunstable against Cork Celtic'. He was the one who shouldn't have been there. He was one of the game's greats. It was a sad situation when you saw that waste of talent."

PADDY CRERAND: "I'll always remember George as a lovely fella and as quiet as anything. The reputation he got from the media was over the top, maybe not at the latter end of his career when he was done but at the beginning of his career he was a great professional, a lovely kid as well. It was just that he lost his way when he got into his late-twenties."

The European encounters between Waterford and Manchester United resulted in a solid and lasting friendship between the two clubs. United came over the following May to play Waterford again in a friendly. At the tail end of his career, Charlton played for Waterford briefly in 1976 while Shay Brennan had a longer and more successful stay as player/manager, arriving as a thirty-three-year-old in August 1970 after United released him. Born to Irish parents, the full-back played nineteen times for the Republic and captained the team. He won League medals with Waterford in the 1971/72 and 1972/73 seasons. The latter title was the last won by Waterford who, in the early 1980s, lengthened their name to Waterford United. The 1973 success was the end of a vintage era that saw Waterford win six Leagues in eight years, but no FAI Cup. Their great rivals, Shamrock Rovers, won six FAI Cups in a row between 1964 and 1969, but no League. Rovers' Cup run was a historic achievement which may never be repeated, but Waterford were truly the team of that generation. In 1970, two years after playing Manchester United, they hit the jackpot again when they were drawn to play Glasgow Celtic in the second round of the European Cup, after beating Glentoran. Jock Stein's Celtic, dubbed the 'Lisbon Lions' on the back of their 1967 European Cup final success over Inter Milan in the Portuguese capital, hammered Waterford 7-0 in the first leg.

JOHNNY MATTHEWS: "For the second leg the Scottish papers did a headline, 'Come and see the massacre of the leprechauns'. We led 2-0 at half-time! Our trainer and kit man at the time was a big Celtic fan. He was late coming out for the second half and Celtic had already pulled one back. They got two more to beat us 3-2 and I'll never forget him jumping up and down at the end thinking we'd got a 2-2 draw in Glasgow! All you could do was laugh. They are great memories and that's what sport is all about. I mean, Waterford played two European Cup champions in the space of three seasons. Sure we'll never see the likes of that again."

EUROPEAN CUP

First round, first leg
September 18, 1968
Lansdowne Road, Dublin
Attendance: 48,000

Waterford: 1
(Matthews 65)

Manchester United: 3
(Law 8, 40 and 55)

Waterford: Thomas; Bryan, Griffin; Maguire, Morley, McGeough; Casey, Hale, O'Neill, Coad, Matthews.

Manchester United: Stepney (Rimmer, 56); Dunne, Burns; Crerand, Foulkes, Stiles; Best, Sadler, Charlton, Law, Kidd.

Referee: W.J. Mullan (Scotland).

First round, second leg
October 2, 1968
Old Trafford, Manchester
Attendance: 42,000

Manchester United: 7
(Stiles 37, Law 41, 47, 60 and 71, Burns 68, Charlton 84)

Waterford: 1
(Casey 69)

Manchester United: Stepney; Dunne, Burns; Crerand, Foulkes, Stiles; Best, Sadler, Charlton, Law, Kidd.

Waterford: Thomas; Bryan, Griffin; Morrissey, Morley, McGeough; Casey, Hale, O'Neill, Coad, Matthews.

Referee: J.P. Campos (Portugal).

CHAPTER 3

ATHLONE TOWN VS AC MILAN
October 22 and November 5, 1975

"1975, that's thirty-five years ago! But I'll tell you a good one. I was down there at a match in Athlone not so long ago and I stayed a few nights. We were in a bar, Nuts Corner, and I was with a friend of mine who has a betting shop down there. He was pointing out the name of a horse in the paper and I said, 'Wait 'til I put my glasses on'. There were two army fellas sitting at the counter. One of them said to the other fella, 'It's a pity he hadn't the glasses on when he took the penalty against Milan!' It was good banter. In fairness, how could you answer that?"
JOHN MINNOCK

John Minnock stooped down and planted the ball in the muck. There was less than an hour left in the 1974/75 League of Ireland season, when Athlone Town were awarded a free-kick twenty yards out. A goal would steady the nerves nicely. Technically, a scoreless draw was all Athlone required to finish second in the table behind runaway League winners, Bohemians. With that, Athlone's highest ever League finish, would come qualification for Europe just six years after being accepted back into the League of Ireland. But, Athlone weren't about to tempt fate by playing for a stalemate, not when their opposition on the final day of the season was Cork Hibernians, the indomitable force of the early-1970s, who could, themselves, leap-frog into second by winning. Minnock placed the ball and backed slowly away as he considered the packed six-man wall assembled in front of him. Regardless of the odds against him hitting the net, the Athlone faithful always fancied Minnock's chances when he took aim. The former Charlton Athletic midfielder-cum-forward had been their prized and revered asset ever since the club shelled out IR£2,000 to bring him home from England in 1970. The fact that Minnock then stuck by the Midlanders when Waterford, Shamrock Rovers and Cork Hibs all made approaches in the subsequent years, only endeared the inter-league player further to the Town. The wall collectively leapt as Minnock wrapped his right foot around the ball and sent it spinning through the air on a right to left flight plane. From just outside the left edge of the penalty area the space he needed to send the ball into seemed little more than the size of a postage stamp. Cork players craned their necks and lunged at air as the ball flashed by their despairing bodies. Minnock watched as the ball then dipped violently into the far corner of the net beyond goalkeeper Joe O'Grady. The ground shook beneath the weight of celebration and, for an instant, it felt like St Mel's Park had just been pulled into the centre of Europe. Cork Hibs won a penalty in the second half of that game but even a 1-1 draw wouldn't have been any use to them. They needed the win. In any case, they missed the decisive kick, failing to do what Minnock had done from nearly twice the distance out with a wall in front of him. John Lawson looked on in anguish as his spot-kick hit the butt of the post and ricocheted away to safety. It finished 1-0 to Athlone. "That Minnock should have the distinction of tucking away the decisive goal was wholly appropriate for over the years nobody has better typified Athlone's fight for identity", wrote Peter Byrne in *The Irish Times* the following morning.

CYRIL BARNICLE: "I remember when John came first. I'd been a young lad watching the games and you could actually feel the excitement rising in the crowd when he had the ball, the same as if you were at a big match in England. He was wonderful."

The revival of Athlone Town as a competitive force was warmly greeted in a garrison town with a rich tradition for football. Athlone initially joined the League of Ireland in the 1922/23 season as the only non-Dublin side in a twelve-team League. They won the Free State Cup, later renamed the FAI Cup, in 1924 before pulling out of the League in 1928. Exiled for over forty years, it wasn't until 1969 that club officials convinced League authorities to re-admit them. In May of 1969, a vote of League of Ireland Management Committee delegates was returned seven to six in favour of bringing Athlone Town and Finn Harps into the League. Athlone secured the Leinster Senior Cup in their first season back with Jackie Mooney scoring a hat-trick in a 4-0 win over Shelbourne. But three consecutive tenth place League finishes more adequately reflected their growing pains in those early years. A consistent turnover of managers – including Billy Young, Mick Dalton, Doug Wood and Jackie Quinn – indicated, in one sense, a burning ambition on the part of the club to improve their lot. But it wasn't until the arrival of Amby Fogarty, in November 1974, following Quinn's dismissal, that things truly began to pick up for them. Fogarty's was a sensible appointment. The Dubliner had managed several clubs since returning from a distinguished playing career in England in the late-1960s. Of particular interest to Athlone was the work he'd done at Flower Lodge, laying the foundations for the League success and back-to-back FAI Cup wins that Cork Hibs would enjoy under Dave Bacuzzi. The notion that Fogarty, a strict disciplinarian, may invigorate Athlone in a similar manner excited club officials. On his first weekend as manager, Athlone beat Limerick 4-0. Minnock scored twice and set up a penalty. The awakening had begun. Such was the pace of change that, by the end of that first season, Fogarty's Athlone had remarkably secured second place in the table and European football, finishing on a high with the defeat of Cork Hibs. It amounted to an increase of nine places on their fourth from bottom finish the previous season. By now, nineteen-year-old Cyril Barnicle was living his dream. The fan had turned player.

CYRIL BARNICLE: *"I really enjoyed working under Amby when he came in. He was a very charismatic manager. He had played with Brian Clough and he modelled himself on Brian Clough, as far as we could see. He was a brilliant motivator. If you can imagine what Clough was like, then Amby was a sort of a version of that – soccer mad and ruthless on a football pitch. He was able to motivate anybody. He could pick up players that wouldn't be hugely well known and get the best out of them in the way that Clough did. That was his main thing, picking up players that mightn't feature on other teams and instilling something in them. Whether it was confidence he gave lads or what, I don't know, but, more often than not, they performed above themselves for him. He came from a very professional background, too, and we'd be doing all sorts of moves around throw-ins and free-kicks, which was pretty much new. It was great. You'd learn so much just listening to him. Then he was a great motivator on top of that."*

Fogarty's first great achievement at Athlone was in pulling a disparate bunch of players together and imbuing them with an unlikely sense of team. Minnock, Barnicle, Noel Larkin and Pauric Nicholson all lived locally, but others came from as far away as Cork, in Carl Humphries' case, and Derry, from where Joe Healy, Andy Stevenson and John Duffy commuted. A clutch of the players lived and trained in Dublin where Fogarty was based. Ironically, Fogarty's desire to commute from the capital was one of the reasons he'd parted company with his previous employers, Limerick United. Ex-Bohemians and Shamrock Rovers striker, Paul Martin, was one of the Dublin-based players.

PAUL MARTIN: "We trained in Dublin during the week but, on Saturday morning about eleven o'clock, Fogarty would collect us and we'd head down to Athlone. Usually there was me, Eugene Davis, Kevin Smith and Terry Daly. We were all fellas that had played for Shamrock Rovers, the four of us. Mick O'Brien was our goalkeeper and he was also part of the group that would go down. We'd head off to Athlone and train in the afternoon, then stay in either a hotel or in this B&B out on the old road into Athlone. On the Sunday you might do a bit in the morning, practise the free-kicks, corners, whatever. Then you'd play the game."

EUGENE DAVIS: "Amby used to bring us down in his car. We'd be wanting a few jars after the match and Amby would be saying to us, 'Be at the end of the road at half seven or you'll be left there – I'm not waiting around'. And he meant it. If we weren't there we'd be left in Athlone. It was a two-hour car journey at that time, so you made sure you were on time. People have compared him to Clough and I would agree with that. If he had something in his mind you weren't going to change it. It's like the famous Clough phrase where he says, 'Yeah, I listen to the lads all right and then we agree to do it my way'. Amby wouldn't have been too far different."

Clough and Fogarty were forces of nature. They played together at Sunderland and, by virtue of their complementory, abrasive, personalities, remained close friends throughout their respective careers. Fogarty was best man at Clough's wedding. On either side of the Irish Sea their management careers unfolded similarly. While Clough was leading a revolution at Derby County's Baseball Ground that would culminate in their first League success, Fogarty was working his own oracle with Cork Hibs. Clough went on to earn legendary status across the continent by claiming back-to-back European Cup titles in 1979 and 1980 with Nottingham Forest. Over in Ireland, Fogarty was turning Athlone around in the mid-1970s. Their relationship paved the way for one of the most successful transfers the League of Ireland has known, that of Dave Wigginton to Cork Hibs in 1968. 'Wiggy' was an apprentice at Derby but the story goes that he fell out with Clough after streaking to first place in a cross country training run. On the pitch, 'Wiggy's' explosive pace cut through Irish defences like a hot knife through butter in the late-1960s and early-1970s and he scored a hat-full of goals. But, it didn't impress Clough who reckoned the teenager must have cheated in the race to finish so far ahead of his team-mates! The suggestion led to a row which Fogarty was happy to defuse by taking 'Wiggy' off Clough's hands. Fogarty worked with midfielder Carl Humphries at another Cork club, Cork Celtic and, when the time was right, signed up the former West Ham United man to the Athlone cause.

An exciting Town team laced with goal scoring potential had been forged, ahead of their opening gambit in Europe. Humphries, Davis, Larkin and Minnock were all capable goal getters while striker Martin, after dropping down to the Leinster Senior League, enjoyed a rebirth of his career in the midlands.

PAUL MARTIN: "Minnock was a great player at the time. They were all good players really and everybody got on well. The Dublin lads got on well with the Derry lads, and so on. There were no real cliques. There was just a good buzz around the club and the people in the town responded to that. They were happy. It's a great feeling when people are happy because you're playing well for their club and when you get a town like Athlone behind you. My football memories, my best memories, are the couple of years I had down there. They were the happiest times of my life."

The UEFA Cup first-round draw was something of an anti-climax. Athlone would face Valerengen of Norway. Few in the Westmeath town had even heard of them. The two clubs actually shared comparable qualification tales. Valerengen also needed a result, a win in their case, from the final round of the Norwegian first division to claim the last UEFA Cup spot. They duly pulled it off, beating Hamarkam 2-1 at home in Oslo, to finish third in the table ahead of Brann who lost their final game. It was a major achievement as, like Athlone, Valerengen had risen from relative obscurity in a short period of time. In 1968, they were relegated from the top flight and achieved that third-place finish in their first season back. Athlone were at home first and, before a ball was even kicked at St Mel's Park, they claimed a mini victory. The game was supposed to be played on Wednesday afternoon, September 17, but they successfully pushed for the game to be put back by twenty-four hours to Thursday to accommodate the weekly half-day in Athlone and the surrounding towns. Club director Seamus O'Brien predicted that, because of the new arrangement, "I am confident that St Mel's Park will hold a record crowd". It wasn't quite a record but 4,000, roughly half the capacity, witnessed a first for Athlone, all the same, as they skated to a 3-1 victory. In a rare accomplishment for a League of Ireland side, let alone European first timers, Athlone outclassed their opponents in virtually all sectors of the pitch. Aside from the three goals they did get, they also struck the woodwork twice and Larkin had a goal disallowed. The missed chances meant that the victory wasn't certain until Davis was shifted from midfield into attack in the second-half and swooped for a brace of goals following Paul Martin's opener. Two weeks later, on a snowy, windswept Oslo evening borrowed from the depths of Scandinavian winter, Athlone finished the job with a 1-1 draw. Minnock's quick pass out of defence set Martin on the way for a brilliant twentieth-minute goal as he outpaced two defenders in a forty yard sprint before burying the ball high into the net. The concession of a fifty-fourth minute equaliser barely took the gloss off a wonderful first excursion into Europe. Athlone had effectively sailed through to the second round on a 4-2 aggregate score line.

PAUL MARTIN: "I scored in both legs. It's something I'm very proud of, one of my greatest achievements, I suppose, in football. When we went one-nil up out there, I knew that was a big thing because it meant they needed to score three then and it was hard to see them doing that."

Pauric Nicholson, now a Regional Development Officer for the FAI in the midlands, was an unused sub for Athlone in Oslo.

PAURIC NICHOLSON: "For me, being local and from the town, it was just incredible, to be playing and winning in Europe. I was in Norway last year at a coaching conference. I visited the Valerengen club and it brought back great memories for me."

At the following morning's draw in Zurich, the name of Athlone Town was tossed into a drum alongside thirty-one other sides. It was an era before group stages and mass qualification so the quality was high even in the earlier rounds. FC Porto, Ajax, Liverpool, Roma, Lazio and Barcelona were all possible opponents. The biggest name of all was the one that was pulled out immediately after Athlone Town – AC Milan.

PAURIC NICHOLSON: "We could hardly grasp it. AC Milan were as big then as they are now and, in many ways, they were even bigger then because Italian clubs were the top clubs in Europe at the time. English clubs have taken over now with the money they have but, at the time, AC Milan and Inter Milan and teams like that, Juventus, they were really the top teams. So, for us to be drawn against them was an amazing thing."

Fogarty initially expressed an opinion that the game should be played at Lansdowne Road. The gate money, he reasoned, could then be ploughed back into upgrading St Mel's. There was little appetite to take the biggest game in the club's existence out of Athlone, however, and the idea died a quick death. The prospect of hosting Milan at their tiny ground was at once thrilling and blood curdling. An inescapable thought prevailed; in 1969, while Athlone had been lobbying for top flight football to return to St Mel's, European Cup holders Milan were in the process of collecting the Intercontinental Cup title making them, effectively, champions of the world. In 1973 and 1974 the black and red team from Milan reached two European Cup winners' Cup finals, winning the first in '73. Suddenly, Athlone's Leinster Senior Cup success didn't seem quite so impressive. Many names stood out from the Milan team sheet but none more so than forward Gianni Rivera, Italian football's 'Golden Boy' and the 1969 European Footballer of the Year. He scored twice in the knockout stages of the 1970 World Cup finals as Italy reached the decider only to be gunned down by the majesty of Pele, Carlos Alberto and the rest of Brazil's dream team. The name of Enrico Albertosi similarly echoed around the continent in the 1970s. The veteran Milan goalkeeper played every minute of World Cup '70, keeping the great Dino Zoff on the bench. Athlone's goalkeeper, Mick O'Brien, couldn't claim to hold the same sort of international renown as

Albertosi but did, in his own unique way, entertain millions of sports fans who tuned into British TV in the mid-'70s. On the final day of March, 1974, O'Brien assumed the position between the sticks as normal for Athlone in an FAI Cup semi-final against Finn Harps at Oriel Park. Athlone took a 5-0 hammering but the score line wasn't what made the occasion memorable. In fact, what sports fans watching ITV's 'Big Match' and BBC's 'Celebrity Sports Quiz' were asked was, "What happened next?" when, at 2-0 down and the ball at the other end of the field, O'Brien trotted mischievously around to the back of his goals. Jim Murphy, in his book, 'The History of Dundalk FC, the First 100 Years', supplies the answer. "He was seen nimbly climbing up the netting from behind, balancing himself for a moment, taking careful aim and then jumping down on the bar – reducing the structure to a pile of kindling wood. Whilst the PA announcer was adding to the comedy by asking, 'Is there a carpenter in the crowd?' referee Mulhall was taking a more serious view of the debacle. Mick O'Brien was getting his marching orders and he made his way to the dressing room to a thunder of boos and a shower of beer cans and apple stumps from the enraged Harps contingent in the stands. While deserving full marks for initiative, it should be pointed out that Mick's demolition effort was not his first argument with the goal structure – on the previous Sunday, he had successfully smashed the bar in a League game against the same opposition in Ballybofey! His Oriel Park efforts were in vain. After a second repair job, the game finished with one of the Athlone outfield players in goals, under strict instructions not to swing out of the crossbar."

CYRIL BARNICLE: "Ah, Mick was great. When I was younger and going to matches in St Mel's, half time would come and about a hundred young lads would storm onto the pitch, seven- and eight-year-olds. Mick would stay on at half time for a penalty competition. Young fellas, eight- or nine-year-olds, would queue up to take a penalty against Mick at half-time. None of the lads were interested in watching the match, they were just waiting for the ref to blow for half time so they could invade the goal nearest the stand. Mick would be there for the penalties, trying to save as many as he could, a great character. I remember another time we played in Drogheda at the Lourdes Stadium. There was nothing going on in the match at all, a real dull match. Jackie Quinn, who was manager of Athlone, tells this story ... he looked around and there was no sign of Mick in the goals. They used to have a running track around the pitch and there he was, sprinting up and down the running track while the match was going on. He was such a character. You wouldn't get a guy like that now. Mick might catch the ball out of the air and do two or three somersaults with it!"

O'Brien never lost his maverick spirit but his predilection for destroying goalposts, thankfully, passed. Athlone had enough to be doing sprucing up their ground for the visit of Milan without having to repair the goal frames. St Mel's Park was a hive of activity in the three weeks between the Valerengen success and the Milan tie. An army of officials, supporters, the local based players and even Fogarty – who cancelled his holiday plans – worked overtime to put a shine on the old ruin. Nobody was in any doubt that the ground was pitifully ill-equipped to host the Italian giants. The grandstand could satisfy two hundred at a squeeze and it took a marathon effort – and considerable expense – to raise the overall capacity to around 9,000. But the joy of it all was the sense of a community proudly pulling together to display its modest home in the grandest possible terms. It also beat playing the game at a Dublin venue which held no connection with fans who'd attended Leinster Senior League games at Mel's in the 1960s and who smiled at the irreverence of even contemplating a game against AC Milan there. Three days before the game, Cork Hibs arrived at St Mel's Park, the southerners inextricably linked to Athlone's European crusade. Athlone were sliding towards their second consecutive home defeat as they trailed 1-0 with six minutes left. Two surging runs down the left from Daly saved the day as he, firstly, set up Martin for a headed equaliser and then, with time almost up, won a penalty kick for Minnock to take. The local hero converted the spot kick with a strong right foot finish and ran away to the embrace of his team mates. Athlone had thieved a 2-1 win. Even more significantly, however, as time would prove, was the fact that a Milan spy attended the game and took detailed notes of Minnock's penalty kick, circling the words 'bottom left hand corner' after the ball flew in between the post and the 'keeper's outstretched arm. The following morning, the Milan team and full entourage touched down at Dublin Airport. They travelled in good mood on the back of a 1-1 draw away to Bologna in the Italian league, a result that kept them one behind joint leaders Juventus and Napoli. Between players, club officials, press and a specialist chef who did all their cooking here, the group spilled over into three figures. Another tangible reminder of the disparity between the two clubs was the list of requirements they'd submitted to Athlone after the draw was initially made; 300 reserved seats for the travelling party and guests as well as twenty working phone lines for journalists to file their copy. After setting them straight about the exact specifications – or, more to the point, limitations of St Mel's Park – Athlone officials hadn't the heart to answer the Italian's next question truthfully: "How far is Athlone's airport from Athlone 'city' centre?" A club official responded that 'Athlone Airport' was located on the periphery of the 'city', about a two-hour drive away! Within moments of clearing customs at Dublin Airport, three coaches whisked the Milan contingent away to their quarters in Athlone, The Hodson Bay Hotel.

PAURIC NICHOLSON: "Seamus O'Brien, he was a director with Athlone at the time. The chairman or the vice chairman of Milan came to him a couple of days before the game. He said he wanted to have a look at our facilities. Seamus was a business man in the town and said, 'No problem'. So he was driving him down to the pitch and, as he was driving along, the car broke down. This guy wouldn't have been too impressed with that for a start. Anyway, they got down to St Mel's Park, our home pitch. They were standing outside and your man didn't really seem impressed. He said to Seamus, 'Your training ground is very small'. That was our main pitch!"

For the purposes of Milan's visit, their training grounds were at the local rugby club. "As far as I am concerned," Fogarty stated, "they will have to make do with that". The battle lines had been drawn. Good news for Athlone came in the announcement of Milan's team. Rivera was available again after a short, self-imposed retirement but would leave it until the away leg to make his official comeback. International striker Luciano Chiarugi was injured and would also miss out so Franco Vincenzi, who scored their goal against Bologna, was named as a lone attacker. Fogarty had done his homework on Milan. He was good friends with Everton manager and future Northern Ireland boss, Billy Bingham, whose side was beaten 1-0 on aggregate by Milan in the first round. Bingham warned Fogarty that Milan's players could be brutal in the tackle and that they weren't unknown to dabble in the black arts of tackling over the top of the ball, flailing their elbows and generally roughing up the opposition. If there was one Milan player who could mix it, it was midfield general and Italian International Romeo Benetti – a cross between Roy Keane and modern-day Milan hard man, Genarro Gattuso. The original midfield 'guvnor' came in at number thirty in a 2007 timesonline.co.uk poll of 'Football's 50 greatest hard men'.

CYRIL BARNICLE: "Benetti was a rough nut, a physically very strong man, very muscular, like Gattuso all right but physically much stronger and much more dangerous. If he hit you with his strength he could break you. Gattuso, now, is tigerish but hasn't the same physical presence whereas this lad was very, very strong, like a little bull."

Doug Wood could only join Athlone on the morning of the game. In the eyes of his employers, his preparations for facing AC Milan came a distant second to his day job. The rest of the team assembled the night before. After a light session, they slept the peaceful sleep of men at ease with what lay ahead.

PAURIC NICHOLSON: "We knew we had a very good team. Amby Fogarty had gelled a good side together, no question about that."

EUGENE DAVIS: "Looking back at the players we had, I mean Humphries had been a few years with West Ham, Minnock was a great player, we had Noel Larkin and Doug Wood, 'Micko' in goals, Paul 'Sniffer' Martin, Terry Daly and Kevin Smith on the left. So, we had a good side. We were knocking around with the best of them in Ireland."

PAUL MARTIN: "My total memory of playing Milan, away and at home, was of having no real fear. Not actually thinking we were going to be tanked. Not believing necessarily that we were going to win but believing that we weren't going to be well beaten. Amby managed to convince us of that and I don't know how he did it. I could never figure out how he did that. I'd love to wake up and for it to go off in my head, or have this marvellous dream where it all comes to me, what he did. He just had confidence in you. I suppose that was really the thing."

CYRIL BARNICLE: "One thing that I remember is that there was no chance of anyone going out, now I was only a sub, thinking they were going to be hammered. Amby was able to gee people up and motivate fellas. It was the feeling that, 'These fellas aren't getting out of here without a good fight'. There was no such thing as, 'We're Athlone. They're AC Milan. They're going to walk all over us'. He had everyone well up for the match."

MICK O'BRIEN: "He had us going. When you were walking onto the park he had you thinking you were the same class as AC Milan."

A famous photo – reproduced on the front page of an *Athlone Voice* pullout in 2005 to mark the thirtieth anniversary of Milan's visit – shows the Italians stepping off the team bus in their tailored garb, casting out measured steps to avoid the pools of mud. A group of scruffy kids wearing wellington boots and bobble top hats gathered to watch, fastening their anoraks tightly as the rain drove in sideways across their cheeks. The Athlone Pipe Band and their mascot, a goat, led the teams onto the field. Gianni Rivera, twice a European Cup winner and a Euro '68 medallist with Italy, surveyed the sight in amusement and befuddlement as he skipped across the muddied surface in his beautiful clothes to the sanctuary of the dugout. There, he joined his old pal, Giovanni Trapattoni, a new addition to manager Nereo Rocca's backroom staff that also included future Italy manager, Cesare Maldini, Paulo's father. Rivera and Trapattoni formed a storied partnership during their playing days with Italy. Rivera was the goal scoring playmaker, Trapattoni the more impenetrable defensive midfield force whose task was to win him the ball. Trapattoni never forgot the scene that opened out before him at St Mel's Park and, thirty-three years later, when he was appointed Republic of Ireland manager, reflected fondly on his previous engagement in the country.

GIOVANNI TRAPATTONI: "It was in a little town, Athlone. I remember the pitch. There weren't many stands. All the people were in a line along the side of the pitch. The day was a very beautiful experience."

The goat was eventually led off the pitch to the sort of boisterous cheering that only a farmyard animal trotting by an impossibly glamorous football team preparing for a UEFA Cup tie can provoke. The players took their positions. Fogarty made just one change to the team that drew with Valerengen in Oslo, preferring Doug Wood to Joe Healy in a back four that also contained right-full John Duffy, centre-half Andy Stevenson and left-full Kevin Smith. When Athlone were defending, they would take a 4-5-1 formation with Carl Humphries, Eugene Davis and Noel Larkin manning the central midfield zone. When they were attacking, John Minnock and Terry Daly would push up either side of attacker Paul Martin. The best-laid plans almost foundered on a rocky first few minutes. A terrible pass from the tip off had Athlone in trouble and they gave away two frees in quick succession. Milan had the gusting wind at their backs and they, too, morphed effortlessly into a fluid 4-3-3 formation when raiding forward in those early stages, with Vincenzi their target man. After a few nervous minutes, the Athlone players composed themselves sufficiently to get to grips with their opponents and impose their own game plan. Those who'd been stunned into silence on the main terrace now came to voice and gave Athlone their full support. Bingham's warning to Fogarty about the ruthless streak that ran through the Milan team was well-founded. Athlone contributed to an entertaining first half by retaining possession and confounding expectation with neat passing movements on a heavy surface. Milan, unnerved by the opposition and their surroundings, opted for cold skulduggery at times.

PAUL MARTIN: *"Joe Haverty was Amby's assistant and before the game Joe had said, 'Close them down but don't get too tight because these guys will just do you with the elbow'. That's what one of them did to me. He clipped me with the elbow and I had to get stitched at half time."*

Eugene 'Pooch' Davis's job was to mark Milan's pit bull, Benetti.

EUGENE DAVIS: *"He gave me a bad auld gash right down the shin. We didn't wear shin guards at the time. They weren't compulsory so I didn't wear them, never did, until after that."*

Nicholson could play left-full or on the left wing, but the form of Smith and Daly in those positions kept him on the bench beside Barnicle. The pair got a perfect view of a spiteful game lowered in tone by the Italians.

PAURIC NICHOLSON: *"He [Benetti] was harder than Gattuso. He was ruthless. He had five or six tackles that were really over the top. He could have broken two or three of our players' legs in the first game. He was a ruthless, ruthless ... but he was a big powerful man, a powerful player. He looked a bit like Roy Keane."*

PAUL MARTIN: "I think, the way he seen it, he had to put his foot in when they were playing over here. In fairness to him, he wasn't a sort of home player. He did his kicking away from home, too."

After half an hour of an exciting game in a tindery, emotive setting, Davis wiggled free of Benetti in midfield and sent Daly haring away down the left wing with a diagonal pass. Daly made some ground and cut back inside onto his right foot, momentarily. Martin was the only man in the box among a battalion of defenders so, Daly, feigning to go right, dropped his left shoulder and darted into the left side of the penalty area. Nevia Scala was caught flat-footed by the turn of pace and an awkward lunge brought Daly tumbling down. The referee pointed to the spot. Athlone had, amazingly, won a penalty.

PAURIC NICHOLSON: "I was really the penalty taker at that time, but Kevin Smith had come in at the start of that season and taken my place. For the previous season I had always been the penalty taker and been very, very successful at taking them. So, John Minnock took the penalty."

JOHN MINNOCK: "Pauric would have taken them all right, but Pauric was out of the team for a while and we got a few so I took them."

The crowd on the grass bank only a few feet behind Milan 'keeper, Albertosi, jostled for the perfect viewing position as Minnock calmly walked up and placed the ball on the spot. Mick O'Brien crouched down on his hunkers at the other end of the field and looked on, putting his faith in Minnock to do what Pele, Gerson, Jairzinho and Carlos Alberto had all done in the 1970 World Cup final, and stick the ball past Albertosi.

MICK O'BRIEN: "Albertosi was a huge man, maybe six foot five. What struck me that day was his massive throw outs and kick outs.

He was putting his kick outs down at the other eighteen-yard box. But 'Minno' was a great player, too. He could really turn it on."

Minnock steadied himself, looked left to the referee and got the nod followed by a whistle which indicated he could proceed with his kick. Adrenaline coursed through his body. The noise around the ground reduced to a barely audible din in anticipation of the most famous goal in the club's history. There was no private debate in Minnock's mind about how he would take the kick. He'd simply shoot the ball low and left, just as he'd done three days earlier when he scored the winner against Cork Hibs.

JOHN MINNOCK: "I just went with what I was used to. I felt confident enough."

Minnock began his run towards the ball, taking three steps on the way to heaven but finding his own personal hell, as Albertosi, tipped off about what side he should dive to after the Cork Hibs game, dropped down low and right and clawed away a weakly struck effort. A Milan defender leapt in the air in celebration as the ball rolled out for a corner. Minnock was rooted to the spot where he stood. He threw his head back in anguish and cursed the heavens. It was a miss he would never live down.

JOHN MINNOCK: "They'd had a scout watching us playing the previous weekend. I'd got a penalty that day and had a habit of putting them to the 'keeper's right. So, when it came to the kick against Milan, Albertosi was nearly down waiting on it. Now, I didn't hit it great, but he saved it anyway."

The silence that followed was eerie, though the crowd soon picked up the chant again as Athlone restarted well and pushed even harder again for the opener. For all of Davis' endeavour, Daly's strong running and Minnock's attempts to atone for the penalty miss, they never truly cut open a disciplined Milan defence again. Larkin sent a cross-cum-shot across the goals early in the second-half, but there was no-one in the goalmouth to turn it home. The tackles continued to fly in hard from both sides, and the Danish referee booked two Milan players. Afterwards, Fogarty claimed four of them could have walked. His own captain, Duffy, was lucky to stay on the field after a reckless second-half tackle on Milan's most potent attacker, Vincenzi. The challenge drew a furious rebuke from the Italian entourage on the sideline.

EUGENE DAVIS: *"I remember John kicking their player. He caught him up around the chest with a boot. John was a tough man, too. He would have been along the lines of Benetti himself. It's actually on a film of the game I have. Trapattoni was part of the management team and they all came up from the dugout. There was nearly a free for all."*

Much of the play was bunched around midfield with Milan breaking out to enjoy their strongest period in the third quarter as Minnock and Humphries tired. Good defending, a dollop of luck and some wild finishing on Milan's part saved Athlone, who bravely regrouped to dominate the last twenty minutes. By that stage, however, they had resorted to long ball tactics from O'Brien which Milan's well-drilled defence comfortably dealt with. A game that deserved a goal finished scoreless. Athlone supporters weren't certain what the right emotion was. They settled on pride. Davis recently found a video of the game and had it transferred onto DVD. He sticks it on regularly to remind his family and friends that Athlone, a collection of postmen, builders, decorators, butchers and trades men, didn't just 'kick and rush' the Italians all afternoon.

EUGENE DAVIS: *"The great thing for me was, all the stories I heard afterwards about the people who'd come to watch us. I live in Dun Laoghaire and all the Italian chip shops from Blackrock to Shankill closed up for the day. They'd all headed down to Mel's. Even lads out of the corporation in Dun Laoghaire just said to the foreman, "Listen,* we're off to Athlone!" I had a busload of family that went down as well."

Con Houlihan described the gallant draw as, "a piece of life stranger than fiction". That evening, BBC TV's six o'clock News reported the insurgency that had taken place in the midlands garrison town. "The mighty Milan have been held." The announcement carried an unfortunate addendum, however, that would follow just about every report of the famous occasion for the next thirty-five years – "and John Minnock missed a penalty".

EUGENE DAVIS: "He's probably more famous for that than anything else. I'm just glad it wasn't me, to be quite honest with you. It's just one of those things, probably a lot of pressure on him, too. It was a pity. But then, who's to say if we had went one up that they wouldn't have come back and hit us for five? As it was, they might have been happy to sit on the nil-all draw."

CYRIL BARNICLE: "To be honest, in terms of John, I don't ever think about that penalty too much. I remember him as a really nice fella who was good me to me when I was a young lad. He was the man that brought the crowds to Athlone when he came back from Charlton. He was Athlone's biggest ever signing at the time. There was kind of a decision to make; would they spend so much money or not? The fact that they did spend the money on him meant they were heading for the big time. If they hadn't signed him, the whole thing mightn't have happened at all. For the four or five years before that, the crowds that John used to bring in were unreal. St Mel's would be packed out at times. It was a very compact stadium and it would be packed out. Literally packed. People would be jammed in like sardines and you could feel the atmosphere in the ground when John would get the ball."

The air was thick with retribution in the days that followed. Fogarty stood by his claim that Milan could have had several players sent off. The *Corriere della Sera* newspaper counter-claimed by stating, "We doubt whether at San Siro they (Athlone) will be able to finish the match with even five players if they use the same violence as in the first game". The verbal joust, coupled with the hung scoreline, lit the touch paper for a potentially explosive second leg. In the meantime, Athlone struggled to refocus on domestic matters. They drew 1-1 with Sligo Rovers, narrowly beat non-League Glebe North in the Leinster Senior Cup before losing 1-0 to Drogheda the day before they flew out to Milan. The Drogheda defeat left Athlone seventh in the table and Fogarty didn't spare the rod when he admitted their display was, "a lot of rubbish". The players' minds were, understandably, on the Milan game the following Wednesday and, when they touched down in northern Italy on Monday morning, they were, at least, finally permitted to give it their 100 per cent focus.

CYRIL BARNICLE: "When we'd played Valerengen we hadn't stayed in such a great hotel. I'd thought it was a fine hotel but Amby wasn't pleased with it. So, when we got to Milan he booked us into the poshest hotel in the place!"

PAURIC NICHOLSON: "We stayed in the Leonardo da Vinci Hotel. For us, at that time, it was something else. It was just outside Milan. There were two absolutely fantastic training pitches at the hotel. We used to train every morning. There'd be three or four hundred people out watching us."

The Athlone players were greeted by a familiar face on their first night in the hotel, actor Omar Sharif, an international icon who had starred in films like 'Doctor Zhivago', 'Lawrence of Arabia' and 'Mackenna's Gold'. Aside from acting, his passion was for the card game, bridge.

PAURIC NICHOLSON: "The night we arrived he was playing in a bridge tournament there. There was no security at that time and we were able to get in and get his autograph and sit with him. It was unbelievable. He was one of the biggest actors in the world. He made our night by telling us he was going to go to our game. He was the Brad Pitt of his day."

PAUL MARTIN: "Mick O'Brien has a photograph with his arm around Omar Sharif. 'Hi Omar, I'm Mick', I can just imagine it! Omar Sharif actually bought us a drink, three oranges. There was a bridge tournament on and, O'Brien being O'Brien, not the shyest man in the world, managed to sidle up to him and, fair play to the guy, he smiled and said, 'Yeah, I read that you were over to play'. Fair play, he bought us a few oranges at the bar and had a few words with us."

MICK O'BRIEN: "It was where all the film stars stayed and we had the pleasure of meeting him. I can't remember what he said to me, a nice man though. I was there with Carl Humphries in the lobby and 'Minno', I think. Someone says, 'There's Omar Sharif'. 'Ah,' I says, 'I'll get a photograph with this fella'. The next thing they all come over! It was a great experience. I don't drink but I had a mineral with him. He was sitting there for a while and then went off."

Everton had stayed in the same hotel when they played Milan and had recommended the facilities to Fogarty.

PAUL MARTIN: "We trained at the hotel, on the football pitches behind it. They gave us an interpreter who basically appeared at every session. It was, 'Hello, Mr Amby' each morning. We arrived on the Monday, trained that afternoon, twice again on Tuesday and were due to train on the Wednesday, something like that. After about three sessions, Fogarty got a bit teed off. He wanted to do his corners and his free-kicks and bits and pieces and thought this guy was maybe a spy. Amby was very paranoid about that sort of thing. So, after one of the sessions, your man says, 'Mr Amby, what time you train in the morning?' Amby says, 'ten o'clock'. Your man goes, 'Fine, I will see you in the morning'. When your man's gone, Amby turns to us and says, 'Right you effers, you're training at eight'. We were up training at eight o'clock and had practised all our set pieces when your man arrives at ten, as planned. He was shocked to see us. Amby just says, 'Sorry. We trained early'."

Sportswriters in Italy christened Athlone 'The Shepherds' on the rather jingoistic assumption that the players were all farmers. The almost light-hearted build up to the second leg took a turn for the austere on the morning of the game when the visiting players came to a shock agreement that they would walk off the field in protest if the sort of tackles, meted out by the Milan players in Ireland, were replicated and went unpunished again. A 'senior member' of the team told *The Irish Times* that if Milan, "are allowed to get away with nasty, vicious fouls by the referee we have already decided, in principle, to leave the field". It was a vow that, thankfully, they wouldn't have to follow through on. For the Milanese, the night held massive significance, not just because a place in the third round of the UEFA Cup was on offer, but because, after six months of isolation, Rivera would make his eagerly awaited comeback. The return of the thirty-two-year-old invested the game with new meaning for supporters as the 'Golden Boy' was idolised by Milan's supporters throughout the 1960s and 1970s in much the same way Paolo Maldini came to be a couple of decades later. Rivera had quit the previous March after being put up for sale but returned, as both player and club President, in November and spent another four years at the club.

CYRIL BARNICLE: "When we were coming into the stadium in the bus there were hundreds of bouquets of flowers at the entrance. We thought it was a memorial for some young person that had died – it was actually a welcoming back thing for Rivera."

The pulling power of Rivera was reflected in the fact that 42,500 Italians turned up for the game when just 20,000 had paid in the previous weekend to watch them beat Ascoli 4-0. The Athlone players listened in their dressing room as the crowd outside began chanting Rivera's name. Suddenly, they realised exactly how the Christians must have felt before they were led out and fed to the lions for the crowd's amusement in ancient Rome.

CYRIL BARNICLE: "I remember going out onto the pitch over there. Milan had beaten Everton in the previous round and this fella in the crowd with a claxon was roaring 'Fuck the Queen!' at us. He hadn't a clue where Athlone was. He thought we were English as well."

PAUL MARTIN: "We knew we were in trouble when they presented flowers to Rivera before the game. It was the referee that actually presented the flowers to him. We were looking at each other saying, 'We're up against it here lads'."

What followed was Athlone Town's finest hour. For sixty-three minutes, in fact, they held Milan scoreless and pooped what was meant to be the homecoming party of the year. Just two minutes in, Davis set the tone for a courageous Athlone display when he revived his personal feud with Benetti and put the big man on the turf with a crunching tackle.

EUGENE DAVIS: "It was near the sideline. The ball was going to him and I came in from behind and took the legs right from underneath him. He went up in the air and back down. I remember the crowd going spare. Peter Byrne (The Irish Times) *commented on it the next week. Somebody said to him, 'So was Benetti up to his old tricks?' Peter just said, 'To be honest with you, Eugene Davis hit him fairly hard and he was quiet after that'."*

Jubilation among the crowd at the sight of Rivera back in action hardened into frustration as Athlone held firm throughout the entire first half with an 'all hands to the pump' approach. Humphries turned in a brilliant midfield display that was lauded afterwards by Milan manager, Rocco, as 'technically' excellent. Disillusioned supporters tossed orange peels onto the field to symbolise their outrage. Pockets of supporters in other parts of the ground roared on Athlone's epic effort and waved blue and black flags. They were Inter Milan fans – delighted that a team bearing the same colours were making a mockery of their great rivals AC. In the sixty-third minute Athlone's padlocked defence was finally picked for the first goal of the tie. In devoting all their energies to chasing down and spoiling Milan's play, Athlone had drained their legs of precious stamina. Back at Mel's the encouragement of the home crowd was enough to fight off fatigue. In a hostile environment far from home they finally caved in. The manner of the concession which derived from a terrible misunderstanding on the left side of defence highlighted their mental tiredness.

PAUL MARTIN: *"Kevin Smith, our left-back, was a really good back and a nice lad. He used to sort of run away, draw his man away, and then check back and take a pass. He'd been doing this all night: run away, lose the man, check back and take the ball. This time, probably tiredness, concentration, whatever but he did the thing again, ran away, only Mick had played him the ball. Kevin didn't see it. The guy stepped in, took the ball and slid it across the box. Bang!"*

Duino Gorin was the player who punished the mistake with a ball across from the right wing. Alberto Bigon missed it but the ball fell to the lurking Vincenzi who hammered it home from five yards. Athlone were still right in it, on paper at least. They always needed to score to progress anyway, and one goal would still put them through on the away goals rule if it stayed 1-0. But, with the humid Milan evening rapidly extracting the pace from their play, an Athlone goal now looked highly unlikely.

PAUL MARTIN: "The game was still on in Milan at 1-0 but they were typical Italians. You knew they felt one goal would be enough. They weren't going to concede."

As Milan celebrated Vincenzi's opener, Athlone brought Nicholson on for a spent Daly. But he was powerless to prevent Milan claiming the crucial second goal, minutes later, that all but booked their place in the next round. Benetti was now patrolling the midfield with real authority and confidently stepped up to a twenty-five yard free kick, which he drove through Athlone's defensive wall and beyond the outstretched palm of O'Brien. Benetti doubled his take for the night from another placed ball, a penalty kick, with ten minutes to go. It was a 3-0 Milan win that told nothing of the tale of the first hour. The goal rush brought an anti-climactic end to Athlone's first European campaign. With the minimum of prompting from Milan, jaded Athlone had eventually mastered their own downfall by gifting a sloppy first goal, failing to defend a twenty-five yard free and then conceding a penalty, when Doug Wood fouled in the box. The irony of a free kick and a penalty settling the issue wasn't lost on a disconsolate Minnock as he trooped off the pitch. His free kick against Cork Hibs a few months earlier had made the whole European run possible. Yet, his missed penalty in the first leg at St Mel's had left League of Ireland followers with that most nagging of questions – what if?

MICK O'BRIEN: "I won't tell a lie, I don't know, did we think we could really beat them out there but I honestly thought in Athlone we had a good chance. For anyone that knows the old Mel's, we were playing down the hill for the second half and finished very strongly. To get the penalty, of course, was the great chance. To go 1-0 ahead would have been unbelievable. But, unfortunately, it didn't work out. Poor auld 'Minno'."

Milan overcame Spartak Moscow in the next round but lost in the quarter-finals to eventual runners up, Club Brugge.

The European run took its toll on Athlone. It had demanded all their concentration and the poor run of form they experienced around the Milan ties reflected how a wretched season would ultimately pan out for them. By the following February, they were a club in crisis after a row between Fogarty and the Board led to his sacking. Serious cracks in the manager/board relationship first emerged in late January when, after a meeting with blazers, Fogarty declared, "All my problems in soccer have been confined to the boardroom and officials". Reports suggested that Fogarty had been outraged by attempts to influence his team selection, prompting him to announce, "I am getting out completely at the end of the season ... I am not interested any more in League of Ireland football. It's impossible". A few weeks later, the Board released a statement through their solicitors, stating that, as Fogarty had still to submit his letter of resignation, they would make up his mind for him. He was sacked. "It seems clear that he has lost all interest in the club and that players have lost all confidence in him", read the statement. Fogarty's assistant, Eunan Blake, took over until the end of the season and Athlone finished seventh. The following season, former Wales international, Trevor Hockey, took over as player/manager but lasted just three months in the job.

PAUL MARTIN: "At that stage, I was about twenty-five or twenty-six and had a bit of experience. This fella [Hockey] was flying into Dublin on a Friday, staying in the Montrose, bringing us out to train in Belfield at five o'clock and basically bringing the lads then for a couple of pints. I didn't drink. I never drank in my life. At the time I was up at seven o'clock in the morning, out to work, then out to training with him and after that I just wanted to go home to my wife and a couple of kids. I knew it and the fellas told me, 'He won't last'. The results weren't great. But Mick O'Brien had left for St Pat's and I jumped at the chance to go to Pat's as well when it came up. It was a bad move. I should never have left Athlone. I'd say six or seven weeks after I left, he [Hockey] left. Such is life. Things happen for a reason I suppose but, definitely, the atmosphere that had been there with Amby left."

After finishing second in Fogarty's only full season in charge, Athlone returned to a mid-table existence for the rest of the 1970s. In the next four seasons they finished seventh, tenth, eighth and seventh before the arrival of Bohemians legend and former Republic of Ireland striker, Turlough O'Connor, as manager in 1979, which prompted a golden period of unprecedented and unrepeated success at St Mel's. That first season under O'Connor, 1979/80, Athlone came third in the league and followed it up with their first title win in 1981. Eugene Davis fired twenty-three goals as a forward and was the League's top scorer.

EUGENE DAVIS: "It's hard to compare that team to the one that played Milan. Individually, I would say the '75 team had better players, the likes of Humphries and Minnock. The '81 team just gelled together. I mean, we went twenty-seven games unbeaten that season. The third game we lost, against Sligo, and went unbeaten right to the end of the season."

In 1983, Athlone claimed their second title in three seasons. The following September they played Standard Liege, backboned by the big German international Horst Hrubesch, in the European Cup. Athlone were beaten by a single goal in a 3-2 loss at St Mel's Park. Joe Salmon missed a penalty. His weak kick quickly passed into historical insignificance, however. Maybe that was because Salmon made amends by scoring an excellent goal late on. Or, maybe the fact that Athlone lost the second leg 8-2 meant it was all irrelevant anyway. But they never forgot the day John Minnock was foiled by Albertosi.

PAUL MARTIN: "It's a terrible thing and it's a terrible thing for a fella who did so much for Athlone, so much good for the club. Say we won 1-0, John Minnock could have dined out until he was one hundred and fifty on the back of that. He deserved the story to have a better ending than it did."

UEFA CUP

First round, first leg
September 18, 1975
St Mel's Park, Athlone
Attendance: 4,000

Athlone Town: 3
(Martin 3, Davis 66 and 85)

Valerengen: 1
(Olsen 12)

Athlone Town: O'Brien; Duffy, Wood, Stephenson, Smith; Humphries, Davis, Larkin, Daly; Minnock, Martin (Healy 54).

Valerengen: Blomfeldt; Hansen (Skojli 48), Brekke, Jorgensen, Haslie; Edner, Eriksen, Hoetvedt, Olavason (Foss 33), Karlsen; Olsen.

Referee: B.L. Hoppenbroueer (Holland).

First round, second leg
October 1, 1975
The National Stadium, Oslo
Attendance: 800

Valerengen: 1
(Eriksen 44)

Athlone Town: 1
(Martin 20)

Valerengen: Blomfeldt; Hansen, Brekke, Jorgensen, Haslie; Edner, Eriksen, Foss, Olavson (Hyving 76), Karlsen; Olsen.

Athlone Town: O'Brien; Duffy, Healy, Stephenson, Smith; Humphries, Davis, Larkin, Minnock, Daly; Martin (Wood 80).

Referee: M. Johansson (Sweden).

UEFA CUP

Second round, first leg
October 22, 1975
St Mel's Park, Athlone
Attendance: 9,000

Athlone Town: 0

AC Milan: 0

Athlone Town: O'Brien; Duffy, Wood, Stephenson, Smith; Humphries, Davis, Larkin, Daly; Minnock, Martin (Healy 60).

AC Milan: Albertosi; Anquilletti, Maldera, Turone, Bet; Gorin, Scala, Benetti, Calloni (Sabadini 45), Bigon; Vincenzi.

Referee: U. Sorenson (Denmark).

Second round, second leg
November 5, 1975
San Siro Stadium, Milan
Attendance: 42,500

AC Milan: 3
(Vincenzi 63, Benetti 69 and 80 pen)

Athlone Town: 0

AC Milan: Albertosi; Sabadini, Maldera, Turone, Bet; Gorin, Scala, Benetti, Bigon; Rivera, Vincenzi.

Athlone Town: O'Brien; Duffy, Wood, Stephenson, Smith; Humphries, Davis (Healy 64) Larkin, Minnock, Daly (Nicholson 75); Martin.

Referee: P. Gheti (Romania).

CHAPTER 4

LIMERICK UNITED VS REAL MADRID
September 17 and October 1, 1980

"To tell the truth it was just another game for me back then. Now, it's a different ball game altogether because I'm getting old and you think back on those games. I was over in Birmingham in February watching Aston Villa against Man United. Four guys came with me and one in particular was mad into his soccer back when I was playing. Sure, after a few pints he was telling everybody in the place, 'Wait 'til I tell you what this fella did against Real Madrid'. I couldn't shut him up!" DES KENNEDY

In the summer of 1979, options weren't the problem for Eoin Hand – picking the right one was the conundrum. The release of the versatile Irish defender from Portsmouth, where he'd won the majority of his twenty International caps, literally opened up a world of opportunities. They ranged from enquiries from Cyrpus and Greece about potential player/manager positions to the possibility of extending his playing career in America. The lure of football in South Africa, where'd he enjoyed a playing spell with Durban, remained strong for the thirty-three-year-old, too. That he eventually settled on a new life in Limerick, a city gorging itself on its reputation as a rugby stronghold after Munster's win over New Zealand there the previous October, came as some surprise. Limerick weren't exactly setting the League alight and their sixth-placed finish the previous season was their best since 1970. Hand, however, had been sold on the potential of the club from his first meeting with chairman Michael Webb in Heathrow Airport that summer and was happy to sign a three-year deal. More than that, he was excited about the future and, as the unseasonably warm rays of sunshine beamed down on the Market's Field on the opening day of the 1979/80 season, it felt good to be Limerick United's new player/manager. That afternoon, two things of note occurred at Limerick soccer's spiritual home: opponents UCD took their first tentative steps in senior League football and, more importantly from a Limerick perspective, Hand kick-started a period of unparalleled success for the host club with a 2-0 victory. The good vibrations from Limerick's solitary FAI Cup success in 1971 – eleven years after their only League win – had long since worn off by the end of the decade when Hand initially pitched up in the city. A final defeat to Dundalk in 1977 was as close as United had come to repeating the Cup win. In the League they hadn't fared much better. Mediocrity became the club's calling card as managers came and left with alarming regularity like the mayflies on the Shannon. The sense of a club in need of real leadership was strong. Any early scepticism from the Limerick players, when Hand laid out his wares and asked them to buy into what he was selling, could be forgiven. Goalkeeper Kevin Fitzpatrick had been at the club since 1960 and reckons he must have seen fourteen managers come and go in that time. But, when the win over UCD was followed by a 3-2 away victory at Sligo Rovers and a 4-1 hammering of Cork United, with Hand scoring all four goals, an unstoppable momentum had built up behind the new boss.

EOIN HAND: *"Those were our first three games, talk about having a great start to things. No matter what your message was to players they were going to believe it now. I was pretty strict on discipline too, though I believed in a time and a place. For instance, we went away for the longer games and stayed in a hotel. I would say to the lads, 'I don't want to see anyone drinking a pint but I don't mind if you have a couple of halves because that will help you to sleep. But if anyone abuses it, it's a week's wages'. There was one occasion where two lads went walking around Ballybofey and I saw them with a pint and I said, 'That's the most expensive pint you'll ever drink in your life'. So, things like that got the message home pretty quickly."*

KEVIN FITZPATRICK: "It was an unbelievable change under Eoin. The first training session we had, he sat us down on the pitch and laid out how things were going to work and what was going to happen. There were going to be fines, which we'd never had before, if we were late. He brought a level of professionalism into it that we hadn't seen in many years."

Hand delved deep into his own playing experiences at the likes of Portsmouth, Swindon Town, Ireland and, briefly, Shamrock Rovers under Johnny Giles, to come up with new and innovative ways of breathing life into Limerick. Set pieces became a tool which they would use to exploit their opponents. Three of those four goals that Hand scored against Cork United came from free-kicks. The other was from a corner. Hand and his dead ball specialist, Joe O'Mahony, were as thick as thieves on the training field, plotting precise set plays which would allow Limerick to steal through opposing defences almost undetected. If Hand was the brains behind the operation it was new physical trainer Dave Mahedy that supplied the brawn. Mahedy was the fitness advisor behind Munster's Heineken Cup wins in 2006 and 2008. Currently Director of Sport at the University of Limerick, he has also trained Cork City and St Patrick's Athletic, the Limerick and Clare hurling teams and guided Shannon to a four-in-a-row of AIL titles in the mid-1990s. Back in 1980, however, he was only fresh out of college and charting new terrain in physical preparation just as Hand was in football management.

DAVE MAHEDY: "I was a newly qualified physical education teacher and I was going to change the world! I had just started the pre-season training when Eoin arrived. I suppose it was cheeky, in a way, but I knew the set-up and the facilities in UL so we used what was available there. It was probably the first time that players used a track and a weights room and stuff like that. I'd say it was the first time, too, that a professional trainer, not in the paid sense, but in the qualification sense, worked with a team. Before that trainers were mostly former players."

The regime change was an eye opener for players, particularly the experienced ones, who'd never known anything like the intensity of the sessions or the sheer volume of them that were crammed into each week. Brutal mountain runs became the norm to invest stamina in the players' legs. Sunday morning training sessions before matches were introduced. The storming start to the League was the sugar that made the medicine go down.

DAVE MAHEDY: *"I remember one player coming in to Mickey Webb, the chairman, and asking for more money because the training was so hard. But we ploughed ahead and, because we were getting the results, people started to buy into it."*

KEVIN FITZPATRICK: *"It was a completely new professional approach. Ewan Fenton was my first manager in 1960 when I joined Limerick. He had a really professional attitude and Eoin brought that back into the club. What happened was that Eoin inherited this group of lads who had not really achieved any great successes but he gave them a new enthusiasm for the whole thing. There was a sense, coming from him, that we were all going to do something together and we just responded to that."*

EOIN HAND: *"The guys were great, they really were. They were part-time players but they trained like full-time players. It was three nights a week and a Saturday morning and then a Sunday. It was nearly like full-time involvement for thirty quid a week, though it wasn't about money, it was, 'Here we are, we're Limerick, we're going to take on the country'."*

Hand barely deviated from the playing personnel he'd inherited, though the acquisitions of Gary Hulmes and John Delamere mid-way through that first season emboldened their title charge. The return of Des Kennedy to the Market's Field after a year at Galway Rovers was significant, too. Hand fancied he could knock the striker into the best shape of his career and use him at the point of the team's attack.

EOIN HAND: "I used mainly what I had, personnel-wise, but I did make an effort to get Des Kennedy back who had gone to Galway. He was a Limerick lad, a centre-forward, a tough lad. I arranged a friendly against a local team and he was to play for the local team. I deliberately played myself against him. I gave him a few wallops early on. He said nothing except he walloped me back. He obviously said to himself, 'That's it, I'm going to get him back,' and he did. He didn't half give me a whack back. At that point I thought, 'Yeah, he'll do'. In fact, it was his test. He passed the test. If he'd started whingeing I would have said, 'Ah, I don't want this guy'."

DES KENNEDY: "Myself and Eoin had a bit of a run-in, all right. He whacked me so I whacked him back. He whacked me again so I whacked him again. That was the end of it. The following day he called into the garage where I worked. He just said to me, 'Do you fancy coming back to Limerick?' I said, 'I don't mind'. 'I'd like if you came back,' he said. So, that's what happened."

With Kennedy back on board, Limerick were a team of near bluebloods. On the final day of the 1979/80 season they needed just one more point to secure their first League title in twenty years and only their second ever. Of the sixteen-man panel that Hand could select his team from, ten players were Limerick lads.

EOIN HAND: "Gary Hulmes was a lad we got down from Sligo. He was an English lad and gave us pace. That was mainly it. Nearly all of the rest of the lads were local; Joe O'Mahony, Brendan Storan, Kevin Fitzpatrick, Pat Nolan at full-back, Johnny Walsh – he was the first name on my team sheet. Johnny Walsh epitomised, as far as I was concerned, the spirit of Limerick because he was only ten stone, if he was even that, but talk about boxing above your weight. He was as tough as nails and very, very skilful. 'Walshy' was the creativity in the team. If he didn't play I thought we would struggle but he was never missing. He was such a tough little so and so."

Hand himself was a blow-in, a product of underage football at Stella Maris in Dublin. His amiable personality quickly won over the hardliners who'd congregate in the 'Popular Side' of the Market's Field and toss caustic comments at managers who they felt weren't up to it.

KEVIN FITZPATRICK: "From the very start when Eoin came in, the crowds went up to five or six thousand in the Market's Field and every week we'd have that. The travelling away support was fantastic as well. Eoin had this ability of bonding with supporters, he was good with the press, he was good with all the people who attended the games. He built up a rapport with everybody."

A cavalcade of blue and white left Limerick city for Athlone on the morning of April 20, 1980, the final day of the season. Having stuffed Home Farm 4-0 the previous weekend, form wasn't an issue for United. Still, nobody could be sure how the players would react to the white heat of battle on the biggest day of their careers. A historic achievement that would polarise their careers as footballers hung in the balance. Athlone were no mugs. Turlough O'Connor was building a side that would win the title the following season and the midlanders needed a result themselves to secure third position in the table. The third team in the mix was Dundalk, the reigning double champions, whom Limerick only needed a point to finish ahead of in the table. Travelling supporters fastened blue and white flags on telegraph poles between Limerick and Athlone. The show of support didn't go unnoticed by the players travelling up on the team bus. A massive visiting crowd set the turnstiles ringing to the tune of IR£6,000, a record take for the venue. At first, they had little to shout about and, when Michael O'Connor curled a thirty-sixth minute free-kick past Fitzpatrick in the Limerick goals to push Athlone into the lead, the Limerick party was well and truly pooped, momentarily at least.

KEVIN FITZPATRICK: "It was a mistake between myself and Pat Nolan for the free. I came out and touched the ball outside the box and O'Connor scored direct from it."

Limerick finally caught a break in the second half as they chased down their sixty-seventhth and most important goal of an amazing season. They were awarded a penalty when Gerry Duggan burst into the penalty area and was grounded by Stefan Feniuk. Tony Meaney, a long time servant of the club like Duggan, stood up to the kick, the most important of that or any other season.

EOIN HAND: "As I recall, Tony Meaney had been in and out of our team, but he was an excellent penalty taker. Tony immediately grabbed the ball. He didn't say, 'Hey boss, I'm not taking this one because there's a League riding on it'. He just took it, cool as you like, and scored it. Then it was just pandemonium. It was fantastic, the celebrations. I think there were a few divorces happened out of all the celebrating!"

Winning the League represented instant success in management for Hand. His punt on Limerick had come good in spectacular fashion. As he wrapped himself in the city's embrace and raised a victory drink to his lips that Sunday night, he couldn't help but marvel at how thoroughly straightforward it had all been. He'd come to the club utterly convinced that he could make them a success and that's how it had worked out.

EOIN HAND: "When it happened so quickly you kind of think, 'Well, this is easy', because all you did was organise and work hard. It was my first year in management. I'd done a bit of coaching with Portsmouth and around other places, South Africa and whatever, but this was the first time I was in charge of a set-up. You become kind of, 'Ah well, sure it's easy to win a League!' So, I won't say it amazed me when we did win."

Goalkeeper Fitzpatrick was older than Hand and had been publicly courting the idea of retirement for several seasons before enjoying the Indian summer to his career. Closer to forty years of age than thirty, it was notions of loyalty and pride and a basic enjoyment of the game that had kept him at the club until Hand's arrival.

KEVIN FITZPATRICK: "Could I have believed that was waiting for me at the end of my career? No. From '64 to '72 we had good times at Limerick but, when you win something unexpectedly in the twilight of your career, it just completely reinvigorates you."

In a city famed for its love of sport, soccer had pushed its way to the top of the public consciousness. Limerick United's home base, the Market's Field, was at the heart of the thriving movement, beating with passion on Sunday afternoons as thousands shuffled down through the arterial lanes and roads into the Garryowen venue. Officially, the Market's Field was the home of local greyhound racing and was owned by Bord na gCon. Any visiting players unsure of the exact landlord/tenant status only had to take a look at the dog droppings left on the pitch from the previous day's racing to realise whose territory they were on. Nonetheless, as a soccer venue it was invested with a new charm and mystique when the silverware from the League success took up residence there. And now, for the first time ever, the famous old ground was poised to host European football. Limerick had competed in Europe three times before. In 1960, they'd played Young Boys of Berne in the European Cup, losing 9-2 on aggregate. Five years later, as beaten FAI Cup finalists, they went down 4-1 to CSKA Sofia in the European Cup winners' Cup. When they met Italian Cup winners Torino in September 1971, they suffered 1-0 and 4-0 losses. The home legs of the Young Boys of Berne and Torino games were played at Thomond Park, while the Sofia match was taken to Dalymount. Supporter Karl Spain, now a renowned comedian and TV presenter, was among Limerick's numbers at the Market's Field in 1980 and picked up on the wit and wisdom of its clientele.

A SPECIAL
EDITION OF
THE OFFICIAL
M.U.F.C.
PROGRAMME
2nd OCTOBER, 1957

Manchester United
VERSUS
Shamrock Rovers

EUROPEAN CUP
COMPETITION
PRELIMINARY ROUND
— SECOND LEG
KICK-OFF 7-30 PM
PRICE FOURPENCE

ESTER CE
GHAM MI
LIGHT REFRESH

BRITISH RAILWAYS

Next Home Match
1st DIVISION
United v.
ASTON VILLA
5 Oct. kick-off 3-0 pm

Shirts Red

MANCHESTER UNITED 3
WOOD
Knickers White

Next Home Match
CENTRAL LEAGUE
United v.
SHEFFIELD W.
12 Oct. kick-off 3-0 pm

Keep d

FOULKES
2

BYRNE
3

BERRY
7

GOODWIN
4

WHELAN
8

BLANCHFLOWER
5

TAYLOR
9

EDWARDS
6

VIOLLET
10

PEGG
11

R

L

Referee:
Albert Alfteen, Belgium

EVENING
NEWS
FOR
RESULTS

Linesmen:
Raymond Lespineux, Belgium
(Red Flag)
Maurice Cumps, Belgium
(Yellow Flag)

"STON

L

R

TUOHY
11

COAD
10

HAMILTON
9

AMBROSE
8

PEYTON
7

HENNESSY
6

KEOGH
5

NOLAN
4

OBTAINAB

DIRECT R
COMP

Kick-off
7-30 pm

MACKEY
3

BURKE
2

Team changes
will be
indicated by
loudspeaker

66 MARKET STRE

Branches in a

Shirts Green and White Hoops

D'ARCY
SHAMROCK R. 2

Knickers White

9-25 am

The Shamrock Rovers and Manchester United team lists for the historic game between 'Coad's Colts' and the 'Busby Babes' which was played shortly before the tragic death of so many of Sir Matt Busby's players; Paddy Coad in his heyday, and the Rovers team which lit up League of Ireland football in the '50s with a wonderful brand of exciting football.

Denis Law scores with his left foot in front of a packed Lansdowne Road in the first leg.

The Waterford team which electrified Irish soccer and won the hearts of fans with their displays against Manchester United.

George Best gets in a brilliant header against Waterford.

EUROPEAN CHAMPIONS CUP COMPETITION

UNITED REVIEW

THE OFFICIAL PROGRAMME OF MANCHESTER UNITED FOOTBALL CLUB

WINNERS OF THE EUROPEAN CHAMPIONS CUP COMPETITION 1968

NINEPENCE 7

OCTOBER 2 1968
KICK-OFF 7·30 PM

16TH FINAL

MANCHESTER
UNITED V **WATERFORD**
(Republic of Ireland)

MANCHESTER UNITED
Shirts: Red   Shorts: White

1 STEPNEY
2 DUNNE
3 BURNS
4 CRERAND
5 FOULKES
6 STILES
7 BEST
8 SADLER
9 CHARLTON
10 LAW
11 KIDD
S.

REFEREE:
Joaquin Fernando Campos
(Portugal)

EVENING
NEWS
FOR
RESULTS

LINESMEN:
Antonio S. Ribeiro   Caetano J. Nogueira
(Portugal)   (Portugal)
(Red Flag)   *(Yellow Flag)*

Next Home Game
DIVISION ONE
UNITED
v.
ARSENAL
OCTOBER 5th
Kick-off 3.00 p.m.

Next Home Match
CENTRAL LEAGUE
UNITED
v.
BOLTON W.
OCTOBER 12
Kick-off 3.00

WATERFORD
Shirts: Blue   Shorts: Blue

THOMAS 1
BRYAN 2
GRIFFIN 3
MAGUIRE 4
MORLEY 5
McGEOUGH 6
CASEY 7
HALE 8
O'NEILL 9
COAD 10
MATTHEWS 11
MORRISSEY S.

The Waterford team list for the second leg at Old Trafford.

Back Row (l. to r.): **P. Nicholson, J. Minnock, N. Larkin, M. O'Brien, J. Duffy, A. McSwiney, A. Stevenson.** Front (l. to r.): **P. Martin, D. Wood, J. Healy, T. Daly, E. Davis.**

The Athlone team which delivered so many great performances in the midlands town and which later measured up to the magnificent AC Milan.

Immaculately dressed Milan players descend from the team bus at a muddied, pot-holed St Mel's Park.

John Minnock places the ball on the penalty spot at St Mel's several decades after missing the kick which would have defeated the Italian giants.

Tony Meaney celebrates the goal which claimed the 1979/1980 League title for Eoin Hand's fabulous Limerick United; Joe O'Mahony leads the Limerick players onto the magnificent Bernabeu playing field, and the Limerick team pose in one of the greatest stadiums in World football.

Argentinian World Cup hero Ossie Ardiles and Ireland's Chris Hughton had their hands full with battling Dundalk at home and away.

THE TEAMS

Tottenham Hotspur		Dundalk
Manager: Keith Burkinshaw (White Shirts, Blue Shorts, White Stockings)		Manager: Jim McLaughlin (Red Shirts, Red Shorts, Red Stockings)
RAY CLEMENCE	1	RICHARD BLACKMORE
CHRIS HUGHTON	2	EAMON GREGG
PAUL MILLER	3	MARTIN LAWLOR
GRAHAM ROBERTS	4	PADDY DUNNING
MIKE HAZARD	5	TOMMY McCONVILLE
STEVE PERRYMAN	6	LEO FLANAGAN
OSVALDO ARDILES	7	SEAN BYRNE
STEVE ARCHIBALD	8	BARRY KEHOE
TONY GALVIN	9	MICK FAIRCLOUGH
GLENN HODDLE	10	JOHN ARCHBOLD
GARTH CROOKS	11	BRIAN DUFF
Substitutes to be announced		Substitutes to be announced
TONY PARKS		WILLIE CRAWLEY
PAUL PRICE		JIMMY REILLY
PAT CORBETT		ROBERT LAWLOR
GEORGIO MAZZON		HILARY CARLYLE
CHRIS JONES		JOHN BYRNE

OFFICIALS

REFEREE
PAUL RION of Obergom in Luxembourg was born 31 July, 1940. His started refereeing in 1969, and attained international status in 1976
In addition to many other important games, he has once refereed ten unconfirmed fixtures.

LINESMEN
Norbert Nollet (Red Flag)
Norbert Roch (Yellow Flag)

Mick Fairclough resurrected his career after an horrific knee injury and starred against Spurs.

The team lists for the game at White Hart Lane when Dundalk scared the living daylights out of one of the most talented teams in British football.

DUNDALK'S F.A.I. CUP WINNING TEAM, 1980-81
Back row, left to right: J. Archbold, S. Byrne, T. McConville, R. Blackmore, P. Dunning, V. McKenna
M. Fairclough
Front row, left to right: W. Crawley, T. O'Doherty, D. Keeley, M. Lawlor, B. Duff, L. Flanagan

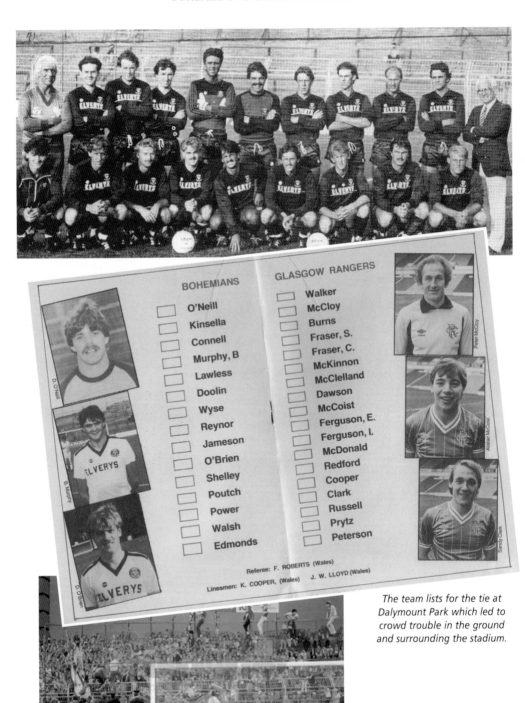

BOHEMIANS

O'Neill
Kinsella
Connell
Murphy, B
Lawless
Doolin
Wyse
Reynor
Jameson
O'Brien
Shelley
Poutch
Power
Walsh
Edmonds

GLASGOW RANGERS

Walker
McCloy
Burns
Fraser, S.
Fraser, C.
McKinnon
McClelland
Dawson
McCoist
Ferguson, E.
Ferguson, I.
McDonald
Redford
Cooper
Clark
Russell
Prytz
Peterson

Referee: F. ROBERTS (Wales)

Linesmen: K. COOPER, (Wales)   J. W. LLOYD (Wales)

The team lists for the tie at Dalymount Park which led to crowd trouble in the ground and surrounding the stadium.

Tension turns into trouble at Dalymount Park.

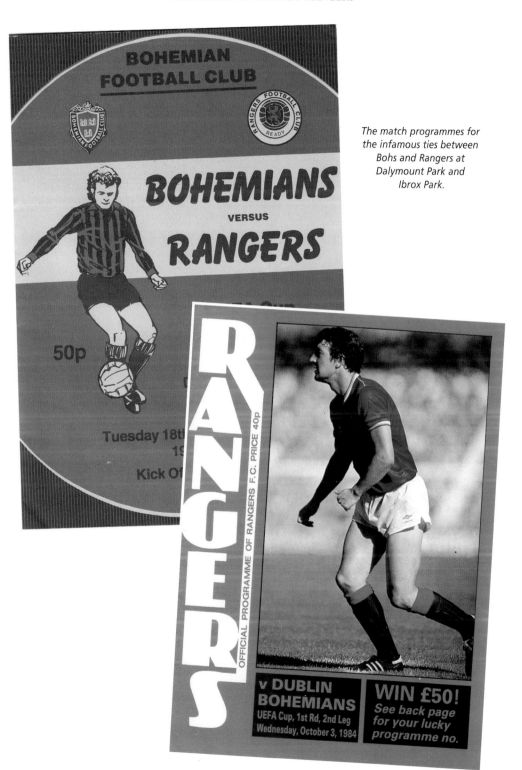

The match programmes for the infamous ties between Bohs and Rangers at Dalymount Park and Ibrox Park.

Houtman scores in the first leg against Galway United.

Houtman in a TG4 story of the famous game.

Paul McGee's performances for Galway against Groningen earned high praise, and later afforded him the move to FC Haarlem.

Pairc an Chatanaigh which came to the rescue of Galway United.

Assembly Deputy First Minister, Martin McGuinness, who was on hand to dispose of a bomb device which almost ruined one of the greatest nights in Derry fotoball.

The team line-outs for the memorable game at The Brandywell.

DERRY CITY F.C.

..... TIM DALTON
..... PASCAL VAUDEQUIN
..... KEVIN BRADY
..... PAUL CURRAN
..... MICK NEVILLE
..... PAUL DOOLIN
..... PAUL CARLYLE
..... LIAM COYLE
..... JONATHAN SPEAK
..... STUART GAULD
..... FELIX HEALY
..... PAUL HEGARTY
..... JOE McBREARTY
..... RAY McGUINNESS
..... JACK KEAY
.....PAUL McLAUGHLIN

Team Manager:
JIM McLAUGHLIN

BENFICA F.C.

..... SILVINO
..... VELOSO
..... ALDAIR
..... RICARDO
..... FONSECA
..... THERN
..... ABEL
..... VITOR PANEIRA
..... VALDO
..... MAGNUSSON
..... CESAR BRITO
..... BENTO
..... SAMUEL
..... DIAMANTINO
..... CHALANA
..... MIRANDA

Coach/ Manager:
SVEN ERIKSSON

1804

⭕⭕⭕⭕⭕ TODAY'S TEAMS ⭕⭕⭕⭕⭕

MATCH OFFICIALS .....

REFEREE:
Mr. GUY GOETHALS

LINESMEN:
Mr. ROBERT HEURISSEN
Mr. FRANK VERNEERSCH

The Programme Committee would like to express their thanks to
G. Anderson. M. Bradley, C. Large, R. Kelly, M. Harkin,
M. McBride, J. Fullerton. J. Clifford and J. Campbell
for their help in this publication.

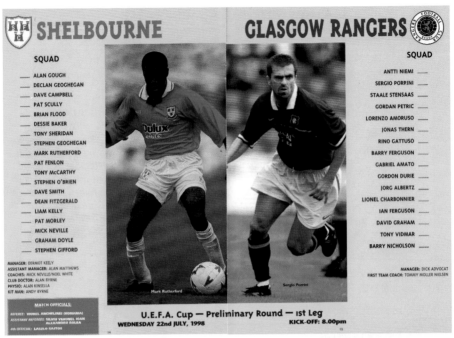

The Shelbourne and Rangers line-outs at Prenton Park in Liverpool.

Liam Kelly, Alan Gough and Pat Morley take the field.

The Shelbourne players visit the home of Glasgow Celtic FC during their Scottish travels.

Tony McCarthy and his Shels team-mates defied and confused their hosts by playing Gaelic football during their training session at Ibrox Park.

Liam Kelly in action against Rangers' Amorosu and Ferguson in the epic battle against Glasgow Rangers.

Shelbourne manager, Pat Fenlon, and Ollie Byrne celebrate their famous victory over Hadjuk Split which earned a tie against Deportivo La Coruña.

Goalscorer Dave Rogers celebrates at the end of Shelbourne's historic victory over Hadjuk Split.

Programme and match ticket for
the game in Lansdowne Road.

Shelbourne and Deportivo players enter the Riazor Stadium during the Irish champions'
epic European journey in 2004.

KARL SPAIN: "There used to be some great stories about what they used to call the 'Popular Side' of the Market's Field. I remember one day, it would have been the early days of when I was going to watch games, there was a guy down injured and he was over getting treatment for a couple of minutes. While they were hanging around, two of the Limerick players started tapping the ball to each other. A guy who was watching shouted, 'That's it Limerick, fucking practise!' Over the years you'd forget the amount of funny things shouted. But that was always the side of the ground where it would happen, the 'Popular Side'. The atmosphere in there was great."

DES KENNEDY: "The big games at the Market's Field were a real boys' day out. You'd have the dinner at home, go up and watch the match and, whatever direction you came home in, there was three or four pubs on your way back. So, there was a few pints had and then home. It was a routine that a lot of people really enjoyed."

The Market's Field never did get to take its place among the list of venues to grace the European Cup. Limerick United being paired off with Real Madrid saw to that. Between its mere 9,000 capacity and question marks that hung over its ability to safely host the previous season's semi-finalists, a line was quickly drawn through the venue. The obvious alternative was rugby's Thomond Park. It could only comfortably accommodate 12,000 (14,000 at a push) which was only marginally better than the Market's Field, but it would keep the game in the city, nonetheless. The sort of sporting ecumenism that would see Croke Park lower its barriers to soccer and rugby in 2005 was still generations away. So, the spacious Gaelic Grounds was out of the question just as it had been when tentative enquiries were made to host Torino there. In any analysis of the pros and cons presented by Thomond, the positives appeared to heavily outweigh the negatives. The ground was 10,000 short of the sort of capacity needed to make serious money at the turnstiles, the sort of money that would sustain the club long-term, but a healthy profit could still be made. The local public would buy into the tie which would be their reward for following the team in leaner times. There'd be knock-on benefits for the business community. Local restaurants, hotels, bars, cafés, traders and hawkers could all expect to get their slice of the pie. From a football perspective, it also made sense. Fitzpatrick, O'Mahony and Meaney had all played there against Torino and knew the lie of the land. A more recent recruit who knew the grain of the rich sward at Thomond better than anyone else was Tony Ward. Mahedy's old college pal had agreed to play on the wing for Limerick whenever he was available. That wasn't often, admittedly, as he was heavily involved in rugby with Garryowen and Ireland at the time. In fact, 1980 had already seen him kick eighteen points for the British Lions – later renamed the British and Irish Lions – against South Africa. Two years earlier, he'd been responsible for two drop goals and a conversion when Munster pulled off a famous 12-0 win over touring New Zealand at Thomond. Now, the same opportunity was being presented to the sons of Limerick soccer to squeeze into sporting immortality alongside their rugby brethren by playing and possibly winning at Thomond. Ward felt the opportunity couldn't be passed up.

TONY WARD: *"We often used the expression 'the umbilical cord' that is there between the players and the fans at Thomond. They're that close, they're right on top of the players and you're very conscious of it. It's very intimidating for the opposition. I think it's that as much as anything else, it's the unique experience for away teams. Obviously, the home team taps into that as well. I've never experienced a ground like it anywhere else, I have to say. It's an amazing place."*

The elephant in the Limerick boardroom was the remaining option for the glamour game; take it out of Limerick altogether, bring it to Dublin and chase the biggest possible pay day. If this was the avenue officials chose to go down, then Lansdowne Road was the obvious choice. In 1968, and again in 1970, Waterford had moved their European Cup games against Manchester United and Glasgow Celtic to the south

Dublin venue. They'd followed the money and been rewarded. But could Limerick really expect Real Madrid to put 30,000 bums on seats at Lansdowne Road, the figure they were aiming for? Both Celtic and United had contested European Cup finals the previous season and, of course, traditionally carried huge box office appeal among football fans in Ireland. Waterford attracted sizeable support themselves in the capital in the middle of a run of six League titles in eight seasons. Could Limerick lay claim to the same backing in Dublin after a one-off title success? It was a barrel of 'ifs', a giant gamble, but one that Limerick eventually decided was worth the risk. After considered debate, they settled on Lansdowne Road. As far as their supporters were concerned, the decision was tantamount to heresy.

EOIN HAND: "Unfortunately, politics came into it, football politics. The wrong decisions were made at Board level, for sure, because the game was taken out of Limerick and brought to Lansdowne and it should never have been. I said, 'Keep it in Limerick, Thomond Park', which they did the next season when Tottenham Hotspur came across for a friendly. It was wrong to take it out of Limerick and to take it away from the supporters who had supported the team brilliantly. When we won that League, every week, as the impetus grew, there were more people coming along to watch. Now, when I look back on it, the stories you hear, there must have been a hundred thousand at every game which, of course, there wasn't. But, there was a great build up of support through the seasons at the Market's Field and all around the country there was record gates and big gates, because of the Limerick support. The Limerick followers were brilliant. Suddenly, to be at home against Real Madrid and to take it to Lansdowne ... it was wrong."

The gamble was based on the fundamental theory that if Real Madrid were the most successful club in Europe then, surely, any genuine football fan would pay to watch them and there were more football fans in Dublin than anywhere else in Ireland. There was a natural logic to it, even if all of Madrid's six titles had come between 1956 and 1966 before TV had afforded their players international recognition. In the autumn of 1980, the best known Madrid player to Irish fans was Englishman Laurie Cunningham. His emergence as a left-winger blessed with blinding pace and agility in the late-1970s had been one of not just sporting but political significance. Ron Atkinson's West Bromwich Albion became the first English club to field three black players when Cunningham turned out alongside Cyrille Regis and Brendon Batson, the 'Three Degrees' as they were affectionately dubbed after the famous American soul band. In an era of race riots and right-wing nationalism, Cunningham's experiences at West Brom steeled him for the media frenzy that erupted when he became the first black player to play competitively for England, months after Viv Anderson had lined out in an International friendly. The 'Three Degrees' were split when Cunningham moved to Real Madrid for Stg£1million in the summer of 1979, but their influence is still felt in stadia across England. Cunningham took Madrid by storm in his first season, winning a League and Cup double and scoring three times in a European Cup run that took them to the semi-finals. They were eventually knocked out by Kevin Keegan's Hamburg who, in turn, lost to Nottingham Forest in the final. In the quarter-finals of the campaign Madrid beat Glasgow Celtic 3-2 on aggregate. The three Madrid players that scored against Celtic; Juanito, Carlos Santillana and Uli Stielike, all competed in the European Championship finals that summer. Spain, with Juanito and Santillana up front, failed to advance from their group but Stielike fared better, steering West Germany from his defensive berth to a 2-1 final defeat of Belgium. At just twenty-six, alternating between defence and midfield for club and country, Stielike was hailed as Germany's new Beckenbauer. Des Kennedy and the Limerick players would get the chance to make up their own minds on that score a few weeks later.

DES KENNEDY: *"There was great excitement about the game coming up to it. Believe it or not, personally, it was just another match. It was against these superstars but they weren't household names, as such, to*

us because television hadn't made them into what they would be now.
But you knew who they were, at the same time."

The biggest gamble by those who took the fixture out of Limerick was actually not how their fans would react, it was the presumption that the market in Dublin was strong enough to fill Lansdowne on consecutive weeks. Exactly seven days before Limerick's game, Ireland beat Holland 2-1 at Lansdowne in a World Cup qualifier. Just 25,000 turned up. Beads of cold sweat broke out across worried brows in Limerick as the morning papers carried action shots of goal scorers, Mark Lawrenson and Gerry Daly, set against clusters of empty seats. The awful thought lingered: if Ireland's first home game in their qualification campaign for Spain '82 couldn't pull in 30,000, against an attractive Holland team, then how the hell were Limerick United going to do it? Nobody sensed what lay ahead more than Hand who, since the summer of 1980, doubled as Ireland's new manager and was on the line for the Holland game. His sensational first season with Limerick had earned him a shot at the International job which he would hold until 1985. The 2-1 win over Holland meant a 100 per cent start to his tenure following an early victory over Cyprus. By game day on September 17, a worrying sense of apathy towards Limerick's European fixture prevailed in the capital. The club's hardcore supporters were putting up and shutting up as they travelled to Dublin in a convoy of cars and vans. But, for the general Limerick public, the cost factor coupled with the sense that an injustice had been done unto them swayed them towards staying at home and tuning in to RTÉ Radio's commentary.

KARL SPAIN: "I can't remember looking forward to the match and all
the stuff like that which you would remember if it had been in
Limerick. I remember when we got into Lansdowne it just being a huge
disappointment, because there was nobody there in this big stadium.
It probably was my first time at Lansdowne Road and I just couldn't
understand how Real Madrid were playing in the European Cup and
it wasn't sold out. For me, this was Real Madrid! The name alone sold

itself. I would have thought if they were playing anyone, didn't matter if it was Limerick, my father would have brought us, myself and my brother, if it was at all possible. So, I remember that being a disappointment. I just couldn't understand it."

The gamble had backfired on Limerick. Badly. Just over 7,000 paid in to Lansdowne Road. Those who had pushed hardest for the move gulped in silent anticipation as the teams ran out into a near-empty stadium to muted applause. To think what it could have been like at Thomond.

DAVE MAHEDY: "Before a ball was even kicked it was just the biggest mistake ever. Ever, ever, ever. I'd say it was probably the smallest crowd that Real Madrid played in front of in a European club game. I'd imagine you could put your house on that. The whole idea was that the Dublin people would turn up, but they didn't. It was one of those crazy, crazy decisions made at Board level that totally backfired. The fans' argument was, 'We'll pay double the price of the ticket rather than going to Dublin'. It was nothing against Dublin, it was just that to get to Dublin you had to get a car or a bus and there was a cost involved with the whole thing. Thomond Park was right there. It wasn't the great Thomond Park that it is now, but it certainly was a better venue to host the game."

The Limerick players resolved to take pride in exhibiting a level of professionalism that went beyond requiring a huge vocal support to perform. The first inkling Des Kennedy got that it may not be such a bad night after all was when he planted his first step down on the manicured green sod that welcomed the players onto the pitch.

DES KENNEDY: "The pitch was absolutely incredible. The surface was just incredible. Now, depending on what way you look at it, we might have been better playing Real Madrid on a bumpy pitch in Thomond. But, don't forget, we were League champions, too. We could knock it around as well."

Real started without injured trio Garcia Ramon, their first choice goalkeeper, defender and future manager Vicente del Bosque and striker Santillana. Jose Antonio Camacho who, like current World Cup winning manager del Bosque, would go on to manage Spain, started in defence alongside experienced international Gregorio Benito, Ricardo Gallego and Perez Garcia. Stielike brought strength and solidity to the midfield while Cunningham's job was to penetrate the right side of Limerick's defence with his hard running. Up front, former Spanish Footballer of the Year, Juanito, represented their greatest goal threat. Limerick hit the pitch with virtually their strongest side though rugby commitments in far off Romania accounted for Ward's absence and he missed the second leg too. The team's form was good. A 4-0 win over UCD on opening day coupled with a 2-1 away win over Sligo left them in top spot in the League. Gary Hulmes scored three goals in those two games while their top scorer in the title winning season, Tony Morris, was up and running with a goal too. The form of Coventry-born Englishman, Johnny Matthews, was notably good. A full fourteen years after joining Waterford in their breakthrough year of 1966, he was still weaving his attacking wizardry. European games were his speciality. He'd scored against both Manchester United and Glasgow Celtic in the European Cup for Waterford. A unique hat-trick was on his mind as referee, Ole Amundsen, set play in motion at Lansdowne Road. Hand was happy with the early performance of his team-mates around him. Four times in the opening half, Limerick set the Madrid defence into a desperate defensive scramble as the hosts chased the opening goal. They were stopped on each occasion, but the intensity of Limerick's play and their intention to trade on skill resulted in an exciting spectacle. Kennedy's aerial power unnerved Madrid from the start, while Hulmes was a ball of energy going forward, narrowly missing with one decent chance.

KEVIN FITZPATRICK: *"We were playing well. Really, really well."*

Limerick believed they'd moved decisively clear with just twenty-five minutes of the contest gone. Matthews had worked some space for himself on the edge of the six-yard box ahead of defender Isidro and was perfectly positioned to slide home Johnny Walsh's cross to the net. The sparse crowd rose to their feet in acclamation of a deserved goal but the roars died in their throats as the referee ruled that Matthews had strayed offside. It was a hairline decision at best.

JOHNNY MATTHEWS: "I'd done two cartwheels and a wave before I looked over and saw the man with his flag up. Good job he didn't understand Coventry English! I was so disappointed."

DES KENNEDY: "I always felt there was nothing wrong with that goal, actually."

DAVE MAHEDY: "We all claimed he was on-side. I remember it vividly, as if it was yesterday. But it was flagged straightaway. There weren't cameras to analyse it afterwards like Sky do nowadays, so we'll probably never know. But it was marginal, that's for sure."

In the context of the overall battle it was still first blood to Limerick. They now knew they were capable of breaching Madrid's defence and, as Hand stood in the middle of the dressing room floor at half time, his words had a ring of simplicity to them: "More of the same lads. If we keep doing what we're doing there's a result here for us".

EOIN HAND: "I remember Dublin people who went to it saying to me they really did think that Real Madrid were the team in blue for a long while. It was because we played very well. Basically, we just went out to play football against them. Early in the game, I was playing midfield, and I hit Stielike, I caught him with a beautiful tackle. It was a bone cruncher but it was clean, it was good, part of the game. That's the way I wanted to play the game and that's how we did. Don't get me onto another thing now: Diving, I can't stand it ... But anyway, after that tackle, Stielike, I never saw him again for the rest of the game. We were determined to give a good account of ourselves."

KARL SPAIN: "It was mesmerising seeing Madrid in the all white. I remember thinking that Laurie Cunningham looked like Pele because all the footage you used to see of Pele was of him playing in the all white of Santos."

Limerick's penetrating start augured well, though the fact that they'd failed to take any of their first-half opportunities rankled. Just ten days earlier, Joe McKenna, Eamon Cregan and the rest of the Limerick hurlers had contributed to an exciting All-Ireland hurling final on the far side of Dublin against Galway, but still came away with nought for their efforts. For them, there was no such thing as a moral victory and it was the same for the soccer team representing Limerick. Hand was happy to see his side retain the same appetite for forward movement as they settled into the second half. Their persistence paid off seven minutes into the half when they finally broke through Madrid's back line, legitimately this time. Walsh was the creative force again, arching in a free kick to the penalty area that Duggan flicked on. Before the visitors quite realised the gravity of the situation, Kennedy had slipped his man in a crowded box and got enough on the ball to steer it to an empty net. As the ball was crossing the goal line, Stielike was racing back after it, his eyes fixed on the linesman for an offside flag that never came. Limerick were one ahead.

DES KENNEDY: "I was on the radio with Des Cahill last year when Real Madrid were in Dublin again to play Shamrock Rovers. He played back Philip Greene's commentary of my goal from RTÉ Radio. I says to Des Cahill, 'Philip made it sound a lot better than it actually was!' And that's the truth. As the ball came in it actually hit my shin, the goalkeeper went down and it lifted over him. It was a scrappy one, but they all count."

Hand belted out the orders to anyone within earshot as the players returned from delirium to their positions: "Keep it tight. No silly mistakes". It was the same solid advice he'd dished out a week earlier to the Ireland players against Holland, and it had done the trick then. Limerick played it cool and calm and kept it tight, as they'd been told to, for the next ten minutes. The adrenaline from the goal wore off and they were back living on their wits again, doing the simple things and the basics right. Kennedy glanced up at the clock on the front of the stand and saw there were seventy minutes gone. "Maybe. Just maybe", he thought. Suddenly, Pineda, only on the field because of an early facial injury to Benito, was put through one-on-one with Fitzpatrick by a deftly weighted Hernandez pass. Drawing on twenty years of experience, Fitzpatrick ushered Pineda wide and away from goals. Then, at the precise moment, he dropped to the ground to try to smother the ball at Pineda's feet like he'd done a thousand times before. Pineda took his cue, making sure there was enough contact with the 'keeper's outstretched hands before tumbling to the ground. The Limerick players knew what was coming before the Danish referee pointed to the spot. They had got nothing off him all evening and sensed things weren't about to change in their favour now. Juanito struck the penalty kick past Fitzpatrick for the equaliser.

GERRY DUGGAN: "I actually had it covered. Kevin, naturally enough, his instincts were to go out for it and go for the ball and he pushed the man wide. But I was coming around the back of Kevin and had it covered but he hadn't seen me and he lunged for it. He didn't make any real connection but the player just dived over him and the penalty was awarded."

KEVIN FITZPATRICK: "Looking at it now I can see exactly why goalkeepers give penalties away on the continent. I mean these guys run at you and as soon as you dive down they're diving over you. I had actually pushed him away from goals, I don't remember anyone around except me so I had to go for it. I didn't think it was a penalty, *no, but sure you would say that, wouldn't you?"*

Limerick's flame burned dimly now. Swamped in midfield where Tony Meaney had come in for Hand, their defence was consequently subjected to a constant barrage. They had sprinted through the first hour but Madrid had come prepared for a marathon over ninety minutes. With just five minutes remaining, the Spanish champions swooped for the winner. Again, Pineda was involved and, like the first, it was a soft goal to concede, from Limerick's point of view. Juanito drilled a free kick at goal, Fitzpatrick blocked it and the ball rebounded kindly for Pineda to knock it in at his ease.

KEVIN FITZPATRICK: "It came from a stupid free kick. What can you say? Just deflating, very deflating to concede like that so close to the final whistle."

A strange mixture of pride in the performance and disgust at the late collapse welled inside the Limerick players as they exited the stage. And, as they embraced their thoughts during the long trip home, it was hard not to wonder how different it might have been at Thomond. Would the referee have been so sure of his offside call for Matthews' goal faced with over 12,000 home supporters in Ireland's most intimidating sporting arena? If not, and Limerick had moved 2-0 ahead with Kennedy's legitimate strike, Limerick would surely have held on for at least a draw. Likewise, would the Scandinavian official have been so content to pull up Fitzpatrick and award Madrid the penalty with derisive cheers, whistles and cries of 'dive' ringing in his ears?

KARL SPAIN: "If we'd played them in Limerick – the atmosphere, everything – it would have been sensational. I think if we'd played them at the Market's Field, or even Thomond Park, it would have been quite a night and maybe we wouldn't have had a dodgy penalty decision given against us."

TONY WARD: "I suppose playing at Thomond would have been like going back to Big Jack's days, it would have been about putting the opposition under pressure, wouldn't it? There would have been a huge element of that. I mean, when we were there it was a case, rugby-wise, of the Garryowen up and under, put them under pressure. So, I'd imagine if Limerick had played there it would have been hitting balls down the channels and pressure them hard, put them under extreme pressure. There would have been a huge degree of that."

KARL SPAIN: "The amount of programmes left over after the Lansdowne game was something else. My family collect football programmes and there were just thousands of them. You could literally take as many as you wanted."

Financially, the first leg had been a write-off, but the tie at least remained in the balance, albeit tipped in Madrid's favour. Hand's thinking on the second leg was simple: to take on professionals and, hopefully, overcome professionals, Limerick must prepare like professionals. In a novel move, the club chartered a plane to bring the team and anyone else who fancied it out to central Spain in style. Those erstwhile fans who'd thought nothing of following their team to Dublin, shelled out two hundred pounds per person for a special package trip to Madrid, not too far off a thousand Euro in today's terms. The Limerick party was well received around the city and particularly at the Santiago Bernabeu Stadium, Madrid's famous home, where they would play the second leg.

DAVE MAHEDY: "We went to see the trophy room in the Bernabeu one of the days. So, we're brought into this room and there are trophies everywhere. We're looking at this, that and the other and then the guide says, 'Are you ready now? We'll go into the trophy room'. We thought we were in it. It was actually just a small annex leading into it. We all looked at each other. The main room was the length of the stand and at the far end were all the European Cups, five or six, whatever number they had at the time. There was one complete section just for European Cups – mind blowing."

The players enjoyed the trip and knocked plenty of craic out of the locals. Each player had been given a new O'Neill's tracksuit for the trip with the brand name emblazoned across the front of all the tops. 'We're the O'Neill family from Ireland,' the players told anyone who was interested, pointing at their tracksuit tops. 'I'm Dave O'Neill, they're all my brothers: Pat, Des, Joe and Kevin.'

EOIN HAND: "The day before the game we went to have a look at the pitch. We walked out with our shoes on and the groundsman came running over, screaming, 'Take off your shoes, take off your shoes'. So, we had to walk on the pitch in our socks. We were kind of saying to each other, 'Sure, we're going to be on it tomorrow wearing studs!' But that was different for this fella. Still, we thought, 'Okay, that'll do'. They took great care of the pitch and you were looking forward to playing on it."

Juanito's strike partner, Santillana, was fit for the second leg and got his start. The experienced Spanish International was rated so highly by the club that he wore the No. 9 shirt, the jersey made famous by Alfredo de Stefano who played in five European Cup finals for Madrid, winning them all and scoring in them all. Reinvigorated and fighting fit, Santillana scored the first two goals of the game in the fifteenth and thirty-first minutes to kill any lingering Limerick hopes of progressing. Trailing 4-1 on aggregate, they were now playing for pride but were determined to win that much. They carried valuable form into the tie with four straight wins to begin the defence of their League of Ireland crown. And, whatever about their late capitulation in Dublin, they'd shown enough over sixty minutes to prove they could open up Madrid's defence. In fact, they almost took an early lead in Madrid before Santillana's brace.

EOIN HAND: "We should have actually gone one up. I got one great chance, from a set piece, a free kick. I had this routine that we practised. It was involving myself and Joe O'Mahony and it worked like a dream. Suddenly, it finished up with me, one against one, with their 'keeper. Lo and behold, I hit it wide. All the other aspects of the free kick had worked perfect. Even afterwards everyone was commenting on that – for an amateur team to come from Ireland and to outfox Real Madrid early in the game and almost go one up, only to miss a sitter. Looking back on it, you know, that was an achievement. But I blew it. I blew it."

Real were operating at least two gears higher than they had at Lansdowne and stylishly swept the ball around the pitch, apparently at ease with their dominance. But they were rocked by a Limerick goal two minutes before half time which changed the complexion of the game at 4-2. It was Kennedy again who picked their pockets, inscribing his name in European Cup history as a scorer in both legs against Madrid. His goal in Dublin was a victory for substance over style but this one was airmailed from his boot with a stamp of class.

DES KENNEDY: "It was a nice goal, all right. We got a free kick on the right, Pat Nolan sent it in, I hit it on the half volley from about eighteen yards. You don't take those ones back. We were losing 2-0 and that made it 2-1, so it gave us a lift at a good time in the game."

DAVE MAHEDY: "Whatever about Dessie's goal in the first leg, when he scored in the Bernabeu I remember the reaction of the Madrid boys, it was just this look of shock on their faces. It was like, 'Who are they to be coming and scoring here?'"

From a position of comfort and control, Real trudged off the field at half time, their shoulders low and burdened by Limerick's redoubled efforts. A full twenty-five minutes of the second half passed and Madrid continued to be locked out in front of goal. Hand was marshalling his men with the authority only a player leading by example can exert until, slowly but surely, his team's energy levels predictably receded just as they had in Dublin. Gaps started to appear in spaces where Jimmy Nodwell, O'Mahony and Duggan had previously patrolled with panzer tank-like efficiency. Morris came on for Hulmes in an attempt to regain ground higher up the field for Limerick. But he, too, found himself tracking back in a frantic bid to plug the holes which were allowing Stielke, Cunningham and Juanito to firstly weave five, ten, then twelve passes together at a time. With twenty minutes to go, exactly as it had happened in Dublin, the Limerick dam burst. Angel de Los Santos raced onto a pin-point through-ball from Juanito. It had just enough bounce left on it for Angel to get his foot underneath and loft it deftly over the head of Fitzpatrick, who could only reach around and swat at air. It was a peach of a goal that opened a pressure valve which had been building in the Bernabeu. By now, 3-1 down and tiring, Limerick's race was run. Only two more minutes passed before they conceded a fourth, Cunningham beating Fitzpatrick from distance with an untypical right foot shot. The English International turned provider six minutes from time when he picked out Pineda for another simple finish, like his goal in Dublin. A 7-2 aggregate defeat felt like an injustice. The gap in fitness levels ultimately told. Hand and Mahedy had brought the team to new levels of conditioning in the previous twelve months, yet they still dipped below Madrid's full-time vigour over the course of an entire game. It was borne out in the stats from the two games: Five of the seven goals Limerick conceded came in the last twenty minutes of the games.

DAVE MAHEDY: "No matter how fit you are it's a mental thing as well when you get towards the last fifteen minutes of a game. Professionals are geared towards really going for the jugular, then finishing off the opponent, whereas part-time players wouldn't have that real cut and thrust. You might get the body fit, obviously you won't get it as fit as the full-time guys, but it's more the mental thing, I think, anyway."

Set in the context of Madrid's whole European campaign, Limerick could be proud of their efforts. The Spaniards went on to beat Honved in the second round and followed that up with victories over Spartak Moscow and Inter Milan to reach their first final in fifteen years. Bob Paisley's Liverpool were the opposition at Parc des Princes in May 1981 but, again, Madrid would rue the interventions of a Kennedy. This time, Liverpool full-back Alan Kennedy struck an eighty-second minute winner from the left of goals to the far corner. It was one of just four goals scored against Madrid in the whole campaign. Three of them were by Kennedys, the fourth by Inter's Graziano Bini. Limerick United never competed in the European Cup again, though the Madrid experience was the first of three consecutive seasons that the Munster club featured in Europe. In 1981 they faced Lawrie McMenemy's high flying Southampton in the UEFA Cup, courtesy of a third-place League finish. With the words 'I told you so' still ringing in their ears, club officials sensibly opted to play the first leg at the Market's Field where they suffered a 3-0 defeat but packed the place out and enjoyed record gate receipts of IR£40,000. Limerick's 1-1 draw at the Dell – thanks to some stunning wing play by Tony Ward and a Tony Morris goal – was one of the great nights enjoyed in the club's successful era. Ward played football when he could fit it in around rugby. He never took a penny in pay so he could keep hold of his independence. In the following 1981/82 season, Ward was an influential figure in the march to a second FAI Cup success. In doing so, he became the first Irish rugby International to hold an FAI Cup winners' medal. On a wet and windy early summer afternoon, Brendan Storan rose above the brutal cup final day elements to volley home a thirty-third minute match winner through a thicket of bodies from Ward's curling corner kick. That afternoon, the gods of football rolled out the red carpet to retirement for Kevin Fitzpatrick. How else can one explain a fresh air kick by a Bohemians player when an empty net begged him to stroke home the equaliser four minutes from time? Limerick escaped and, after the 1-0 win, Fitzpatrick hung up his gloves. On his tombstone they'll etch, 'Kevin Fitzpatrick – The only man to play in every FAI Cup final that Limerick reached'. That summer Tony Ward bade farewell to Limerick, too. His last act was to line out against Manchester United in a high-profile friendly. Those big challenge games excited the city. In August 1981, Glenn Hoddle arrived over with new FA Cup champions, Tottenham Hotspur, and shot four goals in a 6-2 win in front of 12,000 at Thomond Park. In the good days, the Market's Field was the stage where Limerick's footballers came to express themselves week in, week out and to showcase their talents. Pat Grace, who came on board as a sponsor in the late-'70s, and took outright control of the club in mid-1981, viewed the venue differently. For him the rented, bumpy pitch, circled by a dog track, was the very thing that held the club back. He ploughed in thousands to improve the pitch and the spectator facilities, but always dreamt of bigger things. Grace launched an audacious bid, in 1983, to start a new Limerick club with a fresh name and new colours. His efforts to wind up Limerick United and introduce Limerick City – wearing green and yellow in their place – met with resistance. That October, the battle to represent Limerick in the League of Ireland took the owners of the two clubs, City and United, to the High Court and, subsequently, to the peak of farce. Limerick United turned up for one game against Bohemians at Dalymount Park without a clue as to who was going to play for them. Grace was paying the players to play for Limerick City – who weren't yet eligible to play – so United had to cobble together a team at the last minute. Bohs beat them 9-0. The ludicrous story of a city with two teams – one of which wasn't allowed to play and the other which was completely rudderless – gained international attention. The BBC and Channel 4 sent their TV cameras over to investigate. Grace knew he was in a strong position throughout. His City players claimed they were being denied their right to work and won considerable public support as a result. There was also the not inconsiderable fact that Grace, who held the Irish franchise for Kentucky Fried Chicken, was the chief sponsor of the League of Ireland, the 'Pat Grace Famous Fried Chicken League' to be exact. United held their ground for several weeks before a predictable agreement was reached whereby Grace's new incarnation, Limerick City, would replace United in the League. Within weeks, Grace confirmed his intention to purchase the Old Crescent Rugby Grounds in Rathbane, about two miles from the city centre, for his new club. Compared to the City versus United row which played out in the national newspapers, this latest development was barely recorded for posterity. Yet, many people, who followed or were involved with the club at the time, now believe the move was the beginning of the end for Limerick as a national force. Grace wowed locals with impressive plans for a plush new stadium at their new Hogan Park ground in Rathbane, to be partly funded by an innovative new lottery scheme in the city. A promotional brochure was even released depicting families enjoying a day out at the venue. But the best laid plans never came to fruition. By the end of the '80s, local interest in attending games at Rathbane and the enthusiasm of the owners for the project had waned considerably. In 1994, *The Irish Times* reported that, having been declared bankrupt, Grace eventually ceded ownership of Hogan Park to the Bank of Ireland who sold it to its current American-based owner. After Grace's departure, the club changed its name to Limerick FC and returned to its traditional blue and white strip. There was another spell at Rathbane in the 2000s and, for a while, between 2007 and 2009, the club was known as Limerick 37, in recognition of its founding in 1937. Currently, Limerick FC competes in the First Division. It operates out of Jackman Park, a pitch owned by the Limerick District League and, according to the official website, "The spiritual home of Limerick soccer is now Jackman Park". There is hope that, with Bord na gCon taking up residence in a new greyhound stadium on the Dock Road in late-2010, Limerick soccer may finally return to the Market's Field, twenty-six years after leaving. Some believe its status as the 'real' spiritual home of local football is now irrelevant, as many of those who experienced the great soccer days there are either dead or too old to care about the glory days anymore. The counter argument is that Limerick football teams have only ever truly prospered whilst playing there.

TONY WARD: *"In my opinion, the worst move of all was to go from the Market's Field to Rathbane. That was a bad move. I mean the*

Market's Field wasn't the greatest in terms of the distance from the supporters to the pitch but, boy, when you got a good crowd ... I mean, I remember we played Southampton there. I played in that game and the atmosphere in the ground that night was incredible because the place was so packed."

KARL SPAIN: "I was at a match away to Shelbourne last season where there was not even a busload of Limerick fans that went. But they sang from start to finish. Some of the Shelbourne fans, as they were leaving, applauded the Limerick fans. I was blown away by it. The passion is still there at a certain level. I think trying to bridge that gap between starting it and having that bit of success is the biggest chasm of all. If there was a bit of momentum and Limerick were doing well up towards the top of the League of Ireland, I do think you would get people flooding in behind the club again."

EUROPEAN CUP

First round, first leg
September 17, 1980
Lansdowne Road, Dublin
Attendance: 7,000

Limerick United: 1
(Matthews 65)

Real Madrid: 2
(Juanito 70 pen, Pineda 85)

Limerick United: Fitzpatrick; Nolan, O'Mahony, Storan, Nodwell; Duggan (Morris 79), Hand (Meaney 64), Walsh, Hulmes, Matthews; Kennedy.

Real Madrid: Miguel Angel; Perez Garcia (Navajas 79), Benito (Pineda 15), Gallego, Camacho; Isidro, Angel de Los Santos, Stielike, Hernandez, Cunningham; Juanito.

Referee: O. Amundsen (Denmark).

First round, second leg
October 1, 1980
Santiago Bernabeu Stadium, Madrid
Attendance: 50,000

Real Madrid: 5
(Santillana 15 and 31, Angel de Los Santos 70, Cunningham 72, Pineda 84)

Limerick United: 1
(Kennedy 43)

Real Madrid: Garcia Ramon; Isidro, Benito, Gallego, Camacho; Angel de Los Santos, Stielike, Hernandez (Pineda 46), Cunningham; Juanito, Santillana.

Limerick United: Fitzpatrick; Nolan, O'Mahony, Storan, Nodwell; Duggan, Hand, Walsh, Hulmes (Morris 16), Matthews; Kennedy.

Referee: A. Marques (Portugal).

CHAPTER 5

DUNDALK VS TOTTENHAM HOTSPUR
October 21 and November 4, 1981

"Really, there's no way I should have played again. No way. Based on the medical reports at the time: detached medial ligament, badly damaged cruciate. It shouldn't have happened for me again and I had accepted that as fact, and moved on. So, yeah, I do believe Bobby McGregor was gifted." MICK FAIRCLOUGH

Smash! Mick Fairclough's left knee went one way, the rest of his leg the other. Searing pain followed immediately. Nearly forty years on, and the crunching tackle that ended his English League career isn't easily forgotten. Fairclough was on his game for Huddersfield Town that day in September 1973, alive with tricks and flicks, winding the opposing Walsall defence up to breaking point. Huddersfield were in the midst of an alarming relegation slide that would see them drop three divisions in four seasons. Yet only good things were being said about their wiry young forward who'd signed from Drogheda United as an eighteen-year-old in 1971. Fairclough was learning quickly from life at the coalface, against tough as nails defenders like Chelsea's Ron 'Chopper' Harris and benefiting from the wisdom of England International colleagues, Trevor Cherry and Frank Worthington. It seemed only a matter of time before his own international recognition would follow with Ireland. So, as he wove another trademark move with the No. 9 jersey hanging off his slight frame that autumn afternoon, there was no reason to consider anything but his next goal celebration. The rest of his life, he presumed, would simply take care of itself.

MICK FAIRCLOUGH: "I had a full turn on my knee and was about to take off down the line after going by the same guy a few times already. He was probably saying, 'The next time I'll have this fella'. So, I had a full turn on my knee and he came in from the side, hit me on the side of the knee. The knee bent sideways as opposed to bending the way it should do. It shattered. I chipped a bone on the outside of the knee and shattered the medial ligament completely. It completely detached and I badly damaged the cruciate. You can get jobs done nowadays on the cruciate ligament but, at that time, you couldn't. Once you had a cruciate injury, that was it. I was in hospital for a while and then came out with the leg in plaster for a few months. I tried for a while to come back but they took X-rays and did tests and, very quickly after that, told me I was gone. I was finished."

At twenty-two, Mick Fairclough was ordered to quit football forever. Continuing to play the game he loved would risk permanent disability. An insurance assessor investigating his compensation claim agreed he was a lost cause. The money was paid out straightaway. Fairclough was tossed onto football's scrap heap and left to his own devices. Down on his luck, he returned to Drogheda in 1974 and gradually pieced his life back together. He was working away like everyone else a few years later when friends convinced him to take part in a five-a-side tournament. "Okay, it's only a kick-around", he thought, and played. His knee instantly swelled up like a balloon leaving him hospitalised for a week while it was drained. When he bumped into Dundalk manager, Jim McLaughlin, in Drogheda in 1978 thoughts of reviving his football career couldn't have been further from his mind.

MICK FAIRCLOUGH: "I met Jim McLaughlin outside a chemist in the town. He recognised me and we got chatting. He asked how I was doing and about this, that and the other. He asked was I doing anything football-wise and I said, 'No'. He knew about the injury and said, 'Have you been up to Bobby McGregor in Belfast, maybe he could help?' I said, 'Jim, I've been to all the top specialists in England'.

He said, 'Yeah, but this fella is different, you should go up and see him'."

McGregor was different all right. Inadequately titled Physio of Glentoran and Northern Ireland, it did his vast and varied medical abilities a huge disservice. The 'Man with the Magic Hands' possessed no formal physio training but patients who'd visited swore by him. International footballers, champion greyhounds, race horses, athletes, the local public. You name it, they all came to him with strains, ailments and hopeless stories. More often than not, they left with hope in their hearts and a cure in sight. How much they wanted to pay him was entirely up to their own conscience. There was no fee sheet. At the height of George Best's glorious career with Manchester United, he made secret visits to McGregor for help with a knee injury. In Best's autobiography, 'Blessed', he explains how, in the summer of 1966, he travelled home to Northern Ireland for consultations. The club didn't want their most prized asset to be treated by a 'quack' but then they hadn't managed to fix his ailment either. Fearing for his career, Best went with his Dad's advice and stuck with McGregor.

GEORGE BEST: "Bobby was a quiet man, about my height but a bit stockier, with thinning hair and he was, I suppose you would say, a bit quirky. After a few minutes' prodding, he walked away without saying anything. 'What do you think?' I said, but he didn't answer, just came back with a piece of wood, which he handed to me. 'What's this for?' I asked. 'To bite on. What I'm going to do now might hurt a bit.' A bit! As soon as I bit on the wood, he quickly grabbed around the back of my knee, stuck his fingers in and waggled my ligaments around. For a few seconds, the pain was so unbearable that I thought I would bite right through the wood. 'How does it feel now?' he said when he'd finished, standing back. And, though it was sore, the pain didn't last very long. 'It feels a lot better,' I said, feeling the knee. He brought out a jar of sweet smelling cream which he smeared all round the knee. 'What's that for Bobby?' I said. 'It will help the healing process,' he replied. 'Yes, but what's in it?' 'Can't tell you that but it will do you good.' I later learned that this was a cure-all cream, which he administered to every patient, no matter what they were suffering from. You could have had a bad back or a broken leg and Bobby would have given you his cream, though the ingredients were his secret. I don't know whether it was psychosomatic or what, but Bobby's treatment did the trick and a week later I was kicking a ball again."

Dundalk's own bearded warrior, Dermot Keely, got into his fair share of scrapes and was regularly dispatched to Belfast to see the man with the healing touch, too. In time, he'd get even closer to McGregor as a Glentoran player and captain.

DERMOT KEELY: "He was a genius. He was what some people might have called a faith healer. He had a bit of magic in his hands. He treated all sorts; humans, animals, whoever needed him. I mean he had a gift. Absolutely, no doubt about that. He wasn't one of these cranks. He had the gift and was a lovely man."

Intrigued, if not overly expectant, Fairclough agreed to a date with the man of mystery. McLaughlin was the match-maker hoping to spark a romantic return to action. Glentoran were playing Bohemians in a friendly at Dalymount Park and Fairclough was told to meet McGregor in the Glens dressing room afterwards.

MICK FAIRCLOUGH: "He brought me over to the corner of the room and put his fingers in at the back of my knee, twisted it and turned it and said, 'There's fellas with worse knees than that playing. We'll get you right'. I looked at him in wonder because I'd been thinking all along that this was a waste of time – I'm the worst case there ever was. He said to me, 'Go home and I want you to put a poultice of half-vinegar, half-water on the knee every second night. What's wrong is that we have to weaken the knee to make it strong again. The way it's healed is that it's twisted, we need to weaken it to straighten it up'. It *sounded feasible but I was still sceptical. I went home and did what he said. I'd heat the vinegar in a pot and put it on a poultice. I did that for six weeks. Every day I'd smell like an auld chip! The north were playing the Republic in a European Championship qualifier match at Lansdowne, it would have been around late-1978. I rang him and told him I'd done what he said and he told me to come out to Killiney Castle where they were staying. Bobby looked at the knee, sunk his fingers in at the back of it in a really painful way and said, 'Yeah, that's coming along'. He gave me a bottle of lotion and said he wanted me to do vinegar one night, this the other night, for another six weeks."*

The slow process continued for over a year, Fairclough regularly crossing the border to meet McGregor for treatment after Glentoran home games. At the time, he feared the drive north – a single man in an Irish registered car cruising through East Belfast. But, needs must. Often he'd go straight to McGregor's home. Eventually, it was time to put the theory into practise. Fairclough was given permission to start running and training properly again. A weights programme was assigned to build up the muscles in his leg and he stuck to it religiously. By mid-1979, any doubts about McGregor's unorthodox treatment had faded. Fairclough felt like a footballer again. He was a believer. His old club, Drogheda United, were worried about the terms of the insurance settlement and whether he could legally play again, so, a local team took Fairclough on. He played three or four games. One ended in a 6-0 win. He scored all six goals. A national paper did a small write up on it. McLaughlin heard of the heroics and attended Fairclough's next game, a run-of-the-mill 1-1 draw.

MICK FAIRCLOUGH: "Jim asked would I be interested in coming to play for Dundalk. I said, 'Of course, but after seeing that performance I'm sure you're not too impressed'. He said, 'No, I saw enough to see that you still have the hunger, the rest I know about'."

JIM McLAUGHLIN: "I happened to say to him, 'If you're going to play you may as well play in the League as play for a works team'. He said, 'That's good enough for me. I mightn't be able to do the training'. I said, 'That's fair enough', and that's how we got to know one another. There was not a braver footballer in the game."

As it turned out, the terms of the insurance settlement stated that Fairclough could play in Ireland after all, but not England. That suited fine. In March 1980, six years after being officially written off, Fairclough returned to top-flight action with Dundalk, the reigning League of Ireland title holders. His first act was to come off the bench in Milltown and nod home a priceless equaliser against Shamrock Rovers. Dundalk failed to retain the League title but the goal helped secure second spot in the table, a point behind Limerick United. In Dundalk's last six games Fairclough scored four goals. Now almost twenty-eight, his career was stretching out ahead of him once again. The following season he was the Lilywhites' top scorer with twenty goals in all competitions, making his European debut in a terrific 1-0 aggregate UEFA Cup defeat to Porto. In spring, he hit the winner in an FAI Cup semi-final against Finn Harps to book a glamour clash with Sligo Rovers. That felt sweet. Exactly a decade earlier he'd qualified for the Cup final with Drogheda but lost and left for Huddersfield soon after. Now he was determined to make amends, albeit in the colours of Drogheda's great Louth rivals Dundalk.

MICK FAIRCLOUGH: "I remember Dermot Keely and Tommy McConville clashing heads in the first minute of the cup final. The pair of them soldiered on. Keely had a gash that needed six stitches over his eye after the game but played through it and Tommy needed a thing around his head. We were under the cosh that day. The weather was blowing a gale. (John) Archbold was playing on the left wing. He took a corner that swung in and went straight into the net to put us ahead. Late on, Sligo were pushing on and doing very well against us. They had lads like Brendan Bradley and Tony Fagan, good players in a good side, Charlie McGeever as well, a great prospect who nearly went to Spurs. They were attacking and Sean Byrne, God rest him, cleared the ball for us with a long clearance. Sligo had pushed right up to the half-way line and I remember a fella called Paddy Sheridan was marking me. He was a big strong lad but hadn't much pace. A ball was played in between the two of us and I just turned, he tried to take me down from behind because he knew he wasn't going to catch me. I actually felt him clipping my leg but I got away and was clean through one-on-one with Delcan McIntyre in the Sligo goals. Just as I was steadying myself the ball bobbled, Declan came out and went to ground and I just managed to clip it over him. To score in the Cup final at Dalymount in front of a good crowd was great. That was how we qualified for the European Cup winners' Cup."

Jim McLaughlin would pit his wits against the best Europe had to offer again. It was a scenario he savoured. In his eight and a half years as Dundalk manager, between 1974 and 1983, the border club qualified for the European Cup three times, the Cup winners' Cup twice and the UEFA Cup. They were beaten at home only once. That mightn't seem much of an achievement these days when seeding, rankings and coefficients ensure Europe's weakest clubs are pitched in against each other in low-key early rounds. But, by October 1981 and Dundalk's latest European adventure they could boast of either drawing with or beating PSV Eindhoven, Glasgow Celtic, Hadjuk Split and Porto at Oriel Park in the previous five years. Dundalk almost did the unthinkable in 1979 when they came within a goal of knocking Scottish giants and former champions Celtic out of the European Cup altogether. McLaughlin's side beat Linfield first off in an infamous preliminary round clash. The home leg at Oriel Park finished 1-1 and is remembered for the savage sectarian clashes that took place around the game and on the terraces. A report the following day claimed it was the night when, "The concept of All-Ireland club football was killed stone dead," due to, "Two hours of raw, naked tribalism on the terraces," which it took 500 gardai to control. Dundalk were fined IR£900 and

Linfield were stripped of home advantage for the second leg which went ahead in Haarlem, Holland. Dundalk won it 2-0 and, in the first-round proper, beat Maltese champions Hibernians 2-1 to set up the Celtic date. A 3-2 loss in Glasgow meant Dundalk could still dream of joining Europe's elite clubs in the last eight if they could muster a single goal at home, at fortress Oriel. A huge crowd paid IR£38,000 to watch an agonising 0-0 draw. One goal would have secured Dundalk a quarter-final outing with Real Madrid. McConville, charging in at the first post, had a great chance to score from Paddy Dunning's flick on in the eighty-eighth minute but his tame effort was saved by Bhoys 'keeper Peter Latchford. Like most dominant teams the secret of Dundalk's success, both domestically and in European competition, lay in a brilliant defence. Goalkeeper Blackmore forged a near telepathic relationship with his back four of McConville, Keely, Paddy Dunning and Martin Lawlor. As a unit they earned the nickname 'Mean Machine' who, according to McLaughlin, "wouldn't give you a sausage".

TOMMY McCONVILLE: "We'd give bugger all away and probably had the best defensive record in the League at the time."

DERMOT KEELY: "No one could beat us, up there at Oriel. Some of the nights were magic. The Celtic match is one that stands out. We played friendly matches as well. I remember playing Birmingham when Trevor Francis was there, eventually the first million-pound player, but we beat them. No one could beat us. We had a phenomenal team from '79 to '81. It just got together and gelled. It was a very tough, physical team. It wouldn't have compared with the Rovers team that came after it, a lovely passing side. We were uncompromising, that would have been the word. We always reckoned we needed just a goal to win a match. I don't think we set ourselves up like that, it's probably just the way it worked out and the way the players were."

Leo 'Pop' Flanagan and Sean Byrne formed Dundalk's double winning midfield axis along with Brian Duff, while livewire youth international

Barry Kehoe broke into the team soon after and thrilled home fans for almost a decade. Up front, Derry man Hillary 'Hilda' Carlyle top scored in the double winning season. Fairclough's addition improved Dundalk's attacking threat no end, though Keely was a notable absentee by the time the Cup winners' Cup ties of autumn 1981 rolled around. He'd disagreed with the direction the club was headed in after winning the double and made his views known to McLaughlin.

DERMOT KEELY: "I felt the club were taking things for granted a bit and weren't prepared to invest in players. I felt we would slip back if we weren't going to do that and, ultimately, we wouldn't win Leagues."

Keely's flight north meant he, rather ironically, missed out on another League title with Dundalk in the 1981/82 season and, at the beginning of that campaign, a European adventure to beat them all. They were drawn to face Fram Reykjavik in the first round of the Cup winners' Cup, a costly trip that hit the club coffers for IR£11,000 though there was some value for the outlay as they beat the part-time Icelandic team of students, electricians and carpenters 5-2 on aggregate. Fairclough scored in both legs and new signing Eamonn Gregg effectively replaced Keely in a reshuffled back line that now included McConville at centre-half.

MICK FAIRCLOUGH: "When we got to their ground in Iceland it was a bit like the Lourdes Stadium in Drogheda years ago, but in better condition. I poked a goal that put us in the lead but they came back and scored two and beat us, up there. When they came back to Dundalk we beat them 4-0. When we got the first goal in Dundalk they just folded and we beat them well that night. It was another opportunist goal that I got, nothing spectacular about it."

Dundalk's sixth ever European win came with a huge reward – a second-round clash with the aristocrats of the English game, FA Cup holders Tottenham Hotspur, fresh from a 6-1 thrashing of Dutch giants, Ajax.

MICK FAIRCLOUGH: *"The minute we heard about the draw it was just, 'Wow!' We were delighted but also fearful that they may give us a hammering. When you're an underdog you just don't know what will happen. You know you'll give it one hundred per cent, but you never know what way the result will go. The class you would, ultimately, expect to tell in the end."*

JIM McLAUGHLIN: *"It's hard to forget that Spurs team. They had Ardiles, Perryman, Mickey Hazard, the boy that went to Barcelona, Archibald. They had the man that's on the television now, Garth Crooks, Chris Hughton. They were just a class act."*

Eight of the Spurs side that started the first leg at Oriel Park were, or would be, full Internationals, ultimately collecting two hundred and ninety-three International caps between them. Ossie Ardiles had won the World Cup with Argentina in 1978. Glenn Hoddle was rated the midfielder of his generation and displayed all his class just weeks earlier with four goals in a 6-2 friendly drubbing of Limerick United. Full-back Hughton, currently in charge of Newcastle United, was an Ireland regular and wide man Tony Galvin would soon be, too – the green shirt flapping off his waist, the socks typically rolled down.

TONY GALVIN: *"Playing with Spurs was a great experience because we had a very good footballing team with a lot of attacking players. Sometimes we didn't defend as well as we could do which is why we lost games sometimes. But, going forward, we were very positive. We always wanted to win games. Keith Burkinshaw [Spurs manager] instilled that in us. We'd go out to win every game. I know it's not possible but that's how we'd go out to play our football. People like Glenn and Ossie could only play one way – to win."*

Star quality didn't necessarily guarantee humility, however.

MICK FAIRCLOUGH: *"The week before they came over there was a press report, whether it was actually true or not I don't know, but they apparently said they were coming over to play on a pitch surrounded by mud heaps against a pub team. In some of the English tabloids there were some fairly derogatory comments about Dundalk and who they were playing."*

TOMMY McCONVILLE: *"I remember we were called part-timers and that we shouldn't be in the same League as them. We might do well for the first half but they'd take over for the second half, all that sort of stuff. Then they said they didn't want to kill the game in the first leg because they wanted to get a good crowd at home for the second leg. It was all shit, as the fella says. It certainly riled us up, though if anyone needed motivation for a game like that then they shouldn't have been there."*

In the dressing room before the first leg at Oriel Park, McLaughlin held up the newspaper clippings in front of his players. "Is what they're saying about you true?" he probed in his usual measured tones, knowing he'd get his reply on the pitch.

MICK FAIRCLOUGH: *"Jim McLaughlin was a great motivator, not a ra, ra roaring and shouting man, but he'd press the right buttons."*

TOMMY McCONVILLE: *"They were standing in the tunnel before the game. We were coming out of our dressing room and they were already standing there in the tunnel in single file as teams do before a game. They were standing there and giving it all, 'We are Spurs' and, 'We're here to do the job'. We were listening and thinking, 'What a load of shit'. One of the lads went down to the front where their captain Steve Perryman was. Perryman turned around to shake hands and whoever it was said to him, 'Shake hands! I'll shake the bloody throat of ya!'*

He roared it down the tunnel as he said it and the whole lot of them fell silent."

MICK FAIRCLOUGH: *"Believe it or not, even though we were 'no hopers' there was a belief amongst us that we could eke out a result, there definitely was. We did believe, going out onto the pitch, 'We can get a result here'."*

Whatever about the rest of the Spurs players, complacency wasn't going to be a problem for Galvin as he sought to impress Republic of Ireland manager Eoin Hand. While England boss, Ron Greenwood, had advised that Galvin should think carefully before nailing his colours to the Irish mast, the twenty-five-year-old was happy to declare for Ireland, the country of his grandparents, eventually making twenty-nine caps in the 1980s. He sensibly realised that playing in Dundalk represented a great opportunity to impress Hand and kick start that International career.

TONY GALVIN: *"Absolutely, because the Ireland management wanted to see you playing well for your club and expected to see you perform well. That game was just before I started playing for the Republic, so it was also a good experience for me to play in Ireland at another ground outside of Dublin in what was a brilliant atmosphere."*

The official attendance at Oriel for the tie was 17,500. Anyone who was there reckons it was closer to 20,000, with all-but 2,500 of them standing. After the Linfield fiasco of two years earlier, gardai were braced for crowd trouble. Coaches carrying the five hundred or so Spurs supporters from Dublin weren't brought through the town as normal, but took a quieter route and arrived by the Carrick Road before being funnelled into the ground through a specially erected turnstile. Apart from a bout of stone throwing at half time, nothing serious materialised. Dundalk took Spurs by surprise with the power and pace of their early play and forced a third-minute goal chance. Tough centre-half Graham Roberts misjudged a back pass to Ray Clemence which Carlyle intercepted. The angle was too acute, though, and his shot ran agonisingly across the face of the goalmouth. For the first twenty minutes or so it was all Dundalk. They looked like the English First Division side, not Spurs.

TONY GALVIN: *"We knew they'd be tough. We were told – actually by Keith – he warned us, he said, 'This is going to be a really tough game'. He said they were a strong team and they'd done really well and that they were the outstanding team in Ireland. So, we were aware of that. We were expecting a tough game but you know you're still going, 'Oh yeah, it's going to be tough, but we'll be fine'. So, I think we were really taken by surprise."*

MICK FAIRCLOUGH: *"There was a bit of banter between myself and Hillary and the Spurs boys, Paul Miller and Graham Roberts. They were fairly nasty in some of the things they were saying and we were equally as nasty in reply. There was a bit of the 'fenian' stuff thrown at us. But we gave as good as we got verbally and physically."*

Spurs centre-half, Roberts, cultivated a hard man image and, after retiring, brought out an autobiography entitled, 'Hard as Nails'. He met his match in a League game against London rivals Arsenal at the end of the 1980s. Perry Groves was playing up front for Arsenal and felt the full force of Roberts' forearm across his face early in the game. He promised himself revenge. Groves recalled in his own autobiography how, "I launched myself at him with one foot over the ball and another aimed at his knee joint. I was slightly behind him so I was coming in like a stealth bomber. He wasn't expecting it and I remember some dust coming up as he went down. I went over to give him some abuse but then I saw that he was completely still and I thought, 'Fuck it – I've killed him'". Groves hadn't killed Roberts. But the big man must have felt like death as he was carried off the field. Fairclough had been that soldier himself years earlier against Walsall.

MICK FAIRCLOUGH: "You know, I had a lot of respect for Roberts because he did play hard and he did try to wind me up. But that's football. I remember playing against Chelsea when I was with Huddersfield and big John Dempsey was their centre-half. They had a tough side with David Webb and 'Chopper' Harris. It was one of my first games. Dempsey wanted to test my mettle anyway. So, we were running out and the next thing this flash came out of nowhere. He had given me a dig in the side of the jaw. He was testing me and I was the fiery type. I knew I had to react. The next time the ball came in I went in hard, I missed him but if I had made contact I probably would have landed him in the stand or broke his leg or something. I really went in to hurt. I think when he saw that he sort of said to himself, 'This fella is going to kick back, so I'll just play my normal game'. The funny thing is he came to manage Dundalk years later. I was playing with Dundalk at the time and I said to him, 'The last time I saw you, you gave me a dig in the jaw'. He didn't remember. What I'm getting at is that they're the things that happen in games all the time. People test you and they want to see what you're made of."

Back at Oriel, Dundalk's defensive mettle was being tested to the max by resurgent Spurs. After a slow start, the visitors pulled themselves into the contest and soon began to push hard for the opener. Dundalk's defensive dam finally broke in the sixty-third minute when Hoddle picked out Crooks with a rare moment of inspiration. The striker rounded Blackmore and slotted the ball to an empty net. A lesser team might have buckled and allowed the dams to burst completely. But not Dundalk, not with all their European experience, and certainly not Fairclough after all he'd been through to get to this point. Nine minutes from full time, Martin Lawlor played a long ball over the top of the Spurs defence, Fairclough spun Roberts on the half-way line and broke free. Half of Oriel Park lay ahead of him as well as England goalkeeper Ray Clemence, just signed from Liverpool whom he'd won the European Cup with the previous May. As Fairclough bore down on goal, he had time to consider what he was going to do with the ball – to place it or to blast it, that is the question. The answer, he reasoned, was to blast it. "If he gets a hand to it I might score the rebound."

MICK FAIRCLOUGH: *"That was going through my mind very quickly. So he came running out, as all good goalkeepers do, spread himself around sixteen yards from goal and narrowed the angle. I had very little to hit. In hindsight chipping him was probably an option but he'd placed himself so well that I really felt there was little space to aim around him. In the end, I hit it and it went through his legs and in."*

Oriel Park erupted in ecstasy and again when the final whistle sounded a few minutes later to confirm a famous 1-1 draw.

TONY GALVIN: *"When they came back and scored, it surprised us. There was a sort of dodgy period for us right at the end of the game, too. Obviously, you didn't want to get beaten because you'd be really up against it then. We'd been warned it was going to be a tough game, we were warned that they were the best team in the country. We were warned about all these things. We prepared the usual way we would going to any club. But, you know, the ground, the surface, all of that, it's not quite what you're used to. It's a bit of a leveller and, yeah, I would say probably a bit of complacency did seep in to the team."*

A deep sense of satisfaction swept through Fairclough as he considered the long and rocky road he'd travelled to redemption and the greatest night of his football career, so far. He owed it all to one man, Bobby McGregor.

MICK FAIRCLOUGH: *"There was euphoria after the game. I came into the bar afterwards and everyone was saying, 'Well done, Mick' and clapping me on the back. But this reporter came up to me and said he had a bit of bad news. He said, 'Your old pal dropped dead out in Sofia'. It was Bobby McGregor he was talking about."*

In one of football's most cruel ironies, McGregor suffered a massive heart attack close to the same time Fairclough had scored the most memorable goal of his career for Dundalk. He'd keeled over after attending to injured Glentoran player, Alan Harrison, in a UEFA Cup game against CSKA Sofia in Bulgaria. It was his fifty-fifth birthday.

DERMOT KEELY: "I was playing for Glentoran that night. He dropped in front of me. I thought he was messing. It was just coming up to half time and he came in and collapsed. I thought he was wasting time but, of course, he wasn't and it was awful. That was an absolute tragedy. We went in at half time and at that stage, we knew that he was in another room, dead. I remember talking about things at the time and we really didn't want to go out for the second half. But you do what you do."

MICK FAIRCLOUGH: "Talk about bitter-sweet for me. To have scored against Spurs and him having been the reason I was back and then to hear he had dropped dead on the very night I had scored. I was devastated really. It took the good out of it. The next day, on the back of some of the papers, there was a headline about me scoring and Bobby dying. There was an association or link made between the two. I went up to his funeral in Belfast and the vicar held up the paper. He'd been talking about what Bobby had done for players. He said, 'There's a player here today and I'm looking at a report about what this player did as a result of Bobby's help'. He went on to say it was just a testament to Bobby about what a guy had done after his help. I do remember that all right. He specifically mentioned me in that clipping. He was making the point about what a great gift Bobby had given to the likes of myself when he'd been alive."

JIM McLAUGHLIN: "Mick will tell you today, 'Jim, I don't know what he done. I don't know what he done but he gave me belief I could play again'. Mick was a cripple. He was a cripple and had given up playing football in England."

MICK FAIRCLOUGH: "I do believe Bobby was gifted. I do believe he had something that was more than just what you would expect in someone that's treating you. There was just an aura about him. He was such a good man."

In all, McGregor gave twenty-six years of unbroken service to Glentoran, from 1955 until his death. He even managed them for a spell in the mid-1970s and won a League title in 1977. Today, the treatment room at The Oval, Glentoran's ground, is named after him. Fairclough struggled to reconcile his emotions for a long while afterwards. A media circus raged around Dundalk for days after the club's sensational European achievement which outdid any of the great nights of the 1970s. Fairclough was at the centre of it all and should have happily reflected on his unprecedented riches to rags and back to riches tale. But he'd just lost his friend and mentor. The only thing he could do, he vowed, was to dedicate himself fully to finishing the job against Spurs at White Hart Lane, as momentous a task as that sounded in his head. The trouble was, Spurs were forewarned this time. If they'd taken Dundalk for granted in Ireland they wouldn't do so again in north London.

TOMMY McCONVILLE: "Ray Clemence at the time was staying in the same hotel as us over there. He was only after moving down from Liverpool. Spurs were training that day and we were training that morning also. At lunchtime, he was there sitting on his own and he says to the English press, 'This game has had some impact on the manager, Keith Burkinshaw'. All the English press were there and saying, 'But this should be easy and this and that. You should win by four or five goals'. Ray just stopped and said, 'Excuse me, were you over there for the first leg?' The man says, 'No'. 'Well,' he says, 'these so and sos will run all night, tackle all night and they'll still be going strong at ninety minutes. If you think it's going to be easy, I'm telling you now, it's not. If anybody thinks it is then woe betide them'. Half of the English press hadn't even travelled over to watch the first leg and just presumed it would be a doddle in London."

In the intervening two games, Dundalk lost to Bohemians but a hard fought 1-1 draw with Drogheda in the Louth derby set them up for the tough trip to London. Spurs warmed up for the tie with wins over Manchester United and Southampton. They were building a new stand, at the time, so only three sides of their White Hart Lane ground were open for Dundalk's visit. Even at that, 33,500 packed in to see what the Irish were all about. They got one of the first glimpses of eighteen-year-old playmaker Kehoe, who oozed as much class in midfield on the night as his opposite number, Ardiles, and beat the Spurs defence more often than not with his pace and trickery. A Dundalk side, wearing a novel red away strip and carrying several knocks – McConville took a painkilling injection before the game while Fairclough was battling against his knee as usual – rarely threatened the Spurs goal like they'd done at home. Fairclough was a lone attacker and spent most of the night tracking back to help out a midfield under siege. Blackmore pulled off a couple of great saves from Archibald and Hughton. The crossbar saved Dundalk on another occasion. They held out for over an hour before Crooks struck the decisive blow for Spurs, his sixty-third minute goal coming at the exact same time he'd broken the deadlock at Oriel. For all their stout defending it was a soft goal Dundalk's well drilled rearguard conceded. Hoddle's corner kick pin-balled around the Dundalk goalmouth, skidded off Dunning's thigh, whose performance until then had been exemplary, and fell to Crooks who squeezed a shot home. It was 1-0. And that's how it stayed.

TONY GALVIN: *"It was an edgy night. The crowd were very much on edge. They certainly acquitted themselves well. They played some lovely football and gave us a really hard game. We got through by the skin of our teeth. Keith wasn't particularly happy. It was okay away from home because you really want to avoid getting beat. But it was quite disappointing the way we played at home. We really struggled to beat them. That was a testament to how difficult they were to beat."*

MICK FAIRCLOUGH: *"On one of the few occasions that we did go forward I got the ball and was upended in the box. To this day I think it was a penalty."*

But the spot kick wasn't given and Spurs boss, Burkinshaw, was the most relieved man in the English capital when referee, Paul Rion of Luxembourg, blew for full time. His team had made it through to the second round, if only just, on a 2-1 aggregate scoreline.

TOMMY McCONVILLE: "We were walking off and the crowd were cheering and clapping us. We got a great ovation. We said to ourselves, 'We must have done something right'. Mind you, I think it was probably because we had scared the life out of them."

TONY GALVIN: "They made a big impression on the Tottenham supporters with the tough game they'd given us. Maybe they made people in England aware that there actually are a lot of very good players in the Republic. There were a lot of good players out there then, but it's not like these days when there's a lot more coverage on television. You're a lot more aware of players in different Leagues and countries now. In those days, a lot of people in England wouldn't have known much about the League of Ireland and the quality of players in Ireland."

MICK FAIRCLOUGH: "People came up to us, Tottenham supporters, and actually congratulated us. They said it was an amazing performance from a part-time team. That's a memory that a lot of us have because the Tottenham Hotspur supporters would be partisan with the best of them, but they gave us an ovation off the pitch."

Fairclough and Roberts endured a stormy relationship over the two legs but swapped jerseys when it was all over. Roberts clapped Fairclough on the back and said, 'Well done', an unexpected but appreciated gesture. Later that night the two teams met in a local bar and drank the night away. Perryman, Hoddle, Ardiles and Roberts were all there trading tall tales with McLaughlin's men. Bloodied but unbowed, Dundalk's European quest was over. Spurs made it to the semi-finals of the tournament where eventual champions, Barcelona, beat them 2-1 over two legs. The following season the north Londoners retained the FA Cup and in 1984 won the UEFA Cup on their home ground in a two-legged final. They beat Drogheda United 14-0 in the first-round of that UEFA Cup campaign and, in the final against Anderlecht, started six of the players that lined out at Oriel Park, with Ireland's Galvin outstanding. Fairclough's reincarnation continued at Dundalk with his first League winners' medal in April 1982. He was the club's top scorer for three seasons in a row and, against the odds, international recognition came his way in 1982 against Chile, the first of two caps.

TONY GALVIN: "I was quite new to the Irish scene at that stage. Mick had a reputation as a very good player who had been in England. You wonder if he'd maybe had other opportunities he could have had a longer career in England. Sometimes with football you need a bit of luck, sometimes things can go the other way for you with injuries and that kind of thing."

Fairclough learned to accept his lot. He took the road less travelled but eventually reached his destination, albeit without his great companion McGregor, when he pulled on the Ireland jersey in May of '82. 'A good day's work', McGregor must have thought as he looked down from above.

MICK FAIRCLOUGH: "When I went to Bobby McGregor my goal wasn't to play League of Ireland at any level. I just wanted to be able to play. It was almost as if I was trying to prove people wrong, that I could play again. I didn't really care what level it was at, but, as things turned out, it went well for me. I actually couldn't have asked for a better comeback and to play for Ireland as well. From that point of view it's something you dream about really. It doesn't happen for many people."

EUROPEAN CUP WINNERS' CUP

Second round, first leg
October 21, 1981
Oriel Park, Dundalk
Attendance: 18,000

Dundalk: 1
(Fairclough 81)

Tottenham Hotspur: 1
(Crooks 63)

Dundalk: Blackmore; Gregg, McConville, Dunning, Lawlor; Flanagan, Byrne, Kehoe, Duff (Archbold 72); Fairclough, Carlyle.

Tottenham Hotspur: Clemence; Hughton, Miller, Roberts, Perryman; Hazard, Ardiles, Hoddle, Galvin (Smith 76); Archibald, Crooks.

Referee: A. Delmer (France).

Second round, second leg
November 4, 1981
White Hart Lane, London
Attendance: 33,500

Tottenham Hotspur: 1
(Crooks 63)

Dundalk: 0

Dundalk: Blackmore; Gregg, McConville, Dunning, Lawlor; Flanagan, Byrne, Kehoe, Duff (Archbold 65); Fairclough, Carlyle (Reilly 76).

Tottenham Hotspur: Clemence; Hughton, Miller, Roberts, Perryman; Hazard, Ardiles, Hoddle, Galvin (Smith 76); Archibald, Crooks.

Referee: P. Rion (Luxemburg).

EUROPEAN CUP WINNERS' CUP

First round, first leg
September 16, 1981
Laugardals Stadium, Reykjavik
Attendance: 2,200

Fram Reykjavik: 2
(Torfasson 65, Steinsson 70)

Dundalk: 1
(Fairclough 25)

Fram Rekyjavik: Baldursson; Haraldsson, Bjarnason, Sveinjonsson, Hauksson; Thorkelsson, Geirsson, Ormslev, Gudmundsson; Steinsson (Arason 51), Torfason.

Dundalk: Blackmore; Gregg, McConville, Dunning, Lawlor; Flanagan, Byrne, Kehoe, Archbold (Duff h/t); Fairclough, Carlyle.

Referee: M. Rolles (Luxemburg).

First round, second leg
September 30, 1981
Oriel Park, Dundalk
Attendance: 2,600

Dundalk: 4
(Flanagan 4 pen, Fairclough 23, Lawlor 49, Duff 62)

Fram Reykjavik: 0

Dundalk: Blackmore; Gregg, McConville, Dunning, Lawlor; Flanagan, Byrne, Kehoe, Duff; Fairclough (Archbold 65, Reilly 77), Carlyle.

Fram Reykjavik: Baldursson; Haraldsson, Bjarnason, Sveinjonsson, Hauksson; Thorkelsson (Jonsson 68), Geirsson, Ormslev, Gudmundsson; Arason (Steinsson 80), Torfason.

Referee: T. Maanson (Denmark).

CHAPTER 6

BOHEMIANS VS GLASGOW RANGERS
September 18 and October 3, 1984

"I never came across an atmosphere in football as bad as that. Even though it was a relatively small crowd at Dalymount Park, in terms of some of the grounds I played at with Rangers and Dundee United over the years, I have to say that the atmosphere was quite distasteful. I suppose there was an awareness, as Rangers players, that we felt we were going to get a bit of stick from the crowd but I don't think anyone really, honestly believed it would amount to what it did." IAN REDFORD

Broken glass showered Jock Wallace's face like hailstones in a windstorm. He'd tried to duck at the last moment when the bottle came flying towards his passenger seat window but was too late. It crashed through the glass and eventually came to rest at his feet. Outside, Bohemians fans scattered in different directions. "Drive, bloody drive!" bellowed Wallace in his thick Scottish accent as the bus driver found first gear and watched with relief as Dalymount Park disappeared rapidly in his rear view mirror. Wallace exhaled and swivelled his large frame around to check on his Rangers players on the team bus behind him. They sat silent and stony faced, happy to leave a night of religious bigotry behind them. An uneasy atmosphere had welled inside Dalymount all evening as Bohemians supporters chanted the name of their Catholic cousins, 'Celtic, Celtic'. Hard line Rangers fans, mostly from Ulster, who'd travelled down for the first-round European Cup tie, replied with anti-Irish bile. Early in the second half, some of the Rangers fans seized a banner from a group of Raheny Boys Club members supporting Bohs. A regiment of gardai attended to the uprising and frogmarched one Rangers fan out of the ground. Wallace wasn't easy prey to fear. Respect and, regularly, intimidation were the carrots he'd used to extract the sort of performances from his Rangers players that earned them two domestic trebles in the 1970s. He managed Leicester City for a spell in the early-'80s, too. Gary Lineker recalled how once, after scoring two first-half goals for the Leicester reserves, Wallace unexpectedly pinned him against the dressing room wall at half time and, "called me a lazy English this and that!" In October 1975, Wallace wiped beads of cold sweat from his brow and shards of glass from his blazer after the 1-1 draw with Bohemians and prayed he'd never see Dalymount Park again. He meant it with all his heart. Less than a decade later, however, he and Bohemians manager Billy Young would be reunited all over again for a European tie at Dublin's cathedral of soccer. If 1975 was a battle, then what occurred in 1984 could best be described as all-out war. That their rematch was in the UEFA Cup and not the European Cup neatly summed up the positions occupied by both clubs in their respective Leagues as the '70s spilled into the '80s. For all the differences between the two clubs and the fact that their fans loved to count themselves as the best of enemies, Bohs and Rangers actually shared similar tales in this time. Both teams won their respective 1977/78 League titles but then had to watch, with seeming paralysis, as their rivals picked their pockets for all the big prizes. A 'new firm' had emerged in Scotland consisting of Alex Ferguson's Aberdeen and Dundee United to rival the traditional 'old firm' duo of Rangers and Celtic. For Bohs, the enemy also wore green and white hoops – Shamrock Rovers. Out at Milltown, Jim McLaughlin's revolution had just begun and, when all was told, they'd collect four League titles and three FAI Cup wins in the mid-'80s. They'd pilfer from Bohs in other ways, too, as Gypsies defender Dave Connell recalled.

DAVE CONNELL: *"In the couple of seasons before playing Rangers, a few of our key players had gone to Rovers, lads like Mick Byrne, Kevin Brady, Jacko McDonagh, they'd all left. Eventually, Paul Doolin left us too for Rovers. It was a shame really. It was a time of 'nearly getting there' for Bohs. I mean we got to two Cup finals in '82 and '83 and were beaten in both of them. Losing those Cup finals was heartbreaking. Then, we qualified for the UEFA Cup to actually play Rangers by finishing second in the League behind Rovers. So we were kind of the nearly team of that era."*

If second best had become a condition at Dalymount, being drawn against Rangers in Europe presented the chance to be kings, for a night at least. Motivation wouldn't be a problem, not when Rangers were the opposition. Between the four walls of the home dressing room at Dalymount Park the old religious and political divisions highlighted by the champions of Catholic Ireland taking on the Protestant half of Glasgow didn't matter a jot. But the players weren't stupid either. They knew what to expect from the terraces and what was expected of them. They weren't going to walk out into a seething cauldron of furious rivalry and accept second best in front of the eyes of their fans and the entire nation. The first leg was scheduled for Dublin in mid-September, 1984. As the game neared it became increasingly obvious to Bohs officials that what they had on their hands was a ticking time-bomb with the potential for seismic damage. Billy Young was preparing his players to unleash hell. Behind the scenes, the Board were taking their own measures to stop hellfire breaking out on the terraces between both sets of supporters. A fortnight or so beforehand, round-table discussions took place in Dublin involving directors of Rangers and Bohemians, gardai from the Bridewell and a representative from the British Embassy. Early on in the talks, they agreed that segregation of the anticipated 2,000 travelling Rangers fans – many of whom were expected to come from the various Rangers supporters groups in Belfast – was a must. Wallace, now in his second stint as Rangers manager and mindful of the treatment meted out to him when last at Dalymount, travelled over on a separate reconnaissance mission to review the club's security procedures. He was joined by Rangers secretary, Campbell Ogilvie, who met with Bohs secretary Paddy Neville. A logistical plan for getting the away fans in and out of the ground safely was hatched. They would enter only at the Connacht Street side and would be escorted back afterwards to Glasnevin Cemetery where their coaches would be waiting to take them home. A 'no alcohol' policy was decided upon while flagpoles, which could be used as missiles, and large banners that may incite tensions, would be confiscated. "All our discussions will hopefully minimise any crowd trouble," said Neville, who added that, "Segregating the fans should eliminate all the problems". Hostility, however, brewed around Dalymount Park throughout the morning and afternoon of the first leg. Rangers supporters gathered around the forecourt of the shopping centre that backs onto Dalymount Park and multiplied quickly with each coach-load that was dropped off. Local pubs shut, in line with the gardai's zero alcohol policy, but it wasn't hard for enterprising young men to lay their hands on enough booze to fuel an idle day in Dublin. Many brought their own supplies. As the evening encroached on an afternoon's supping, the mood darkened around Phibsborough. Gardai took a 'kid gloves' approach to the situation, opting for a policy of containment and a general marshalling of the area to avoid a riot. An hour or so before kick-off, the gates were thrown open and the away fans piled onto the terrace behind the goals at the shopping centre end of the ground. Bohemians supporters, many wearing Celtic jerseys, green and white hats and scarves, filled the opposite end – the school end. Where the two sets of fans might be expected to meet in the middle, a couple of thirty-foot high barriers were erected to segregate them with a no-go area in between. The first flashpoint occurred when a Union Jack flag was set on fire by home fans banked behind an array of tricolours. Minutes before the game was scheduled to begin, Wallace had to be summoned to beg for calm among the Rangers fans who sought revenge. He pleaded with them to remove a Union Jack that had been hung provocatively from the fencing. It was taken down to ironic cheering from the Bohs fans. It was to those strains of hate-filled sectarian chanting that the two teams emerged. Bohs midfielder Paul Doolin was only twenty at the time and braced himself for a position on the front line of battle.

PAUL DOOLIN: "It was my first game in Europe, and I remember coming out onto the pitch in Dalymount and I couldn't believe the amount of people down at the shopping centre end of the ground. I couldn't believe it. It was unreal. We heard that, because of who we were playing, there could be trouble. It didn't really bother me beforehand but, coming out onto the pitch, I just couldn't believe it. That's being honest. It was an intimidating atmosphere."

Goalkeeper Dermot O'Neill had his back to the 3,000 Rangers fans in the first half and, as missiles rained down on him, he got a sense of what it must be like in the trenches with bullets whizzing by your head.

DERMOT O'NEILL: "In the first half there was a garda behind the goal and at one stage the ball went wide. One of their supporters put a hand through the wire and kind of looked at me very menacingly. I turned to the garda and I said, 'Will you get that ball?' He just said, 'No way. I'm not getting it'. So, I said, 'Right, I'm leaving it there. I'll get another ball'. I actually do remember, because I counted, that I got twelve pounds sterling in coins thrown at me that night. I gave it to the groundsman at the time. It was funny because when I went over to Scotland to play in the return leg I got 10p. They were far more charitable over here!"

That either team was able to concentrate on the game itself was a wonder. That Bohemians served up one of the great performances – perhaps the greatest, in the circumstances – by a League of Ireland team in European competition was nothing short of a miracle. The 'nearly men' tag which Bohs assumed in the '80s by losing back-to-back FAI Cup finals to Limerick United and Sligo Rovers in 1982 and 1983 and finishing in the League's top three on five occasions was gloriously cast off in a setting that inspired the spectacular. Full-back Dave Connell set the tone for a resolute display as he got the toughest task of all – marking Rangers' best player, international winger Davie Cooper, in the right-back position in front of the away crowd – and thrived.

DAVE CONNELL: "They certainly weren't intimidating me, not at all. I was just focusing on keeping Davie Cooper quiet. He skipped by my first tackle or two but then I kind of got to grips with him and felt I did well."

Paul Power, who'd only just arrived with a rising star reputation from Home Farm, took the other full-back position, while Barry Murphy and John Reynor manned the centre of defence. Reynor replaced Ronnie Murphy who was ruled out because of a two-year-old suspension picked up while playing for Shamrock Rovers in Romania against Universitatea Craiova in the UEFA Cup. One of the defensive pairing's primary tasks was to muzzle young Rangers striker Ally McCoist. These days McCoist is an Ibrox legend. His prolific strike rate backboned the club's nine-in-a-row of SPL titles in the late-'80s and early-'90s. But he was still trying to make his name at the club in 1984 after a miserable spell at Sunderland. Midfielder, Ian Redford, arrived at Rangers for a Scottish record fee of Stg£210,000 in 1980 and remembers the early days of McCoist's fifteen-year playing career with Rangers.

IAN REDFORD: "The supporters got on his back and they made life difficult on him, which didn't help. The one thing that you can't take away from Ally is that he had the chance to leave Rangers, and they actually wanted rid of him, but he didn't want to go and he refused to go. He decided that he wanted to battle for his place. He turned his situation around."

McCoist ingratiated himself with the Rangers fans at Dalymount by scoring after just seven minutes. It was the worst possible start, from a Bohs perspective, and appeared to signal a long night of suffering. But a young team full of youthful promise drew on the atmosphere and the occasion to launch an inspired comeback. In the twenty-fifth minute they drew level with a poacher's goal from David 'Rocky' O'Brien which laid down the marker for a wonderful game of tit-for-tat scoring.

DAVID O'BRIEN: "Craig Paterson was playing for Rangers and I took the chance that he was going to back pass it to the 'keeper. He did and I caught it in between them. Basically, I went around the 'keeper and put it in with my left foot. It was a bad goal to give away, from their point of view."

Bohs' callow defence, none of which was over twenty-four, conceded again just three minutes later and to a set piece they should have defended much better. Cooper tossed in a corner kick that should have been meat and drink for the backs, but big Dave McPherson headed in comfortably for Rangers. Youthful exuberance ensured, at least, that nobody in a red and black shirt panicked. In an open game they would continue to get their chances. In fact, only another seven minutes elapsed before they dramatically equalised for a second time. Again, it was a bad error at the back from Rangers and, again, 'Rocky' was the man who took advantage with a crushing blow to the solar plexus of the opposition. Connell floated in a hopeful cross and Rangers 'keeper, Nicky Walker, under pressure from Bohs winger Mick Shelley, dropped the ball for O'Brien to tap in. Rangers had conceded just one goal in seven Premier League games beforehand. Now, in thirty-five minutes, they'd leaked double that amount to the part-timers.

DAVID O'BRIEN: "They were two tap-ins I scored, to be completely honest. Nicky Walker kind of palmed the second one out to me and I headed it in. I didn't get too many of them! In fairness to Walker, he didn't do himself justice against us at all. Both of my goals I would put down to bad defensive errors but, I suppose, you have to be there to put them away, too."

In the Bohs corner, 'Rocky' weighed in at only ten stone and stood just five feet, seven inches. The Rangers match programme for the second leg described him as an, "Irish U-21 star," whose, "lack of weight makes life just a little difficult as a striker but his astute passing skills more than make up for that handicap". At his best he was a split atom, all flair and energy. By his own admission, he regularly capitalised on the extra attention given to his forward colleague, Jackie Jameson, whose princely skills earned him just about every moniker possible from the Bohs fans. For a while, he was called, 'The Irish Stanley Matthews'. By the time he passed away, suddenly, in 2002 those who'd followed his career had settled on 'The Great Man'. Jameson was an instant hit at Dalymount and was adored from the moment he knocked back Jim McLaughlin's advances – and almost certain silverware with Dundalk – to join from St Pat's. He scored soon after joining in a 2-0 win over Sligo Rovers in September 1981, the same day midfielder, Doolin, who also scored, made his debut. Doolin went on to enjoy a trophy laden career and picked up medals at Rovers, Derry City, Shelbourne and Portadown. Jameson devoted the best years of his career to Bohs in the '80s but, unlike Doolin, never won a thing of note in one of football's great injustices. A modest, shy man, he was Bohs' silent assassin who'd turn up, play his football and slip off into the wilderness. At twenty-seven, he was the elder statesman of a young team when they played Rangers, but was in his prime and frustrated defenders John McClelland and Paterson with his mazy dribbles, close control and endless wizardry.

DAVID O'BRIEN: "McClelland was a Northern Ireland International at the time but Jackie was exceptionally good for us. He played up front and was absolutely superb, in both legs. Certainly, he should have played at a higher level. Jackie was just a pure ball player, the ball would nearly have been talking to him in training. He had a special ability all right, I'd certainly say that."

DERMOT O'NEILL: "At the end of the day, what a player. You can't take anything away from him, what a player, just brilliant. He had skill to burn. He was like a pre-Liam Coyle. He was the quietest guy you could come across but, once he crossed the white line, he was different class, absolutely different class."

The sight of the combative Doolin winning a crunching tackle in midfield or of Larry Wyse slipping a pass to Jameson for another trademark run enraged the Rangers fans. Red mist clouded the terraces. They'd watched in horror as their team twice threw away the lead in the first half to a bunch of part-timers and, when the whistle went for half time and the teams departed to the sanctuary of their dressing rooms, it all kicked off. Rangers fans spilled out onto the pitch and fought a prolonged battle with gardai. Bohs fans got stuck in, too, on the terraces. Vicious fighting broke out as supporters scaled the partition fences and locked horns. Gardai intervened but had to retreat from the terraces when two of them were knocked to the ground and pelted with coins, bottles and stones. A unit of riot police was summoned from Mountjoy to quell the violence and baton charged the rabble, pulling the worst of the offenders out and arresting them. In all, five gardai had to be taken away to hospital, four were released but one stayed in overnight. In former Celtic player Paulo di Canio's autobiography, the Italian describes the old firm derby between Rangers and Celtic as the greatest derby in football, even bigger than the rivalry that exists between his beloved Lazio and Roma. Redford played in several old firm derbies, including one the previous month in front of 43,500 and, three years later, competed in a UEFA Cup final for Dundee United against Gothenburg. The decisive second leg of that final was played at a heaving Tannadice Park in Dundee. But he never experienced intimidation like the night Rangers played Bohemians at Dalymount Park.

IAN REDFORD: "It's quite vivid, even now. It was frightening. It was scary. I remember standing in the penalty box waiting on a corner kick and a dart landed right at my feet. I didn't come back up for the corners after that. I stayed up on the half-way line. There was actually talk in the dressing room about the game being abandoned at half time. As usual, the lunatic fringe were getting a bit carried away that night, which was a shame. It was a pity. Yeah, looking back, it was quite intimidating. I never came across as bad as that. Even though it was a relatively small crowd in terms of some of the grounds I've *played at over the years I have to say that that atmosphere was quite distasteful. I suppose there was an awareness that we felt we might get a bit of stick from the crowd. But I don't think anyone really, honestly believed it would amount to what it did."*

DAVE CONNELL: "I suppose you'd have to say, in this day and age, you'd be looking at a game being called off with all that kind of stuff going on."

For the second time in the evening, Rangers boss Wallace was forced to march out onto the field and appeal to the Rangers supporters for calm. He was joined by his centre-half, McClelland and, between them, they restored some semblance of order. The pitch was cleared and the fans were separated again. Amazingly, the game resumed.

DAVID O'BRIEN: "Going out for the second half, you could feel it was a rather intimidating atmosphere, all right. But we were probably on the safest place of all – on the pitch."

The devil had made work for idle minds at half time but a gripping second-half of action kept both sets of supporters glued to the action, save for a few bouts of missile throwing. Rangers had more of the ball but Bohs had more of the chances. After a shaky first half, Bohs' back four tightened up noticeably and formed an impenetrable unit that wouldn't be breached again. McCoist and Stg£200,000 strike partner Iain Ferguson were both replaced by the seventy-first minute. Rangers only really threatened a third goal when McPherson beat O'Neill with a shot but Connell got back to clear the danger. At the other end of the field Jameson didn't get the goal he deserved though he cleverly retained possession and consistently brought those around him into play. He could mix the steel with the silk too. One of his dribbles from the half-way line was eventually halted at the edge of the penalty area but, just as full-back Ally Dawson was about to clear the danger, Jameson came sliding across with a heavy duty tackle that claimed man and ball. On a night of drama lifted straight from the fiction books it was fitting that the game was, ultimately, decided in typical Roy of the Rovers fashion – by the captain of the home team scoring a wonder goal from twenty yards. The second half was only six minutes old when Gino Lawless, Bohs' skipper and their most experienced European player, added another crucial rider to his name that will follow him to the grave – 'The Man who Scored that Goal'. At first, there wasn't a whole lot on when the ball crept loose to Lawless on the left wing from a tangle between Doolin and Dave McKinnon. But he ran diagonally at goal and, while Jameson commanded the full-back's attention with an overlap towards the left corner flag, space opened up inside, allowing Lawless to cut onto his right foot. Like a darts champion he took his back lift and let fly from just outside the left edge of the penalty area. Bullseye! Walker wasn't unlucky in goals this time – he had no chance as the ball dipped in over his head into the far corner of the net.

GINO LAWLESS: "Everything is still vivid. The goal, the game, the crowd, the build-up, the importance of it. Every week and every year that's gone by, the goal came from further out. I think I scored it from the half-way line last week! But I saw it on tape and it was only just outside the box. Over the years it's been exaggerated – going from twenty yards out to forty yards, or whatever."

DAVID O'BRIEN: "It was a super goal, worthy of winning a game like that. Like I said, my goals were two tap-ins, Gino's goal was the best of the night, by a mile."

PAUL DOOLIN: "It was a brilliant goal, an absolutely brilliant goal."

DERMOT O'NEILL: "Gino just gave himself half a yard, that's all it was, and the 'keeper had no chance with the shot. I was behind it watching from the other end of the field. To see it going in and the crowd just erupting was some moment. It's one of those moments you'll always remember and still makes the hairs stand up on the back of my neck. It was amazing stuff, absolutely amazing. When you take the tension and the fighting and all that negative stuff out of it, the game itself was end-to-end. I mean, they went 1-0 up, then it was 1-1. Then they went 2-1 up, then it was 2-2. Then Gino bangs it in the top corner to win it! That was just the stuff of dreams."

IAN REDFORD: *"Maybe there was a little bit of lethargy on the part of our players in the first leg. We just treated the game a little lighter than we should have. We treated it more like a League game than a game against tougher opposition. When you start a game in that frame of mind, quite often it's tough to get yourself out of it. Then when you go a goal behind, as we were for most of the second half, it's hard to lift yourself."*

DAVE CONNELL: *"People may argue that it wouldn't be the strongest Rangers team ever, but the likes of McCoist was there, a couple of Scottish internationals, John McClelland played in the 1982 World Cup, Davie Cooper was a fantastic player, Dave McPherson the same, so it wasn't such a bad team."*

JOHN REYNOR: *"I felt afterwards that we should have beaten them by more. I thought that we were the better side by a long way. After Gino scored to go 3-2 up, Rangers just seemed to give up. I think they were happy enough to take it over to Glasgow at 3-2. I thought we were the better side on the night, by a mile, and should have probably hit them for four or five."*

DAVID O'BRIEN: *"In fairness to Jock Wallace he came in afterwards and he was very gracious. He said well done and all the rest of it. For a part-time team to beat Rangers at the time would have been a fair kick in the teeth, so he was quite gracious."*

The remarkable 3-2 win was manna from heaven for the statisticians. It was the first time Bohs had ever scored three goals in a European game, and none of their players had scored a double in one game before. O'Brien's brace also put him top of the club's all-time scorers list in Europe. All eleven goals they'd racked up until then had come from different players. In the club's twenty-first game in Europe, they'd spectacularly come of age, grabbing the keys to unlock a first win for an Irish team over British opposition. The great underachievers of the '80s had finally found their niche. Inside the Bohs dressing room, the party kicked off. Outside on the mean streets of Phibsborough the rioting resumed. Several hundred gardai in full riot gear were waiting at the shopping centre end of the ground and, for a while, managed to keep the crowd in check. There was a skirmish when a gang of local youths tried to attack the departing Rangers fans and the windows of the former Gaywear store in the shopping centre were smashed. The worst of the disturbances were saved for the route from Dalymount Park to Glasnevin Cemetery where most of the coaches for the Rangers fans were parked. Rampaging hooligans smashed everything and anything around them. Residents cowered in their homes as stones, bricks, bollards and bottles were hurled through their windows, their cars overturned. Local businesses, including Ranks Flour Mills, Des Kelly Carpets and the Brian Boru Pub, had doors and windows smashed and missiles pelted at them. Over a quarter of a century later, the fear instilled by the mob and the prospect of a possible reprisal attack – as unlikely as that is – prompted several business owners still trading in the area to turn down interview requests for this book. One anonymous shopkeeper, whose premises was open when the mob rolled by, recalled events: "It was horrific to be completely honest. You're not just talking about hundreds of them coming down the road but thousands, a lot of them chanting fairly obscene religious stuff. You certainly got the feeling that a lot of these guys were well used to acting in this way. One shopkeeper recalled, "I remember there used to be a bus stop outside our premises and there was a girl standing there, she was a nurse who we knew from the shop. She just had this startled look on her face when she saw this huge group coming her way. We pulled her into the shop and shut the door and waited until they went by. It was probably only fifteen or twenty minutes until they were all gone but it felt like an hour. Just about everything you can think of was thrown at our windows. We were lucky because we had more wood than glass in the shop front so we were safe enough inside. A guy who I was friendly with owned another shop nearby and had gone home. He asked me to ring him if his windows were put in. When I rang him to tell him it had happened he picked up the phone and the first thing he said was, 'Ah, I expected this call'. The next day he called me in to look around his shop. His place was in bits and, in the middle of the floor, was the entire flashing lights and siren off the top of a garda car. I don't know, the police must have abandoned the car and they ripped this thing off and put it through the window. Basically anything that could have been used as a weapon or a missile was; bins, signposts, rocks, bottles, anything that was handy. Of course, most of the traffic lights along the way were smashed to bits as well." In the shopkeeper's opinion, the gardai were partly to blame for tacitly allowing the all-day drinking binge that fuelled much of the aggression. Whilst the majority of the carnage was wreaked by Rangers supporters, Bohemians followers clearly weren't entirely blameless either. Some Dubliners, who weren't at the game, took matters into their own hands, stoning the Rangers buses as they stopped at traffic lights in Finglas on the road out of Dublin. The rocks and missiles that broke the coach windows were kept as ammunition by those onboard to shell cars, businesses and houses in towns like Slane, Collon, Ardee, Castlebellingham and Dundalk. A garda spokesman described the road north after the last of the convoy had passed through as resembling, "a Vietnam battlefield". The next morning Gino Lawless, a postman, was up at six in the morning for work, as usual. He hadn't got much sleep but was still buzzing. 'Rocky' O'Brien was in early, too. He'd got off early from his engineering job to play the game and had time to make up. It was only when the players picked up the papers that morning that they realised the full extent of what had taken place the previous evening after the final whistle. The front page of the *Irish Independent* was dominated by three separate pictures of gardai restraining rioters on the pitch at half-time. There were details of the bedlam between the ground and the coach stops. The headline screamed, 'Rangers fans leave trail of destruction'. 'Chaos at Dalymount' was the lead story in *The Irish Times*, too. 'Gardai injured as Rangers fans riot at match.' Wallace told reporters, "One can tolerate a certain amount of boisterous enthusiasm but what we saw here tonight was a disgrace to football and a sad reflection on Rangers".

DAVE CONNELL: "It was only after the game that we realised what had gone on at half time, let alone afterwards. The next morning in the papers it said that buses had been bricked all the way back to Larne, or wherever, on the way back to Belfast. It was pretty scary when you thought about it the next day."

The Dublin District Court convened less than forty-eight hours after the game. Just one of the rioters was actually Scottish, five hailed from Northern Ireland and the other six were from Dublin. Despite the fact that Rangers fans were largely blamed for the anarchic scenes, a Finglas man received the heaviest punishment, a three-months suspended jail term and a IR£250 fine. He was charged with possessing an offensive weapon, a chain, which he explained he needed because, "I was afraid for my life". The court heard that the lone Scot and a Belfast man, waved a Union Jack in front of a man on a bike, pushed him off the bike and kicked and punched him. A man from Newry pleaded guilty to throwing a bottle at a passing CIE bus and escaped with a IR£2 fine. The other charges included breaching the peace, riotous behaviour while drunk and urinating in a public place. A major security operation lay ahead for the away leg in Glasgow. An appeal to the fans for good behaviour before the first leg had obviously fallen on deaf ears. The next logical step of banning Bohs' fans from attending Ibrox Park altogether was taken. It mirrored the decision taken by Shamrock Rovers to refuse Linfield a ticket allocation for their European Cup game at Milltown the following evening, which passed off peacefully. Remarkably, all three League of Ireland teams competing in European competition in the 1984/85 season drew British opposition. Champions Rovers faced Irish

League winners Linfield while FAI Cup holders UCD took on FA Cup victors Everton. It was a security nightmare for the gardai as the home legs of all three games demanded a considerable increase in normal policing levels. Bar some trouble with travelling Everton fans on a B&I Line boat, and some stone throwing after the game in Milltown, the UCD and Rovers ties were without incident. Bohs paid a heavy price for the shameful scenes in and around the first leg. Locals were left traumatised and many, naturally, blamed the club for bringing a rogue element into their community. Some claimed a right to compensation from Bohs for damage to their businesses and personal possessions. As for the UEFA Cup itself, it was a huge setback for the team to be stripped of all travelling support for the second leg. Rangers posted a warning in the match programme under the headline, 'BEHAVE!' but what chance of a riot was there really, or of serious disturbance, when everyone in the ground supported the same team? Into this supercharged atmosphere of an entire stadium baying for their blood, the Bohemians players prepared to go.

DAVID O'BRIEN: "I could only speak personally but I wouldn't have had an inferiority complex going in against any team. When we beat Rangers at home I was going over there thinking that I wanted to do my very best. There was none of this, 'Keep the score down' mentality. Without sounding smug, we were quite a good side. That's not being arrogant. Really, I'd put a lot of it down to the media, they were the ones who were billing it as 'David versus Goliath'."

Bohs stayed at the Albany Hotel in Glasgow, a hangout of the rich and famous over the years. The build-up was trouble free, in every sense, and Billy Young saw no need to change a winning team.

DERMOT O'NEILL: "They were great to us over there, in fairness. Some of the lads had a tour of their trophy room and all that kind of thing. They were very nice, no problems at all."

DAVID O'BRIEN: "There was a fair bit of media interest over there. It was such a shock that we'd beaten them, so there would have been a fair amount of interviews and people at the hotel and that kind of thing. I think they were presuming it would be six or seven-nothing over there, but that certainly wasn't the case."

Rangers replaced error-prone goalkeeper Walker with thirty-seven-year-old Peter McCloy who'd won a Cup winners' Cup medal for them way back in 1972 and also played in the European Cup ties against Bohs in '75. The travelling Gypsies had no fears about their own 'safe hands', O'Neill, who received a timely boost on the afternoon of the game – his big brother's lucky gloves. The previous night, Dermot's brother, Alan, had played his heart out for UCD against Everton in the Cup winners' Cup. Alan let in just one goal at Goodison Park and had kept a clean sheet in the first leg in Dublin wearing the same gloves. He asked a couple of journalists travelling on to Glasgow from Liverpool to pass the gloves on to Dermot and they duly obliged. When the last man into Ibrox had been accounted for, the attendance figure peaked at 33,000. About twenty of them were Bohs fans who huddled together like sheep in a wide open field.

DERMOT O'NEILL: "The three sides of the ground were full and there were fifteen or twenty of our supporters in a whole two-tier stand. I think UEFA decided that there had to be a stand for the few of our supporters that were allowed to go. In the first half, looking up at them was the weirdest thing. You had something like 30,000 Scottish fans baying for you. Then you'd look up and there were the fifteen or so poor souls! It was weird, all right."

PAUL DOOLIN: "I remember someone saying to me, 'You thought it was bad over here in Dublin – wait 'til you get over to Glasgow'. When we came out that night at Ibrox, there were about 35,000 at the game. I have to say, the atmosphere was, well, I think someone threw a bottle at us and then you had the usual songs they were singing. One of the lads got a bit intimidated and he wasn't sure if he was all right to play, because it was intimidating. Everywhere you looked it was red, white and blue, bar one end of the ground. Funnily enough they felt that if Celtic hadn't been playing in Europe that same night we might have got 10,000 of their fans at the game supporting us."

A draw was all Bohs required to qualify for the second round because of the 3-2 win in Dublin. But sitting back and waiting for the play to come to them was anathema to players like Jameson who contributed wonderfully to a game that, if anything, was even more exciting than the first leg. Rangers enjoyed a patent on possession but found it tough to make it count. O'Neill was a frustratingly impassable obstacle in the Bohs goals. Jameson was inspired again as a lone striker and, with two men struggling to mark him, a sense of grudging admiration emerged from the stands as he flicked, tricked and shimmied his way through the evening. After surviving a series of near misses in the first quarter of an hour, or so, Bohs enjoyed a brief respite. 'Rocky' O'Brien shot wide from a good position and, in the eighteenth minute, Jameson's header wasn't too far off target. The tempo of an already exciting game increased in the run-up to half time when only the agility of O'Neill saved Bohs from conceding the goal that would have put Rangers, already with two away goals, in the whip position. The big Dubliner put his brother's gloves to good use when he tipped away a crashing drive from McCoist and then denied Ferguson. Bohs were also lucky to escape a penalty call when John Reynor got his body and, specifically, his hand, in the way of Bobby Russell's shot.

DERMOT O'NEILL: "John Reynor handled it and put the ball out for a corner. It was in the box and he would never have got near the ball! They were baying for our blood but the ref gave it as a corner and that was great. Everything was going for us. We kind of thought, 'Jesus, we might do something here'."

Bohs hoped they'd weathered the worst of the storm but, if anything, bolts of blue lightning struck with even more ferocity in the second half. Twice Rangers hit the woodwork in desperate bids to claw back the goal they needed. Redford hit the crossbar with a header from Russell's fiftieth minute corner kick and, with just sixteen minutes left, substitute David Mitchell – who surely holds some sort of record for playing professionally in Australia, Scotland, Turkey, Germany, Holland, Hong Kong and England – clipped the post with a shot.

IAN REDFORD: "We just had a very frustrating night. I think in these situations, quite often the pressure can start to work against you because the longer the game goes on without you scoring the more tense and uptight you start to get. You feel the pressure from the crowd and you feel, within yourself, that you've got to get that goal. You start to get a bit wound up so, yeah, the longer it went on the harder it became that night, it really did, and in the last ten or fifteen minutes a bit of desperation crept in. You've really then got to do what you can to get that breakthrough – or you're out."

Cooper's industry, in particular, threatened to make the belated 'Gers breakthrough. Yet, as they committed men to attack and replaced both their forwards in a frantic search for a goal, they left gaps at the back. Barry Murphy seized possession for Bohs and burst out of defence, eating up the space ahead of him before releasing O'Brien who darted between Dawson and McClelland. 'Rocky' shot wide and cursed his errant footwork but was gifted an opportunity to make amends with only eight minutes left. An away goal would have meant game, set and match to Bohs but, as history beckoned, the two goal hero of Dalymount hesitated and put a poor header on Jameson's nonchalant chip pass. McCloy easily gathered. At around the same time, the small band of brothers supporting Bohs were ushered from the ground by police. It was for their own safety, to make sure they'd be well away when the main gates opened and turned the local roads a royal blue colour. The group were only a few hundred yards away when, with just six minutes to go in the game, guttural roars rose up from Ibrox behind them. No explanations were necessary apart from which Rangers player had scored – it was Craig Paterson. The skipper had seen Lawless' 'Captain Fantastic' intervention at Dalymount and raised him. Cooper, of course, was the provider with a curling free kick that begged just the slightest of touches. Paterson was happy to oblige and O'Neill was beaten in cruel, cruel circumstances.

DAVE CONNELL: *"On the night the wet ball just skidded off his head into the corner. It was a good finish, in fairness. Dermot had been top class up to that but he had no chance with it."*

It only levelled the tie 3-3 on aggregate but Rangers had those two precious away goals. In the end, they didn't even need to use that 'get out of jail free' card. A second goal in the eighty-eighth minute secured a 2-0 victory and a 4-3 win overall. Redford showed his class with a diving header from Cooper's cross that rippled the rain sodden net.

IAN REDFORD: *"I've actually kept a photograph of that goal. That's how I remember it so well. I've got a folder that I keep a lot of photographs from past games in and it's in there with them all."*

The mental picture of the late goals is still etched in the minds of the Bohs players, too. The term 'so near but yet so far' was never as apt. The visitors trudged off the field with not a single fan in situ to praise their gargantuan efforts. Alone with their thoughts in the dressing room, the sound of silence was only broken by a familiar Scottish brogue, Rangers manager Wallace. He picked out Jameson and slapped him on the back. "You almost cost us a million pounds tonight, son", he said, in reference to what he believed a money spinning second-round draw with Inter Milan was worth to the club.

DAVE CONNELL: *"There were a lot of tears shed in the Ibrox dressing room that night. I'll always remember Jock Wallace coming in and saying he was six minutes away from losing his job. That's what he said to us but, you know, at the time we didn't really care because we were just heartbroken. I remember Dermot [O'Neill] was badly affected by it that night. He was in tears actually. We were very, very close to something amazing. It was heartbreaking."*

DAVID O'BRIEN: "That dressing room was very low. I've never seen a dressing room like it. I've lost Cup finals and things like that but this was absolutely, well, there weren't too many that didn't have a tear in their eye. We were all gutted."

There were crumbs of comfort in seeing Rangers beat Liam Brady's Inter Milan 3-1 in the next round at Ibrox, having moved heaven and earth to put just two past Bohs. Brave Bohs, the team that won nothing only the imagination of a generation.

DERMOT O'NEILL: "Other than the President's Cup or the Leinster Cup we never won a major honour. It's a travesty really. You had the likes of Rovers playing against us who went on to do the four-in-a-row. Then again, you can't always put it down to luck. With all due respect to Sligo and Limerick, we should have beaten them in the two Cup finals we played. That goes down in the history books and you can't get it back."

DAVE CONNELL: "I suppose, when you think about the result in Ibrox as well, it was another 'nearly there' situation."

UEFA CUP

First round, first leg
September 18, 1984
Dalymount Park, Dublin
Attendance: 12,000

Bohemians: 3
(O'Brien 25 and 35, Lawless 51)

Rangers: 2
(McCoist 7, McPherson 28)

Bohemians: O'Neill; Connell, B. Murphy, Reynor, Power; Shelley, Doolin, Wyse, Lawless; O'Brien, Jameson.

Rangers: Walker; McKinnon, McClelland, Paterson, Dawson; Fraser, Redford, McPherson, Cooper; Clark (Ferguson 71), McCoist (McDonald 78).

Referee: R. Roberts (Wales).

First round, second leg
October 3, 1984
Ibrox Park, Glasgow
Attendance: 31,000

Rangers: 2
(Paterson 84, Redford 88)

Bohemians: 0

Rangers: McCloy; McKinnon, McClelland, Paterson, Dawson; Russell, Redford, McPherson, Cooper; Ferguson (Mitchell 58), McCoist (Fraser 71).

Bohemians: O'Neill; Connell, B Murphy, Reynor, Power; Shelley, Doolin, Wyse, Lawless; O'Brien, Jameson.

Referee: M. Moffat (Northern Ireland).

CHAPTER 7

GALWAY UNITED VS GRONINGEN
September 16 and October 1, 1986

"We went in the bus and went to the pitch in Galway [Carraroe] and what the hell! I think, 'Where are we going to? Maybe we're on the moon!' We were on a route at one stage and we had to stop because there were all kinds of donkeys walking across the road. The pitch was in the hills if I remember. I couldn't believe the pitch was flat but it was flat. It was very Irish and I liked it very much." HENK HAGENAUW.

The clouds didn't exactly darken their hue or collect menacingly over Croke Park to a background of thunderous noise. There were no reports of the soil shifting around the grave of Michael Cusack in Glasnevin Cemetery. But there was no denying that the great Irish sporting institution that is the Gaelic Athletic Association took a direct hit on a late June afternoon in 1977 and from its oldest foe – soccer, the garrison game. The old bones of Semple Stadium creaked that Sunday as Cork fans sprang to their feet in celebration of a late goal from Ray Cummins that secured victory over Waterford in the Munster hurling championship. The cries of relieved Rebels echoed a mile or so away around the main square in Thurles where Cusack and the other founding fathers of the GAA bore a sporting son in 1884. While Cummins was applying the finishing touches to another masterful display at the birthplace of the GAA, Thurles was the subject of a separate discussion in Dublin's Merrion Square at the FAI's Annual General Meeting; Thurles Town wished to join the League of Ireland and after some debate their request was granted. The home of Gaelic games now possessed a new tenant. An application by a second non-

League club, Galway Rovers, to play with the big boys was also received by the FAI that day and got the green light. As it turned out, the admission of Thurles into the League of Ireland was chiefly a psychological blow for the GAA. The soccer club rarely impinged on the resources of hurling hot beds like Thurles Sarsfields. In fact, their League of Ireland existence lasted just five years before consecutive rock bottom finishes ensured they were deemed unfit for re-election. The FAI's decision to include a Galway soccer team for the first time proved to have a more lasting impact on the GAA. Unlike Tipperary, Galway churned out senior hurling and football teams with realistic All-Ireland ambitions each season. In future, they would have to battle a strong adversary for the full commitment of talented youngsters. The new soccer club, in time, would also present the GAA with a second major headache by instigating a heated national debate about the issue of playing 'foreign' sports on GAA pitches. Galway Rovers' first steps in senior football took them to the Sportsground for a pre-season challenge in July 1977 against Scottish side East Fife ahead of their maiden League of Ireland campaign. Traffic restrictions on College Road where the sides played out a 2-2 draw weren't necessary. Just 400 turned up. The road to revolution and mass approval, as manager Amby Fogarty well knew, is seldom smooth and inviting. Rovers officially became United at the start of the 1982/83 season though the name change didn't stop them from hitting serious financial difficulties that almost sent them tumbling in the same direction as Thurles Town. In December '83, the entire board was cleared out and replaced by successful local businessmen Joe Hanley and Mattie Greaney, the new chairman and treasurer respectively. The white knights assumed IR£36,000 of the clubs' IR£42,000 debt and constituted a new, more efficient, slimmed down board. They installed professional structures off the field that allowed players like Eamonn 'Chick' Deacy, Paul McGee, Stephen Lally and Ricky O'Flaherty to inspire the club's on-field fortunes. Galway finished sixth in the 1984/85 season, their first time inside the top eleven, and qualified for the European Cup winners' Cup as runners up to Shamrock Rovers in the FAI Cup final.

RICKY O'FLAHERTY: "Joe had a number of men's clothes shops around the town and the other fella was involved with Greaney Glass. The two guys stepped in and they pumped a bit of money into the club and brought stability you could say. Before that, the committee had been there from the start and I suppose they were a little bit naive when they started off in the club. These two guys came in as prominent businessmen. They were used to running businesses and dealing with businesses. They kind of ran the club more as a business rather than being supporters like the previous committee were. They stood back and looked at the business side of things before they looked at how the football was going."

Terryland Park in the city was home to Galway United. It wasn't the most salubrious of settings, however, and was deemed unsuitable by UEFA to host their first ever European game. They took on Danish side Lyngby at the Sportsground instead, eventually losing 4-2 on aggregate. Hanley had applied for the use of the GAA's Pearse Stadium in Salthill but was knocked back on the basis that the GAA rulebook didn't permit soccer being played at their grounds. The availability of the Sportsground softened the blow that year. But when the Sportsground was also taken out of the equation a year later by UEFA because of a lack of adequate fencing around the pitch – one of the reasons Terryland couldn't be used – the issue of the GAA extending a helping hand shot to prominence. Galway qualified for the 1986/87 UEFA Cup after their highest ever league finish, second. Only for an end of season speed wobble, Tony Mannion's side might have even stolen the title and ended Rovers' four-in-a-row odyssey. With six games to go Galway were unbeaten and just two points behind leaders Rovers with a game in hand. They also had to play the Hoops at Terryland Park so their destiny was very much in their hands. But a 3-1 home defeat to Rovers in what proved a title decider meant Galway ended up having to settle for second place. Groningen of Holland would provide the first ever UEFA Cup opposition for Galway. Martin Moran, an FAI Cup winning full-back with UCD in 1984, knew no more about Groningen than the next Irish man, pretty much nothing, but fancied the idea of playing in Europe again and agreed to join Galway.

MARTIN MORAN: "I was really attracted by the prospect of playing in Europe for a second time because the first time against Everton with UCD was such a magnificent experience. I was newly married and newly qualified as a solicitor and there were a few players from Dublin playing for Galway and travelling down so the whole thing looked a good prospect. I thought they could win something and was excited about the whole challenge."

Groningen had emerged as strong challengers to Holland's traditional big three of Ajax, PSV Eindhoven and Feyenoord with a fourth place finish in the Dutch Eredivisie. They'd displayed their intention to compete at the very top level by re-signing prolific striker Peter Houtman. His 30 goals for Feyenoord had earned him Europe's silver boot award as the second highest scorer on the continent in 1983. Young forward Rene Eykelkamp was a Dutch International-in-waiting while, years later, midfielder Johan de Kock would help Holland get the better of Ireland in a play-off at Anfield to reach the Euro '96 finals. Galway's pressing problem was that they had nowhere to play the second leg, their home leg. The local community put pressure on the GAA to intervene. Mayor of Galway, John Mulholland, wrote to GAA President Mick Loftus asking him to make Pearse Stadium available for a one off UEFA Cup game. The 'miracle' Mulholland said he was hoping for was dashed at an early stage, however, as he was directed to review the letter of the GAA's law. It's Official Guide stated that, 'All property including grounds ... shall be used only for the purpose of, or in connection with, the playing of games controlled by the Association, and for such other purposes, not in conflict with the aims and objectives of the Association, that may be sanctioned from time to time by the Central Council'. The push to make certain GAA grounds available for other sports had become an irksome issue for the amateur organisation long before the Groningen situation arose. As far back as 1957, there were calls for a crucial World Cup qualifier between Ireland and England to be played at Croke Park instead of Dalymount Park. More recently, in 1980, they'd been accused of scoring a spectacular PR blunder by not opening the Gaelic Grounds for Limerick United's European Cup tie with Real Madrid. Limerick played the game at Lansdowne Road and a pitiful crowd of 7,000 turned up. Mayor Mulholland told RTÉ TV news what he thought of the 'our hands are tied' reaction from the GAA regarding the Groningen game. "It's their pitch. It's money they raised themselves albeit the money was raised from the people of Galway city who weren't necessarily associated with the GAA in any way. There were a lot of businessmen, professional men, ordinary working people who put the money in and I'm certain the majority of them aren't all members of the GAA. So, therefore, I think they could soften their attitude a little". But there would be no softening of attitudes and no one-off arrangement. The GAA's rules simply didn't allow for it and their message to Galway United was clear – you're on your own. Club officials sat back and considered the alternatives. They could play the game in Athlone at St Mel's Park or maybe in Sligo or Limerick. But the mood of all concerned was to keep the game in the county. That way, at least, the local economy would benefit. They got their wish as, in a most ironic twist, they eventually settled on playing the game out in Carraroe in west Galway. And on a GAA pitch, of sorts. Out in the Gaeltacht village of Carraroe, about twenty-five miles from the city, the local community had just opened a redeveloped sports field and complex following a IR£150,000 makeover. Most people presumed that Pairc an Chathanaigh, in the heart of Irish speaking Galway, was owned by the GAA as it was home to the Carraroe, Rosmuc and Carna GAA clubs. But it was actually a community ground. The MacDara soccer club played there too while there were plans to construct an athletics track around the pitch and build tennis courts on the site. The idea of bringing the UEFA Cup to Carraroe was the brainchild of Galway Rovers secretary Bernie O'Connell.

BERNIE O'CONNELL: "At the time I was teaching in the Irish college in the area so I knew of Pairc an Chathanaigh. Seeing as this was a public pitch I thought it would solve the problem. You must remember that it had just been renovated. It was as good as any pitch in the country. I thought this over for a while. One Saturday I met with Joe Hanley. I said, 'Don't call me crazy but I think we can solve this problem'. He came out with me to take a look at the pitch that evening. He thought it was a great solution."

Galway United would play their first ever UEFA Cup home game on what was for all intents and purposes a GAA pitch – even though the GAA had barred them from entering one of their grounds. Sean Kelly, President of the GAA when the decision to open Croke Park to other sports was taken a couple of decades later, took a keen interest in goings on in western Galway in the mid '80s.

SEAN KELLY: "There was a lot of discussion on it and people were saying, 'Should it be played there or should it not?' Essentially, the rule was against it but the fact that Carraroe was a community ground meant there was a little loophole there that they were able to avail of. That probably suited everyone in the sense that there wasn't as much stick flying around, particularly in the local area of Galway over it. But if it was fully vested in the GAA it wouldn't have happened."

Ricky O'Flaherty took particular stick for what was viewed in certain GAA quarters as an opportunist move by Galway United. The United forward was also a strong Gaelic football player with both the St Michael's club in the city and the Galway county team. He won two Connacht SFC titles in the 1980s. He should have known better than to rile his own, or so the claim went.

RICKY O'FLAHERTY: "I think Carraroe was nearly blacklisted from the GAA for letting us play out there. There was a huge hullabaloo altogether. There were die hard GAA guys and they just couldn't get over it. They thought it was a disgrace. I played for the county as well around the same time. I used to play the soccer during the winter and the GAA during the summer for the county. For myself, playing in Carraroe was great. I thought it was a fantastic idea but there were some die hards that couldn't get over it at all. Sure I got it big time. Guys from my own club, St Michael's here in the town. One of the guys used to call into the house nearly every day and he was fuming about the game. He was going off the head. He thought it was blasphemous to have a soccer team on the hallowed turf of a GAA pitch."

Aside from the odd blow-in like Martin Moran it was a largely home-grown Galway United side that took to the skies for Holland and the first leg of their UEFA Cup tie that September. Stephen Lally, Kevin Cassidy and O'Flaherty sat together on the flight. A quarter of a century on they're giving back to the soccer community what they once received; O'Flaherty takes the Galway U-11 team, Lally has the U-12s and Cassidy is with the U-14s. Another native, Eamonn 'Chick' Deacy, was the star defender of the era. He won the English league with Aston Villa in 1981 and played four times for Ireland before returning to his roots in 1984, to work in the family shop. In October 2009, NUIG awarded him an honorary degree for his achievements in the game though he sat out the Groningen ties with a pelvic injury. Fellow International Paul McGee was Galway's stand out striker. The Sligo native would go on to set a club scoring record of seventy-four goals. He arrived at Galway in 1985 with sixteen Ireland caps under his belt, the majority picked up while playing for QPR and Preston in England. Having swapped jerseys with an eighteen-year-old Maradona after Ireland played World Cup champions Argentina at Lansdowne Road in 1979, McGee wasn't daunted by the prospect of meeting Groningen.

PAUL McGEE: "I suppose I'd been out of professional football for, I'm not sure, a year or two by the time of Groningen so I was really looking forward to playing those games. In Holland, the press people were looking into Galway United and I was getting a bit of headlines as an

International. Going out to Groningen was great. They were a club putting a push on to get up there with the likes of Ajax and the PSVs. They'd spent a lot of money that year. They had a super side in fairness."

MARTIN MORAN: "They were typical of a team that got on a roll at a particular time, a little like Kaiserslautern did in Germany a while back. These days I often watch Dutch league football on TV but I don't think Groningen have come to any great prominence since then. I think that was their best period. I stand to be corrected but they had beaten Ajax the previous season and given the likes of PSV tough games as well. A very close knit and homely club they were. Houtman was an outstanding talent for them."

The lone Englishman in the Groningen team was attacking full-back Paul Mason. The former Everton trainee was picked up by the club while working locally in the town and playing for an amateur team. The move would revive a career that took Mason on to Aberdeen and, 158 appearances later, to Ipswich Town where he finished his career in 1998.

PAUL MASON: "The Galway United game was my first in Europe. It was a big occasion for me and I have vivid memories of it for that reason. I'm a Liverpool man so I'd obviously heard the Fields of Athenry *sung but that was about as much as I knew about Galway before then! I'd never been there before or anything like that. Naturally we did a bit of checking on the opposition before they came over and Paul McGee was their man striker who could score goals. He was a player we were wary of at the time."*

Tony Mannion and his Galway players flew into Amsterdam before boarding a coach for the two hour journey north to Groningen. There they booked into the Euromotel where the hostelry was far more accommodating than the quarters Lyngby had arranged for them the previous year beside a busy railway track in Copenhagen. Groningen's local newspaper *Nieuwsblad van het Noorden* described Galway as 'unknown opposition' and stated that the home team can 'expect a clear cut win in opposition to the Irish part-timers'. The media's confidence, despite not knowing anything about Galway United, was based on the fact that Groningen had assembled a star-studded side with ambitions of going far in the competition.

PAUL MASON: "Houtman was a top player. He scored goals all through his career wherever he went. He was a player who knew where the net was and played as an International. Eykelkamp, I would say, was a player like Peter Crouch, very awkward to play against. I played with him, obviously, but I'd imagine he was very difficult for opponents to mark. He was unpredictable and very tall, just a really good player. De Kock was strong and as the seasons went by he matured and excelled and just got better and better. It wasn't until after I left that he really progressed. I was full-back but more of an attacking defender. I was never a good defender, to be honest. I was more of a midfielder or even an attacker. When I got in the team the manager picked me at right-back and I said, 'I can't play right-back'. But he had something in mind for me as an attacking full-back with a good engine. He must have seen something in me because half the time left-wingers or forwards were more worried about me going forward than the other way around. If you imagine the style of Roberto Carlos bombing forward, I think that was the style that the manager had in mind. It was an excellent team to play in."

Things were looking good for the 'unknowns' at half-time though as Galway held their own in front of 16,000 Dutch fans at the three-quarter full Oosterpark Stadium. United had fallen behind after just four minutes when a Mason cross sat up perfectly for Eykelkamp to deliver a delicious volley to the net but a 37th minute penalty conversion from McGee left it level at the break, 1-1.

PAUL McGEE: "I really enjoyed the night because I was up against a man called John de Wolf who played in England afterwards and I gave him a good running. I was on my own up front. I got into the box with de Wolf and he kicked me. I was giving him a good chasing and he brought me down."

Groningen masseur Henk Hagenauw gave a couple of players a rub down at half time in the corner of the dressing room. He got on with his work in silence as manager Rob Jacobs unleashed a torrent of abuse at his underperforming players.

HENK HAGENAUW: "At half time our coach was rather pissed because the score was 1-1 then. He came in the dressing room and he was shouting at the players. 'Hey, what the fuck are you playing at? They don't understand anything about football. Kill those guys!'"

RICKY O'FLAHERTY: "Before we went out to Holland at all for the first leg our manager, Tony Mannion, sent two of our club committee members out to watch Groningen the previous weekend. They were playing Ajax in a League game. They told us, 'Listen lads, they're not very good in the air, knock it in high, use the high ball'. So we said, 'Grand'. We formed a game plan to keep the ball knocked long and high. It wasn't until we walked out onto the pitch before the game that we saw every one of them nearly was over six foot! There were only two guys I think playing with them who were under six foot; Paul Mason was about five foot nine and they had one other guy of about five foot eleven. Everyone else in their team was between six foot and six foot five! We were looking at each other saying, 'How the fuck are these not good in the air?' We played the game and it was 1-1 at half time. We're saying, 'Great, let's keep this going'. We went out in the second half, they started knocking the ball in high to their forwards and got four goals, three from headers! It wasn't until after the game when we were having a beer and the two boys came in that we said, 'Jesus, what's the story lads? You said these guys weren't any good in the air but they were bloody brilliant! They were all giants!"

MARTIN MORAN: "They were huge, absolutely huge. They were the biggest team I've ever played against and probably the strongest team I've ever played against."

RICKY O'FLAHERTY: "De Wolf was a big tall man with long blond hair and a beard. He looked like a fecking Viking. He was playing centre-half and I was playing in the forwards. I thought 'Fucking hell, this fella is going to eat me never mind kick me'. Eykelkamp was another massive man, about six foot four, with long, curly hair."

PAUL McGEE: "Tactically we were very naive out there. We got hit for five. I suppose we tried to play ball with them instead of closing up the gates at 1-1. In those days, when you talk of coaching and systems, we weren't professional enough but those were the times. League of Ireland as a whole wasn't professional enough and Galway United certainly wasn't professional enough to cope with what we were going into. We had a very good team on paper when you look at it but, tactically, I suppose we were just a bit unaware. We had a very good first half out there, played well, matched them, but fitness wise they were full-time professionals and that helped them."

PAUL MASON: "We were a bit scared thinking they might put on a good show when they pulled the goal back. But we were able to relax when we got the few goals in the end. Galway were a part-time side so they wouldn't have been expected to go through to the next round. I think they would have been happy just getting into Europe, the occasion and having a good time in Holland."

RICKY O'FLAHERTY: "We went into the bar out in Holland, the players' lounge, after the game. A few of us went up to the bar and called for a beer. The Dutch boys were there as well and being purely professional they were calling for beers but in these small glasses, about a third of a pint. Us being pure amateurs it was almost like being on a school tour. We went up and spotted these small glasses and ordered three at a time! The bar man couldn't get over it. He pointed at the glasses and he said, 'I see now why it was 5-1'. It was a great trip."

PAUL McGEE: "That game kick-started me again because I was still young, not young in football terms, in football terms in those days you were dead when you got to thirty. People said when a guy is twenty nine or thirty, 'His legs are gone', and, to be honest with you, it almost felt like a stigma for anyone to play over thirty. It was like, 'What are you doing?' I remember thinking, 'I'm thirty now, should I be slowing down, should I be stopping, should I be struggling?' But I still felt fit and able to score goals. So it was exciting out there, brilliant. Big crowd, beautiful pitch and it did excite me again. It kick-started what I'd been missing."

The disappointment of the 5-1 drubbing faded with the prospect of taking Groningen deep into Gaeltacht Galway for a historic and most bizarre second leg. With a four goal deficit there was little chance of Galway actually progressing or even winning the game. Nobody at the club was admitting that, of course, though they privately accepted that the game was now a matter of historical significance more than anything else. It was, after all, only 15 years since the GAA had deleted Rule 27, or 'The Ban', from its Official Guide. Admittedly, the conditions at the turn of the century which gave rise to the GAA enforcing a ban on its members playing or encouraging 'foreign' sports like soccer had long since improved but the rule still lasted until 1971 all the same. Now Galway United were going to take a UEFA Cup game and play it in a Gaelic football heartland. While GAA men on bar stools across the country cried foul play in the west, the villagers in Carraroe were busy sprucing up their Irish-speaking haven and community grounds for a new audience. They were requested to make provision for twenty Dutch reporters including three live radio broadcasters from RTÉ, Raidio na Gaeltachta and a Dutch station. A car park was resurfaced to accommodate an anticipated 5,000 crowd. New fences were erected in the ground. Old ones around the town got a lick of paint. A half hour of traditional Irish music and dance was organised before the game at Pairc an Chathanaigh, just one facet of a mid-week festival that was organised around the tie. There were dances arranged in the local hall for the Tuesday night before the game and the evening of the game itself. The Conquerors and Brendan Mulhaire would bring revellers to their feet each night.

RICKY O'FLAHERTY: "It's just the whole carnival atmosphere that was out there at the time that stands out. It was like something you'd see in Brazil rather than the back end of Connemara. It was fantastic. The hospitality that the people of Carraroe showed us was amazing."

Gaelic football was Carraroe native Sean Og de Paor's first love. A decade later he'd play a blinder for the local club, An Cheathru Rua, in their only county SFC final success. In 1998 and 2001, he was Galway's All-Ireland winning left half-back. He played at Pairc an Chathanaigh more times than he can remember and reckons the sod was never as lush or inviting as it was for the visit of Groningen.

SEAN OG DE PAOR: "The pitch was actually redeveloped that year, '86, and it was in great shape around that time. I remember before it had been officially opened that summer, I snuck in with another fella for a kick-around. At the time it was top class. The area around it wouldn't be known as the Golden Vale or anything but the pitch itself was like an Augusta golf green. I do remember seeing a few guys in blazers, I thought they were from UEFA or the FAI, looking at the pitch before the soccer game to check it out."

Aidan Gallagher was sent by the FAI to inspect the pitch and the facilities. The dressing rooms were top class, curiously described by Hanley as on a par with Arsenal's set-up at Highbury. As for the pitch, Gallagher deemed it suitable to host the tie.

AIDAN GALLAGHER: "When we first came to see the pitch the Gaelic posts were up. There was no grass around the goalmouths. But I knew that a soccer pitch is smaller than a Gaelic pitch and that the goal posts could easily be pushed forward at either end. The pitch itself was great. It was situated in a lovely location. It wasn't a stadium but it was a lovely pitch."

For locals like de Paor, the prospect of a bunch of Dutch men knocking a piece of leather around maroon shirted Galway players wasn't, funnily enough, the strangest thing they'd ever witness on that particular plot of land.

SEAN OG DE PAOR: "A long time ago, the circus used to come and pitch up on the field. They always had a few horses with them and part of the show would be the horse being walked around in a circle. I'll never forget afterwards, when the circus would have packed up and went away, there'd be a big ring left in the pitch from the horse walking in circles. More recently, in the Celtic Tiger era, you'd have helicopters landing on the pitch. It was parents maybe from Dublin with kids in the Irish colleges for summer and they'd be coming down for the day. I heard a story that one parent landed on the pitch, picked up his son and flew off to Ashford for dinner."

One stretch of road outside Carraroe is flanked by rock encrusted hills as far as the eye can see. Look sideways or down and it's either bog or stone that will meet your gaze. It was here that the thought first crossed Hagenauw's mind that he and the visiting Groningen squad may have landed on the moon as the team bus snaked its way through the sort of rugged landscape that must have felt like climbing Everest for those more used to the Dutch low lands.

RICKY O'FLAHERTY: "These guys couldn't believe where we were bringing them. Some of them got travel sick on the bus going out to it. They thought it was a ploy."

MARTIN MORAN: "I remember the Dutch team bus having difficulty in making its way to the ground. They had no idea of what they were going to face because there was just this barren landscape all around them. Then, suddenly, they would have turned into this ground and seen this pitch just like an oasis. It was absolutely perfect."

PETER HOUTMAN: "I have played in many stadiums in the world from the biggest stadium of Real Madrid to I don't know where else. It was so nice to come to a 'stadium' like that. There was not much of a crowd there because they have a lot more popular sports in Ireland. But, yeah, it had something. I don't know how to explain it but it was something special."

PAUL MASON: "I came to Groningen from amateur soccer so I was actually used to grounds like that. At the time I was playing for Groningen for two or three years and was playing in decent grounds but I was an amateur before I became professional so I was certainly used to those type of grounds. I remember Galway had a temporary stand put up for the game because there wasn't a proper one there. The whole ground was wide open. I actually didn't realise it wasn't their main ground. Maybe I was preoccupied or whatever but I just thought this was normal and this was their main pitch."

A wet afternoon, coupled with the lost cause aspect of a 5-1 aggregate deficit, meant only 3,000 turned out to witness the peculiar spectacle. Spectators filed into the ground below the tricolour which flew alongside the maroon and white of Galway. The flags were buffeted by a breeze that begun out over the Atlantic Ocean and whipped in through the picturesque village between Casla Bay and Greatman's Bay. Minister for the Gaeltacht, Padraig O Tuathail, and Mayor Mulholland, met both teams before kick-off. Local children from Carraroe and nearby Tuairin were ball boys. An enterprising Dutch visitor gave one of them a few bob to hang an advertising banner up inside the ground. Officials of both clubs sat side by side and enjoyed the corporate facilities – on the back of a lorry which had been reversed in along the sideline. The teams took their positions and Groningen prepared to attack the end of the ground that proclaimed in the best of Gaeltacht Irish, *Failte go dti Pairc a Chatanaigh*. Unfortunately for the locals, they didn't get to witness a famous 'home' win for Galway. The unstoppable Houtman had scored a hat-trick in the first-leg and scored the first and the third in Carraroe, sandwiching a de Kock strike late in the first-half that made it 3-0 to Groningen. Paul Murphy – the man who scored Galway United's first ever goal in Europe, against Lyngby – gave the fans something to cheer about with a 63rd minute consolation. McGee intercepted a miscued back pass, drew Groningen goalkeeper Sjaak Storm away from his goal line on the left and crossed the ball to the unmarked Murphy who fired a volley past a despairing de Wolf on the goal line. True to the unique occasion, Murphy raced away in delight and punched the air like a southpaw jabbing an imaginary opponent despite still being 8-2 down on aggregate.

RICKY O'FLAHERTY: "The whole occasion was one of the high points for Galway United. It was a great couple of years under Tony Mannion. We had the likes of John Mannion, Denis Bonner, 'Chick' Deacy, Kevin Cassidy, great players. There was an awful lot of good local talent and we had some really great times."

MARTIN MORAN: "The travelling, for me, was a huge inconvenience really. Very often we'd get the train down on a Saturday morning, train on a Saturday afternoon, stay overnight, play on a Sunday afternoon and then get the train back. Then, of course, you had to work on the Monday morning. When I think of it now it was some commitment. It was hard on my wife and two children because they didn't see much of me. But that's the commitment you make. If you want to play at that level those were the things you had to do. It was great for a year or so but I couldn't do it any longer. It wouldn't have been fair because we had two children under three at the time."

Like Moran, McGee left the club soon after for what proved to be the last big move of his career, to Holland. FC Haarlem had sent scouts to both legs of the UEFA Cup tie and liked what they saw in McGee, *The Connacht Tribune* Sports Star of the Week after his performance in Groningen. It was a full seventeen years since he'd first turned out for boyhood idols Sligo Rovers. But he'd proven by winning and scoring the penalty in Holland and playing in Murphy for Galway's goal in Carraroe that he could still break down and expose top level defences. He would spend two years with FC Haarlem who cut him a great deal, IR£500 a week in wages and a IR£6,000 signing on fee.

PAUL McGEE: "I'd have loved to have joined Groningen, to be honest, and there was a whisper at the time of them being interested. They were spending big money on the likes of Houtman and Eykelkamp and these guys. It was a real English type stadium they played at too. It always reminded me of Goodison Park, it would have been very like that. They were an English-type club, a lot moreso than Ajax or PSV, so I would have liked it there. My deal with Haarlem was being brokered around the time of the second leg in Carraroe. Galway got paid. I think they paid a fee of IR£20,000 or something which was great. Galway had got me for nothing. So they were happy."

Playing for Galway United in Carraroe helped McGee secure his dream move to Holland. Years later, he would be drawn back to the village. If his first visit was business, this time it was personal.

PAUL McGEE: "It's amazing looking back now and talking about my first time out in Carraroe playing in the UEFA Cup. I'm now married to a Carraroe woman! So something obviously happened to me out there. She remembers being at the match that day and seeing all these soccer heads about the place. She would always say the people out there got a great kick out of the occasion. Fair play to Galway United too because they really made something out of the tie. They made it an occasion when there wasn't really much to play for after the first leg."

Groningen played Swiss side Neuchatel Xamax, home to Irish striker Don Givens, in the next round. They drew 1-1 overall and progressed on the away goals rule to face Vitoria Guimaraes but were knocked out by the Portuguese. The following April, Sweden's Gothenburg beat Dundee United in a two-legged UEFA Cup final. In European terms, Galway United were small fry. Their first taste of UEFA Cup action yielded an 8-2 hammering that barely raised a ripple of recognition outside of Ireland and Holland. Yet the Carraroe occasion is enshrined in Irish history as a point in time when sport rose above ancient political divisions and closed old wounds, for an afternoon at least. John 'Kerry' O'Donnell surely smiled wryly when he learned of the accommodation of soccer out in Carraroe. Labelled the 'Don of Gaelic Park', New York, in a list of the GAA's 125 most influential people ever, O'Donnell was a self-made businessman driven by a touch of the maverick.

MARTIN MORAN: "It's a little known fact, and I stand to be corrected on the year, but I think it was 1978 or 1979 when I was at UCD. We were on a soccer trip in the United States. We were playing in New York and it was the John 'Kerry' O'Donnell era. I don't know how Tony O'Neill [UCD General Manager] managed it but we played a soccer game there in the GAA grounds, Gaelic Park in New York, against a local team. John 'Kerry' O'Donnell ran Gaelic Park and was trying to be controversial at the time, I think. He got the right man in Tony. He even provided the beer afterwards! The local GAA people were very angry that soccer had been played there. But John 'Kerry' O'Donnell was in charge of the Gaelic grounds and he put his mark on it that day. We were going to play soccer there and that was it."

Terryland Park remains Galway United's base though they've never played European football there. They qualified for the 1991/92 European Cup winners' Cup after Johnny Glynn's match winning FAI Cup final goal sealed victory over Shamrock Rovers at Lansdowne Road. But UEFA stadium restrictions once again forced them to play the home leg at a GAA ground that, again, wasn't technically owned by the

Association. This time, Ballinderreen Hurling Club came to United's rescue though they went down 7-0 on aggregate to Danish side Odense. The GAA finally embraced change at its 2005 Annual Congress. Sean Kelly was in the middle of his Presidency when delegates voted 227 to 97 in favour of opening up Croke Park to soccer and rugby for four seasons between 2007 and 2010 while Lansdowne Road was being redeveloped. The decision drew immediate support from all the major political leaders. In 2010, the GAA revealed that all €35m of the rental income generated from the use of Croke Park by the FAI and the IRFU would be invested back into capital developments around the country, providing for the future of the organisation. The current position, since April 2010, is that the GAA's Central Council retains the power to open up Croke Park to other codes on a case by case basis. Rival games are strictly prohibited from all other grounds.

SEAN KELLY: *"There'll always be an occasion when a generous gesture is required. People are often afraid that a once-off will set a precedent for ever more. The evidence doesn't stack up though. I mean when did Galway United ever play in Carraroe again? Never. Just because a GAA ground, or what was seen to be a GAA ground, was used it didn't mean it was going to be taken over. For me, it's about looking at the situation and saying there's an opportunity to do something helpful here without compromising our basic ethos. That's really all it comes down to in the end."*

UEFA CUP

First round, first leg
September 16, 1986
Oosterpark Stadium, Groningen
Attendance: 16,000

Groningen: 5
(Eykelkamp 5, Houtmann 47, 57 and 74, Mason 72)

Galway United: 1
(McGee 37)

Groningen: Storm; Boekweg, van de Berg, de Wolf, Gall; Mason, Bakker (de Kock h/t), Riekerink, Roosien; Houtman, Eykelkamp.

Galway United: Blackmore; Cassidy; Naughton, Ashton, Moran, Carpenter; McDonnell, Murphy, O'Toole; Mernagh (O'Flaherty h/t), McGee.

Referee: J.P. Schon (Luxemburg).

First round, second leg
October 1, 1986
Pairc an Chathanaigh, Carraroe
Attendance: 3,000

Galway United: 1
(Paul Murphy 63)

Groningen: 3
(Houtman 23 and 57, de Kock 36)

Galway United: Blackmore; Cassidy, Ashton, Moran, Carpenter; McDonnell, Murphy (Killeen 72), O'Toole, O'Flaherty (Lally 85); Mernagh, McGee.

Groningen: Storm; Mason, van de Berg (Gall h/t), de Wolf, Verkuyl; van Dyk, de Kock, Riekerink (Waslander 68), Roosien; Houtman, Eykelkamp.

Referee: G. Biguet (France).

CHAPTER 8

DERRY CITY VS BENFICA
September 13 and 27, 1989

"I did say to Sven Goran Eriksson, and this is absolutely true, after the game at the hotel I was talking to him and I said, 'What did you think of our team?' He said, 'I liked your No. 8'. Liam Coyle was playing at No. 8 that day. I said, 'Would you like to buy him?' Eriksson said, 'Well, not this year anyway, we'll see'. Those were his exact words'. IAN DOHERTY

It all began on a Sunday morning in 1984 with feverish knocking at Tony O'Doherty's front door. Awoken suddenly from his slumber, the former Derry and Northern Ireland player raced out to see what the commotion was. Outside stood pals Terry Harkin, another former International, and Eddie Mahon, a long time League of Ireland goalkeeper, both proud Derry men. "We need to get Derry City into the League of Ireland," said a breathless Harkin, Mahon nodding in agreement beside him. O'Doherty pulled on his clothes, grabbed his car keys and the trio headed for Ballybofey to put the idea to FAI President, Fran Fields. "And we got Fran out of bed," recalled O'Doherty. "I remember going into Fran's bedroom, waking him and saying, 'Willie,' – everybody called him Willie – 'we need to get into the League of Ireland'. 'Jeezus, you've got no chance.' That was his opening remark." Though not initially convinced by the idea, Fields soon threw his significant weight behind the cause. He could see the logic of it. If the Irish League didn't want Derry back then why not simply cross the border and join the League of Ireland? Momentum soon gathered and tireless trio Harkin, Mahon and O'Doherty became the indomitable 'Gang of Four' when former Derry and Sunderland player, Eamonn McLoughlin, joined them. They were in complete agreement that twelve years without League football in Derry, Ulster's second city, was twelve years too long. The impact of the Troubles had forced them to give up their Irish League membership in October 1972, six years after they'd been champions. The beginning of the end came in September 1971, when Ballymena United's team bus was seized and burnt out by a mob at the Brandywell. Banished to Coleraine for the rest of the season, Derry's support dwindled. When they were denied their return to the Brandywell for the following season, officials saw no option but to remove the club from the League entirely. Their absence suited the Irish League's authorities. The Brandywell is based in the predominantly Catholic/republican Bogside area that experienced the worst of the Troubles in the late-1960s and 1970s. Fulfilling fixtures in a largely Protestant League became like a deadly game of Russian roulette. All too often, the bullet aligned with the chamber and triggered incidents like the Ballymena bus hijacking. Derry reapplied for their Irish League status each season but were consistently knocked back. It led to the 'Gang of Four' and some local businessmen eventually considering the alternative, the League of Ireland. The beauty of the idea was its sheer simplicity – a predominantly Catholic club competing in a predominantly Catholic League. A year after that first rap on O'Doherty's front door – a year that included a friendly against Jim McLaughlin's Shamrock Rovers which raised Stg£5,000 for the cause – football finally returned to the Brandywell on September 8, 1985. The PA announcer belted out the record 'Derry are Back' as 7,000 locals watched them beat Home Farm 3-1 in a League Cup tie. Former England winger, Denis Tueart, got the Man of the Match award and made the cross for Barry McCreadie to score their first goal. 'The Wilderness Years', as they'd been known, were over. It became fashionable in the Maiden City to support the local club. Candystripe jerseys were in vogue. Armies of fans piled into transit vans and crossed the border for new and exciting trips to Dublin, Cork, Athlone and Waterford. The 'Gang of Four' was now a vast band of brothers.

Lifelong fan and soon to be club chairman, Ian Doherty, was among their early numbers and sensed both power and purpose in the movement.

IAN DOHERTY: "It took off in a way that I think nobody would have predicted. I remember being at the first game against Home Farm. I got a season ticket because our company supported the club. It was a great day. Huge numbers of people came and the whole thing just snowballed. It just caught the imagination. I suppose people in Derry were fed up after a lot of trouble in what was a pretty grim time or what certainly had been in the previous ten or fifteen years. It just caught the imagination of the people. It built up from then."

Life in the League of Ireland began at the foot of the First Division under Jimbo Crossman. Inside two seasons, and under the guidance of Noel King, they were promoted as First Division winners in April 1987. The arrival of players like South African Owen da Gama, Brazilian Nelson da Silva, Yugoslav Alex Krstic and Tueart not only strengthened the side but underlined the all-inclusive nature of the club. A significant revenue stream from sponsors and big gate receipts funded the arrivals. Following promotion, their support swelled again.

IAN DOHERTY: "The gates were great in the initial years, fantastic gate receipts. You would have got six or seven thousand at games. There was a cup game against Finn Harps, our neighbours from Ballybofey. There was real local rivalry there, and there were over 10,000 people at the ground. There was a feel-good factor about the whole thing."

The good vibes would lure former Coventry, Notts County and Bradford City goalkeeper Tim Dalton to the Brandywell revolution.

TIM DALTON: "The support Derry got was fantastic and it was a real shot in the arm for the League of Ireland at the time. I remember, when

I was being courted by Derry I went to watch them in one of the cup semi-finals. I was just gob-smacked by the crowd that travelled down to the game in Athlone. I can't remember who they played but I remember being in awe of how many people travelled down. I thought, 'This'll do for me, this is okay'."

Under King, the club established itself as a credible League of Ireland force. A difference of opinion between him and then General Manager, Jim McLaughlin, led to McLaughlin taking over completely during the 1987/88 season. A split developed between those who supported King, the man who'd led them to promotion, and those who backed McLaughlin, the city's famous son who'd cemented his status as the most successful League of Ireland manager ever in the previous decade with Dundalk and Shamrock Rovers. McLaughlin's relatively instant success made it hard for those in the King camp to continue the fight against him. With an inherited team, he guided Derry to the 1988 FAI Cup final. They lost 1-0 to double winners Dundalk and qualified via the back door for the European Cup winners' Cup where they went down 4-0 to Cardiff City. It was tangible progress early in the evolution of the club but, for a manager like McLaughlin who'd won six League titles and five FAI Cups before returning 'home', second best wasn't nearly good enough. So, he overhauled the team in the summer of 1988. His first act was to bring twenty-year-old striker Liam Coyle back from Finn Harps.

LIAM COYLE: "I was at Derry when I was eighteen when Noel King was the manager. Jim was the General Manager at the time. Me and Noel King never got on. I was only eighteen. At the time I wasn't the best trainer in the world. I wasn't the strongest. Noel just couldn't have been arsed with that. I was happy with playing on the Sunday, I didn't want to be going training three or four times a week. I wouldn't really blame Noel. At the time I said he was wrong but, looking back ..."

JIM McLAUGHLIN: "I remember going to get him back because I knew what Liam's potential was. I knew what he was about and I knew he wanted to be back. I was delighted when he did come back from Finn Harps. As a footballer I think he had one of the quickest and best brains that you could have come across on the football field. His touch was exemplary. He wouldn't have been the fastest but he didn't have to be because his brain compensated for his lack of pace."

Rovers were in terminal decline in mid-1988, their Milltown home controversially sold for development the previous year. McLaughlin picked at the carcass of his old club, signing defenders Mick Neville and Kevin Brady, veteran striker Noel Larkin and midfielder Paul Doolin from the Hoops to further strengthen his squad. Former Rovers player, John Coady, signed from Chelsea and could play in defence or midfield. The experienced quintet possessed eighteen League winners' medals between them and would add nine more before retiring. McLaughlin knew he was onto something big approaching the 1988/89 season.

JIM McLAUGHLIN: "I felt that, once we got the team we wanted together, we were always going to win the League that season. We were a bit special. If you think about it, it included four or five of the Shamrock Rovers batch who'd won four Leagues in a row. There was Mick Neville, Kevin Brady, Noel Larkin, Paul Doolin and John Coady. So, you had those four or five players and then you put in the likes of Felix Healy, Tim Dalton and Liam Coyle – who was just emerging as a player – Johnny Speak, too. What I'm saying is that it was such a strong, experienced squad. They were really exceptional."

McLaughlin's instincts about his team were confirmed in spectacular fashion as Derry swept the board and won an historic treble, a feat not achieved by any other club before or since. Coyle's seventeen goals – fourteen in the League – were crucial. He hit a hat-trick on his debut against Cobh in November.

IAN DOHERTY: "I remember Paddy Daly handing Liam the ball at the end of that game. Paddy was the referee and was one of the top referees. I'll always remember him giving the ball to Liam that day because it was the start of a magical couple of years."

By January, Coyle had effectively displaced Larkin, a five-time League winner with Athlone and Rovers.

LIAM COYLE: "Noel Larkin is a much better man than I am. At that time, I was only around twenty. Noel had been around and had won everything. For somebody to come in who was really taking your place in the team, you could have been a bit bitter towards them. You certainly didn't have to help them out and stuff like that, but he just looked after me so much. He used to come over to me before and after every game and tell me things, bits of advice. He was an absolute star."

IAN DOHERTY: "Derry were undoubtedly the best team in the League that year. Teams have won the League since and certainly they're not head and shoulders above everybody else. That Derry team was."

LIAM COYLE: "I never played in a better Derry team and I never played against better players. We only won the League by two points and won it on the last day of the season. So, that shows you how tight it was. But I know what Ian is talking about. We were head and shoulders above Dundalk, Athlone, Shelbourne and St Pat's back then. Dundalk kept winning matches. We were winning matches 4-0 and 5-0 and they were winning them 1-0 and scraping out results. Between January and March we won thirteen games in a row, yet we still only won the League by two points. I do know what Ian is talking about football-wise because it was a different standard even as I went through my career. I spoke to 'Dooler' about it and I spoke to Mick [Neville] about it and they won titles with Shelbourne and a couple of other teams. 'Dooler' said to me, 'That's the best team I ever played with', and that includes the Rovers team he won the doubles with."

JIM McLAUGHLIN: "In that [Derry] team no one would have escaped with an ego and no-one would have wanted to escape. When you had that kind of a squad of players ... I'll give you an example, say Paul Doolin and Noel Larkin, this is actually a true story – if Paul Doolin didn't bring Noel into the game as a centre-forward Noel would have ate him alive. Noel was a big man, a lovely man and a gentleman but when you're on a football field you must communicate and do what you have to do. Felix and Paul Doolin were the two midfield players and they weren't afraid to say to each other, 'What are you at? You're not doing this and you're not doing that'. They could communicate. They communicated for the best and there wasn't an ego. You simply weren't allowed to have ego trips."

Coyle was sipping sangria in a Tenerife bar in the summer of 1989 with team-mate Paul Carlyle – brother of McLaughlin's former Dundalk striker, Hillary – when the draw for the first round of the European Cup was made.

LIAM COYLE: "We heard from someone in the bar that night that we'd got Benfica. We couldn't believe it. It was just a massive thing for all of us. I had only turned twenty-one, Paul Carlyle was twenty-two. We had a great time out there when we heard that."

It was just the high-profile draw Coyle needed to focus the mind again. A dream move to Manchester United, and a chance to get in on the bottom rung of Alex Ferguson's ascent with the club, had just fallen through. After emulating his father, Fay, by playing up front for Northern Ireland the previous May, just days after his twenty-first birthday, he was led to believe the move to Manchester was a done deal.

LIAM COYLE: "As far as I was concerned the deal was written and on the table. Harry Gregg would have been friendly with my father, the two of them played together for Northern Ireland. Harry told me I was going to United at the end of the (treble winning) season. Apparently, a deal was struck for Stg£150,000. It was going to build up another Stg£100,000 with appearances, and such. I think I was going for a quarter of a million in all, at that stage. For someone that had just one season under their belt, I thought Derry should have just taken the money and said, 'There you go'."

The deal stalled, though United promised to keep an eye on Coyle. Years later he learned that a secret meeting took place between Derry officials and another top English League team at around the same time which almost saw him transfer there. He wonders if all the interest in him didn't prompt Derry to hold out for more money from United.

LIAM COYLE: "We played Galway the season we won the treble at the Brandywell on St Patrick's Day. I only found this out years later, but Derry officials met (the English club) in the Everglades Hotel before it and a deal was struck, Stg£100,000, I was signing at the end of the season. Apparently, Derry were asked to bump the price up by fifty grand by one of the negotiators – 'We want to make fifty grand, we want you to bump it up by fifty grand, we'll split the fifty grand'. Ian Doherty, who's a very honest man, said, 'We don't do business like that'. The deal was struck and all – it was Stg£100,000, but it suddenly became Stg£150,000. I don't know what else was going on. When I heard that news I wasn't happy. Guys were messing with my career. That's exactly what it was. In fairness to Derry the guys that ran the club were trying to do things right. They weren't saying, 'It's all right to put money into my back pocket'."

Several other clubs took a peek at the Brandywell sensation. Glasgow Celtic, Liverpool, Everton and Derby County all sent their spies but none of them made a firm offer. The Benfica ties would, at least, put Coyle back in the shop window for potential suitors. The Lisbon giants were only beaten on penalties in the European Cup final two years earlier and commanded the respect of the entire continent. Under the guidance of Sven Goran Eriksson – the future Manchester City and

England manager – and with Brazilian stars Ricardo, Aldair and Valdo on their books, they were installed on short odds to win the tournament outright. In Eriksson's first stint as Benfica manager they'd lost the 1983 UEFA Cup final. Second time around, he was making no secret of his European ambitions. On the Sunday before the Derry game Eriksson displayed where his priorities lay by heading to the Brandywell to watch the Candystripes play Shelbourne while, back at home, he left his own team to find their way in a 5-0 win over Beira Mar. Derry were workmanlike against Shelbourne but no better than that, perhaps distracted by what lay ahead. Felix Healy scored the only goal, *á la* his FAI Cup final replay winner against Cork City. Asked what he'd made of Derry, Eriksson said, "I was very impressed. You tell me that they were not at their best but they struck me as a very aggressive side that could cause us problems. They have good organisation and are fighting all the time. The man who scored the goal (Healy), I think he is the brains of the team". Healy was approaching thirty-four but still looked every bit the goal-poaching midfielder who'd commanded international recognition and featured in the 1982 World Cup finals with breakthrough team, Northern Ireland.

JIM McLAUGHLIN: "Felix could have played for Brazil and he wouldn't have been out of place. You may say that's an exaggeration but Felix Healy was as good a player as I've seen or played with. That doesn't mean that he's the greatest player ever but he was a hell of a footballer and, as a person, he was pretty good with me. I gave him the respect that he deserved."

TIM DALTON: "He was quality. He had two good feet. Bear in mind he was in his thirties at this stage. In all honesty, he was hardly training because he'd had injuries and all the rest of it but he was still a class apart. A fit Felix Healy would have been, my God almighty, he was certainly beyond the League of Ireland standard at that time, with no shadow of a doubt. I'd always say the two players that made the difference in quality, as far as I'm concerned, were Liam Coyle and

Felix Healy, two Derry men. The likes of Felix probably didn't get the credit he deserved. I just think that sometimes the Derry crowd were particularly hard on their own, if you know what I'm saying. But, by golly, those two were the difference in that treble-winning team. They were just on another level."

LIAM COYLE: "Felix was a different class, the best I ever played with, great on the floor, scored goals, either foot, from twenty-five or thirty yards. He played for Port Vale but he came back and played most of his football with Coleraine. Derry were out of the League at that time. I found myself playing a lot with Felix, you know, one-twos around the box. I should have been in the box myself, I should have scored more goals but I became a better player because of it."

Little did the Derry team know but, just eight hours before the biggest game in the club's history, there was a very real danger of it being called off. That morning a massive bomb was found one hundred and fifty yards from the ground, in the cemetery next to the Brandywell. Estimated to be around one hundred pounds in weight, the device was described as being a, "beer keg with wires leading from it". Whatever about destroying Derry City's European ambitions, it threatened to cause carnage by blowing a gigantic hole in the very spot where it lay. Standard practice would have been to alert the police. But, given the club's troubled history, the words 'standard practice' and 'Derry City' were rarely uttered together. Instead, lifelong fan, prominent nationalist and then Sinn Fein Vice President Martin McGuinness was tipped off about the gruesome find. In an interview with the *Guardian* newspaper in 2001, headlined "My Team", McGuinness revealed, in startling detail, his role in events that Wednesday afternoon twelve years earlier in City Cemetery.

MARTIN McGUINNESS: "Some senior representatives of the club came to see me and said there was a major problem. They explained that explosives had been found in the cemetery close to the ground.

The club's view was that if the British Army and the RUC were brought in they would, as they usually do, make a meal out of the whole thing, stretch it out for a week and inconvenience everybody. The game would have been called off and that would have been a disaster from Derry's point of view. This was pretty much the biggest game in Derry's history remember. Myself and some of the club's directors went up to the cemetery. I remember them hiding behind the headstones while I tied a rope around the device – which, I think, was a substantial device of maybe one hundred pounds – and pulled the thing out. Nothing happened, but it was a device of some description. We opened a manhole in the cemetery and threw whatever material was in it – I don't know if it was explosives – down the drain and flushed it away. Between the directors and ourselves we managed to avert what would have been a disaster for Derry City."

IAN DOHERTY: *"To tell the absolute truth, I asked, 'Is it gone?' 'Yes, it is gone', was the reply. So I said, 'I just don't want to know about it'. What could I do? I only know what I was told at the time that the device turned up. Somebody went to Martin McGuinness when it happened. He decided, and I hold no brief for Sinn Fein, [to dispose of the bomb]. If he did that, in all the circumstances, it was a decent thing to do, a courageous thing to do."*

Following McGuinness' revelation in 2001, it was claimed in media reports that the device was originally planted by the Provisional IRA and aimed at an army patrol.

TIM DALTON: *"As far as we were concerned, it was a hoax. I didn't think at that particular time that somebody would have wanted to follow through with something like that. Maybe I'm being naïve but it wasn't the impression we got at the time. So, did it phase us? Not in the least."*

When the bomb scare had passed and the game was cleared to go ahead

Doherty sat back in his director's chair, breathed out and surveyed the occasion before him, the fruits of an entire community working in harmony.

IAN DOHERTY: "The local hotel, the Everglades, looked after Benfica in terms of accommodation. We'd dedicated all our members of the Board to look after them. Senior people connected with football in the city were also there as minders, guides, helpers – just providing any assistance that they needed. Myself and the rest of the Board of Directors didn't do much work that week, I can tell you. It was just a big thing for Derry. Remember what we were coming out of in terms of being a city pretty much on its knees through the destruction and bombing and violence of the 1970s and early-1980s. This was a very positive thing. It got tremendous buy-in from the whole of the local population."

Coyle craved the big occasion but had been taken off the previous Sunday against Shels when Jonathan Speak, the League's top scorer in the 1987/88 season, had come on to partner Krstic.

LIAM COYLE: "I had been in and out of the team and not in good form. I thought I was going away and then I didn't get away. So, I started the season a bit sluggish and I thought I might have been left out, to be honest. 'Larko' was gone at the time, Jim had sold 'Larko' and brought Alex Krstic in. I thought he was going to leave me out and start 'Speaky' up front. But he named the team and I was in it."

McLaughlin gave a final stirring address and then the dressing room door burst open. A thousand studs clattered on concrete as the Derry players raced out onto the field, their movements tracked by the RTÉ TV cameras. The capacity crowd of 12,500 had just been greeted by Eusebio, the Black Panther of Benfica, who won back-to-back European Cups with the club in 1961 and 1962. After retiring, he became an ambassador for The Eagles.

IAN DOHERTY: "I'm old enough to remember him (Eusebio) playing. He was one of the great players of the 1960s, without a doubt, maybe the best. Himself and Georgie Best were the big guys around that time. Before the game, he walked out onto the Brandywell pitch, marched up and down and got a huge ovation."

LIAM COYLE: "The atmosphere was unbelievable. I remember walking out and it was one of the first times a League of Ireland game was on RTÉ. It was just TV cameras, noise and the crowd cheering like mad. I remember thinking, 'This is what it's all about. This is why I'm a footballer'. It was fantastic."

JIM McLAUGHLIN: "It was just a pleasure. There was a great atmosphere in Derry, no matter which match you were playing in, but probably extra special that night because it was Benfica. We didn't know it at the time but Eriksson was going to go on to become the England manager and all the rest of it. It was all the things that you want in a European night."

McLaughlin made just one change from the Shels game, bringing in Scottish midfielder Stuart Gauld for Paul Hegarty. Five minutes in, Coyle picked out Healy but his shot on the run clipped the post. Soon after Gauld found Krstic but he couldn't finish the move. Approaching half time Krstic went even closer with a header that Benfica's Brazilian goalkeeper, Silvino, somehow parried onto the angle of post and crossbar and away to safety.

LIAM COYLE: "We were pounding them, absolutely pounding them. We made about four or five real chances. Their 'keeper pulled off a few great saves. We went in 0-0 at half time and we went in thinking, 'We have a chance to beat them'."

PAUL DOOLIN: "We played really well against them. And, in fairness to ourselves, our team was a good side. I would even say a brilliant side. The two in my area of midfield that evening were Jonas Thern, a Swede, and Valdo, a Brazilian. For the most part, we competed well with them."

In the sixtieth minute, Benfica broke through. Thern collected Neville's headed clearance, evaded Doolin's tackle and drove a shot that deflected off full-back Pascal Vaudequin past Dalton. They doubled their lead soon after in what amounted to a disaster for Derry. Dalton and Paul Curran blocked shots from Valdo and sub, Vata, with despairing tackles before Ricardo had a go. He drilled his kick at goal, Brady headed it clear but the linesman claimed the ball had already crossed the line. Brady argued the toss but the referee backed his linesman. Benfica led 2-0. Justice for Derry finally arrived in the seventy-fourth minute when Carlyle struck their first European goal as a League of Ireland team. Coyle set up Healy whose shot rebounded off the post to Carlyle to hammer home from the edge of the box. The Derry fans raised the roof at the Brandywell. Derry pushed on for the equaliser but Krstic couldn't turn home the best of the chances four minutes from time. When the final whistle sounded, Derry's players struggled to fathom how they'd suffered a 2-1 defeat.

LIAM COYLE: "You wouldn't believe how open Benfica were that night but we were a really good side too and we could play. We could keep the ball better than most Irish teams at the time. We made a good few chances in the second half. That's the only down side about the game, that we were beat. If we had come out of it having won or drawn people would have thought a wee bit more of us. It was the only downside, if I can put it like that, because we performed very well. Remember, every one of their team were stars. Ricardo, the Brazilian captain, Aldair, they had another wee Brazilian international, Valdo. They had Thern and another fella playing for Sweden called Mats Magnusson. They were all quality players, fantastic players."

TIM DALTON: "They beat us 2-1 in the first leg but we actually didn't think they were anything special. Overall, I just remember thinking they weren't as good as I thought they would be."

Goal scorer, Thern, would go on to captain Sweden to third place in the 1994 World Cup finals and finished his career with Glasgow Rangers. He recalls mitigating factors in defence of Benfica's lacklustre display against Derry.

JONAS THERN: "I remember I felt we had a big problem with the pitch. It was, of course, quite a difference when you're used to playing on perfect grass in the Estadio da Luz where we played our home games. We had to play very well and to fight physically during the whole ninety minutes to get the result. That's what I remember of that game. The Derry players worked very hard and made life difficult for us during that game. When I was playing at the Estadio da Luz you were talking about 120,000 people. Playing against Derry City was a bit different. I remember that, like the British teams, they were physically very strong. They worked very hard but, of course, we were a bit better team so we managed to get through that first leg."

As disappointing as the defeat was, it was by no means a disgrace. An uphill task awaited them at the Estadio da Luz – better known worldwide by its English name, the Stadium of Light -- but it wasn't 'Mission: Impossible'. Coyle was elated with his own performance in the home leg. If any English teams were watching him they couldn't but be impressed. He'd been struggling for form but had found it when it really mattered on the big stage.

LIAM COYLE: "Ricardo and Aldair were marking me at the Brandywell. I was playing up front and everything that was played up to me just stuck, the ball just stuck, I never wasted a pass. I was turning and twisting. It would be great to be like that all the time and I remember saying to myself after it, 'Why can't I play like that all the time?'"

Afterwards, Eriksson told Doherty he fancied Coyle as a player and promised to keep his eye on the big man. A six-month trial was suggested but Coyle was told to forget about any possible move until after the second leg. The following Sunday afternoon in Dundalk disaster struck, altering the course of Coyle's career dramatically. Brady played a routine pass across midfield to Coyle, who was about to collect the ball, when a thundering tackle came in from the side, catching him square on the left knee.

LIAM COYLE: "Bam! I went down and I knew, I just knew it was bad. You know yourself when it's an injury and when it's a knock. Initially, I thought it was my cartilage gone. I got up and played on and played well after it, actually. I was starting to get my touch again after Benfica and scored my first goal of the season that day. Then with about five minutes to go I put a ball through Joey Malone's legs and had a shot with my left leg. I just felt something go in the knee. That was about an hour after the original incident. I got up in the morning and the knee was an awful size so they sent me up to Altnagelvin (Hospital). I just remember the doctor turning around, he says to me, 'I'm a bit worried about this, I'm a bit worried'. I says, 'Ah, it's just a knock, I'll be grand', but he said he could see some black spot in the X-Ray of the knee. Apparently, there was a wee hole in the knee. A piece of bone broke off from the tackle and got lodged in the knee. They sent me to Hull to see a top specialist over there."

Football being football, Hull realised that opportunity was knocking on their door and took the opportunity to invite Coyle for a look around the stadium while he was over. When the news from Hull's medics was relayed to the club, however, their interest in Coyle immediately ceased. He was told that the knee injury was so bad he'd have to give up football completely. Instinct convinced him to play on through the pain barrier. Before the second leg in Benfica there was another domestic game against Rovers. Coyle started but felt a twinge in his knee and came off. The following Monday he jetted out to Lisbon, hopeful that things would somehow come good for him. Healy joined him in the sick bay and sportingly received physio on an ankle injury from Benfica. It led manager McLaughlin to claim that, 'Football could do with more like Benfica', adding that, 'If we have to lose, then I will be proud to lose to them'.

LIAM COYLE: "We went to watch Benfica train one of the days out there. There were about 3,000 supporters there to watch them train. It was like a cage they were training in. They just cleared off when we came in and we were left to our own devices, except for one or two. The support for them was pretty fanatical. When we were going to the ground itself they were cutting the heads off chickens. Unbelievable! I presume it was to intimidate us, no word of a lie, cutting the heads off chickens they were. We had to go right through them all to get into the ground."

Doolin and Dalton had played at the Stadium of Light with Shamrock Rovers and Coventry City and retained fond memories.

TIM DALTON: "Bobby Gould was the manager at the time and we went over and I played there as a seventeen-year-old. I actually got Man of the Match and played very well so I had some very good memories going back to the place. I was really looking forward to it."

At nine o'clock in the evening, the players ran out into one of the world's great arenas, the 120,000 capacity Stadium of Light. Even thought it was just over half full, the crowd of 65,000 ensured a raucous atmosphere. Derry braced themselves for battle as they made the long journey from the dressing room to the pitch.

TIM DALTON: "There was a long, long walk from the changing area to the pitch. All the way we were humming this tune. I can't remember the name of it but I remember how it goes, it's a kind of death march. The Benfica boys were looking at us like we all had two heads."

PAUL DOOLIN: *"I remember the walk out. It took about five minutes to get from the dressing room to the pitch. It was all up steps, down steps, down tunnels. It was only half full but you were still talking about 65,000. The atmosphere was great. We were well away from the supporters but there were still 65,000 or so out there and they were very passionate and made some noise. I've been at games there since and the passion is just as strong."*

Unfortunately for Derry, the decibel levels in the crowd increased as Benfica tore into them. Coyle got the nod to start but, between his battered knee and the fact McLaughlin deployed him as a midfielder, he never got the chance to shine and was taken off.

LIAM COYLE: *"I was playing right in between Felix and 'Dooler'. The three of us just said we need to get on the ball and just pass it and keep it. We were going to get slaughtered if we went 4-4-2. So, we played five in the middle. It was a football lesson that night at the Stadium of Light. We had chances again just like at the Brandywell – two or three good chances before they scored – but, once they scored, and the first goal went in, that was it."*

Derry lost 4-0. Magnusson hit the first after thirty-two minutes, dodging past Brady and chipping Dalton. Prolific Angolan striker Vata doubled their tally in the sixty-first minute and central defenders, Ricardo and Aldair, completed the rout with one each. Ricardo's third was the pick of the bunch, hit with typical Brazilian flair from twenty-five yards out.

TIM DALTON: *"They were spraying the ball all over the place and were full of football at that stage. In fairness, they had a good few Brazilians on the pitch, the likes of Aldair and Ricardo, and they had the pick of the Portuguese Internationals at the time. Jonas Thern was a handy player too."*

JONAS THERN: "Aldair had a great career so, if I had to pick one player from that team, it would be Aldair. He was there for one year only and left for Roma. I joined him at Roma a couple of years later. He was one of the best Brazilian players for many years."

With six minutes to go, Krstic missed a penalty to cap Derry's woes. A bad end to a bad night, or so one would think.

TIM DALTON: "That was probably the best match I played in all my time for Derry City, I felt. You see I had so much to do that night. Normally, because I was with such a good team, I didn't really get that much to do. Performance-wise I was probably most pleased with that match in all my time. How ironic is that? To get beaten 4-0 but to be so pleased with how you performed. It was the fact that we were on a big stage and, as far as I was concerned, I hadn't let myself down. That's how I always felt. I either let myself down or I didn't and I felt, that night in Lisbon, I didn't. Every single one of the Derry lads performed in their own way that night."

Derry's 6-1 aggregate defeat became more palatable in time as Benfica blazed a trail to the European Cup final against AC Milan. Unfortunately for Thern, a solitary Frank Rijkaard goal ensured Arrigo Sacchi's Milan retained their crown. The money raised from Derry's European venture made the rest of the year 'comfortable' for the club, according to Doherty. The previous few weeks, however, had cost them their priceless asset, Coyle. He battled on for a few months with the knee injury but eventually heeded blaring medical advice that he should quit the game at just twenty-one. A testimonial against Newcastle was organised to drum up a few pounds for his rehab. Coyle took off to America with vague notions of a miracle cure. He didn't find it. Instead, he played semi-pro football for a few months, ate and drank the good life and returned two stone heavier and disillusioned with life. After a two-year gap, and two knee operations, he returned to football with Omagh Town in 1992.

LIAM COYLE: "I think Jim and one or two others at the time should have been a wee bit more verbal with me and should have said, you'll be all right, keep him out for a year or so, rehabilitate his knee. But they just left me with doctors and you know doctors – we're not having this on our conscience if he goes and ends up in a wheelchair. I thought they were doing what was right for themselves, not what was right for me. Then when I left I just cut loose. I was twenty-two years of age at that stage, didn't know what to do with myself."

JIM McLAUGHLIN: "I couldn't have managed Liam knowing the consequences of that knee injury. I was told about it and that's why I had to say, 'No Liam, you can't play any more'. I couldn't be part of it. The specialist that we went to in England said, 'Look, if he gets a bang on that knee do you know what will happen? The bone shatters and he will be in a wheelchair. Do you want to live with that?' I said, 'I do not, I don't want that and I never could have come to terms with what could have happened'. At the same time Liam didn't have much in life outside of football. Therefore, he said, 'I'm prepared to play, come what may'. It's so grand and easy when a disaster doesn't happen. It's so easy to say, yes, that was what we should have done, Liam should have been kept playing. But we were not medical people. The medical people said, 'You could ruin that boy's life'. You take the choice. If we'd won a League or a Cup would it have mattered if a fella had ended up crippled as a result? That's exactly what they said to us, he can end up in a wheelchair and that'll be it. How the hell could you ignore that?"

McLaughlin also left Derry in April, 1991. A year and a half after guiding the club to the peak of its powers as treble champions, playing eventual European Cup finalists Benfica at the Brandywell, he stepped down citing, "personal abuse and a lack of support from certain sections of the local media". Almost two decades on, he simply admits that after winning the treble in his hometown it became a 'pretty demanding place'. The demands at Dundalk and Rovers were never as great on

McLaughlin, even though they won more trophies but, then, the adulation in Derry was unparalleled. So, how did managing Derry compare to the other two?

JIM McLAUGHLIN: "I could sum it up in probably one sentence but you'd have to fill in all the details after that – Derry was the only team that won the treble."

Coyle returned to Derry for the 1993/94 season and devoted the rest of his career, save for a brief stint at Glentoran, to the town he loves so well. He collected a multitude of personal awards and a second League winners' medal in 1997 proving that, whatever about the injury, he never lost his ability. In 2002, at the age of thirty-four and with his knee heavily bandaged, he hit the winner against Shamrock Rovers in the FAI Cup final. He retired in 2003, ending his career as he began it, with a bang, scoring the goal that saved Derry from relegation in a play-off against great rivals Finn Harps.

LIAM COYLE: "To get ten more years with Derry wasn't bad. From what I was told, that if I kept playing by the time I was thirty I'd be in a wheelchair, it wasn't bad at all."

EUROPEAN CUP

First round, first leg
September 13, 1989
The Brandywell, Derry
Attendance: 12,500

Derry City: 1
(Carlyle 74)

Benfica: 2
(Thern 61, Ricardo 66)

Derry City: Dalton; Vaudequin, Neville, Curran, Brady; Carlyle, Doolin, Healy, Gauld; Coyle, Krstic.

Benfica: Silvino; Veloso, Aldair, Ricardo, Fonseca; Paneira, Thern, Valdo; Abel (Chalana 72), Magnusson, Cesar Brito (Vata 52).

Referee: G. Goethals (Belgium).

First round, second leg
September 27, 1989
Stadium of Light, Lisbon
Attendance: 65,000

Benfica: 4
(Magnusson 32, Vata 61, Ricardo 69, Aldair 81)

Derry City: 0

Benfica: Silvino; Veloso, Aldair, Ricardo (Paulinho 73), Fonseca; Abel (Chalana 80), Thern, Valdo, Pacheco; Magnusson, Vata.

Derry City: Dalton; Vaudequin, Neville, Curran, Brady; Carlyle, Healy, Doolin, Coyle (Coady 66), Gauld; Krstic.

Referee: U. Azpitarte (Spain).

CHAPTER 9

SHELBOURNE VS GLASGOW RANGERS
July 22 and 29, 1998

"There were definitely people looking down on me saying, 'This guy has always wanted this and always wanted this to happen – now it's going to happen'. There was no way, once I scored, I wasn't going to bless myself in front of the Rangers fans. That was my night and forever more." PAT MORLEY

In football, there are those who subscribe to the bottom line theory that winning is all that matters: First is everything. Second place is a set of steak knives. Damien Richardson came to a different conclusion about the beautiful game early in life. As much as it's a results driven business, he always got his kicks from the excitement of the journey through ninety minutes more than from the destination. Watching Shelbourne win the League in 1962 strengthened his conviction that football is a game played by artists on a blank, green canvas. The deft touches of Freddie Strahan, the sweeping movements of Jackie Hennessy, the finishing of Eric Barber, all master craftsmen doing justice to their trade. When Richardson took over as Shelbourne manager in 1995, little about his outlook on the game had changed. In fact, being part of the Shamrock Rovers team that won six FAI Cup titles in a row in the 1960s and playing up front for Gillingham and Ireland had only developed in him an even greater affinity with flair and style and the subtler aspects of the game which he, naturally, carried into management. His football faith would be put to the ultimate test approaching the final day of the 1997/98 season. Shelbourne needed just a draw in Dundalk to win the title – Richardson's first as a manager or player and only the club's second since that 1962 success. They were also going for three FAI Cup titles in a row with Cork City waiting in the final. Before the Dundalk game, Richardson received correspondence from the FAI revealing that an error had been made regarding player suspensions. Key midfielder Pat Fenlon and winger Dessie Baker had both been overlooked for one-match bans which were left to serve. An agreement was reached between League authorities and Richardson, whereby he'd decide which game the duo would miss, either the crucial League match or the equally critical Cup final. Now, Richardson wasn't about to happily forsake a League title but, when it came to a straight choice between the romance of a Cup win – the pinnacle of the beautiful game, as he saw it – and a possible League win, there was only going to be one outcome.

DAMIEN RICHARDSON: "I felt that three cups in a row would have been more momentous than winning a League title. I spoke to the players, they left it up to me. I decided to let them miss the League game. It spoiled our preparation to a great extent in a very important week but the alternative was to tell two players they're out of a Cup final, the third of three wins in a row, possibly, and a serious part of history."

Some may view it as madness to prioritise the cup over the League but there was method in Richardson's gamble. Shelbourne had played Dundalk six times that season and beaten them five times, drawing the other game. Dundalk hadn't scored against them once in all those games, while Shelbourne had knocked nine past the border club, in total. So, he put together a patched up team for their latest meeting, with defender, Mick Neville, covering for Fenlon in midfield. Shelbourne lost 2-1. Elsewhere, St Patrick's Athletic beat Kilkenny City 2-1, leapfrogged into top spot in the table and stole the title with the most daring of final day raids. The following weekend Shelbourne lost the FAI Cup 1-0. Just for good measure they were beaten in the League Cup final by a single goal, too. Forget the FAI Cup three-in-a-row,

Shelbourne were treble runners-up and it cost Richardson his job. Sacked, resigned, quit, walked away – take your pick. For the record, he planned to leave anyway as his relationship with chairman Ollie Byrne, he claims, had reached breaking point. Given his time again, Richardson insists he'd make the very same decisions – Fenlon and Baker would be saved for the Cup final.

DAMIEN RICHARDSON: "I would, because in Shelbourne's history to look back on three Cup wins would be something that would be a source of enormous pride. I was a member of the Shamrock Rovers team in the 1960s that won six Cups in a row. Then Shamrock Rovers won four League titles in a row in the 1980s. They were the points of fortitude that sustained Shamrock Rovers through the difficult times that followed. They could always say, 'We won six in a row and four in a row'. Having been part of the six-in-a-row and then to go to Shelbourne I was thinking that, if we can get this three-in-a-row that's something that'll never be forgotten. To me, in my opinion, that was more important than the League."

Chairman Byrne clearly didn't share Richardson's viewpoint and made a strong statement by hiring Dermot Keely to replace him as manager for the 1998/99 season. The difference between the two was like night and day and indicated where Byrne felt Shelbourne had gone wrong, they lacked steel. As players, Richardson scored goals while centre-half Keely spilt blood, his own and others, to prevent them. The pair's managerial styles followed upon similar lines, Richardson the talker, the cultivator, the Cup specialist. Keely the general, the old dog for the hard road, the authority on how to win Leagues. Fittingly, the Keely era began with Shelbourne staring into the Alamo in July of 1998, a position the new boss was used to and relished. They were drawn to play big-spending Glasgow Rangers in the Preliminary round of the UEFA Cup having missed out on a Champions League qualifier after finishing second in the League. The July 22 tie, ostensibly a home game, would be his first match in charge. Because of security fears, the first leg couldn't be played at Tolka Park: When Rangers last visited Dublin in 1984, their supporters ran amok in nearby Phibsborough after a UEFA Cup tie with Bohemians, causing thousands of pounds in damage and leaving lasting psychological scars on the community. Gardai swore they'd never risk a repeat scenario. Disturbances at Drumcree ahead of the Shelbourne game, in the midst of the Orange Order's marching season in the north, heightened the anticipation of sectarian violence breaking out in Dublin if Rangers did arrive in the capital city. Officials from both clubs, the FAI, gardai and the British Embassy put their heads together over several days. A number of alternative venues were considered, including Lansdowne Road, Kilmarnock's Rugby Park where Shelbourne played the previous season in the European Cup winners' Cup, and Carlisle United's Brunton Park in the north of England. It was finally agreed to meet in the middle at Tranmere Rovers' Prenton Park outside Liverpool. Fenlon was well aware of the sensitive political issues at play. He wasn't long back from a spell at Irish League side Linfield, a Belfast club closely aligned with Rangers who also draw from a predominantly Protestant support base.

PAT FENLON: *"From playing at Linfield, there's always the worry that people attach themselves to occasions who you don't see on a regular basis. They're the worry rather than the genuine supporters who would go and watch their team week in, week out. When you have a big occasion like Shelbourne/Rangers with a lot at stake, people will attach themselves to it who have different agendas."*

Shelbourne centre-half and PFAI Player of the Year, Pat Scully, relished the opportunity of returning to Prenton Park. The former International had played there several times before with Southend United and Huddersfield Town after leaving Arsenal.

PAT SCULLY: *"The pitch was always beautiful, gorgeous. I thought it was a big disadvantage going there but I'd played there before so I knew it was a nice ground, at least. Tranmere was a good club and they always kept the pitch well. They were doing reasonably well as a club at the time, too. So, I knew it was going to be a nice set-up. It was disappointing from the point of view of not playing at Tolka because we always did reasonably well there. We played Kilmarnock the year before in the UEFA Cup there and they drew with us 1-1. We gave them a real run for it. Going through the years, we always did well at Tolka. It was a disadvantage but you get on with it."*

The disappointment of giving up home advantage was tempered by the excitement of working alongside European Cup champions in waiting, Manchester United, at their training ground, The Cliff, in the lead up to the first leg. Shels chairman Byrne called in a favour from a United contact to train there, and United manager Alex Ferguson agreed straightaway, sharing several conversations with Keely while both sets of players trained. Shels striker Pat Morley met a few of his old Cork pals at The Cliff.

PAT MORLEY: "Denis Irwin was a good friend of mine and he came over for a chat. Roy Keane was just coming back from his cruciate injury as well, so I was talking to them. I knew them personally because they're Cork lads."

Aside from being Cork natives, and both wearing the No. 16 jersey for their respective Reds, Morley and Keane had another huge thing in common, their dodgy knees. Morley would go on to become the second highest scorer in League of Ireland history, with one hundred and eighty-two goals, but just the previous winter he feared his career could be over at the age of thirty-two. A seemingly innocuous clash with Packie Lynch of St Pat's, in March of 1997, led to him requiring surgery later that year for the same knee injury that Keane suffered.

PAT MORLEY: "I had the operation in November of '97 – five days after Roy Keane's – and my goal was that I wanted to get back playing football before him. A friend of mine was great friends with Roy

Keane, luckily enough, so there was rehabilitation programmes coming back and forth and updates and stuff."

With a full pre-season behind him, Morley was desperate to convince Keely to give him a start against Rangers, the great rivals of his beloved Celtic.

PAT MORLEY: "I actually played for Celtic in a reserve game in 1984 against Rangers. I played up front with Alan McInally and we won 5-0. There were about 25,000 at Parkhead that night. I'd been brought over on trial when David Hay was manager. Basically, they said they liked me but felt I needed to beef up and get bigger so they sent me back to Waterford to get better. I was in the Waterford reserve team for two or three months and then Alfie Hale brought me into the first team for my League of Ireland debut in 1984. I scored a hat-trick on my debut and the rest is history. I went back over to Celtic again a few years later but, by that stage, David Hay had been sacked as manager. Billy McNeill came in and the move never happened for me."

Despite shifting the UEFA Cup game out of Ireland, the Shelbourne/Rangers tie was still classified as a Category A security risk by British police, so a major security operation cranked up around Prenton Park. Merseyside Police Superintendent, Paul Forrester, promised that misbehaviour by fans could lead to a, "five-year suspension from these competitions," for their club. His fears were rooted in experience. The previous summer, Rangers fans had clashed with police at Goodison Park at Everton defender Dave Watson's testimonial. Several arrests were made. On the day of the Shelbourne game, police conducted random stop checks of fans and dog handlers and mounted police were deployed to keep the peace. Furthermore, the 6,000-strong crowd that filed in for the game was laced with under-cover 'spotters'. Not even the best laid plans could account for those who travelled to the game intent on causing trouble, though. This was borne out as the Shelbourne team bus came under attack yards from

Prenton Park. Only the glass windows of the team bus separated the Shelbourne squad from their attackers, many of whom had spilled out of the local Mersey Clipper pub. Winger Mark Rutherford ducked for cover inside the bus as bottles, rocks and beer glasses flew from all angles.

MARK RUTHERFORD: *"There were supporters on either side of the bus throwing bottles at us. They ended up throwing a lot of them at their own supporters because they'd fly over the bus and hit their own supporters on the other side. There were hundreds of them on either side as we were driving in. I couldn't believe the hatred in their faces, shouting at us through the windows. That was the ugly side of the game. They were really trying to intimidate us."*

Liam Kelly had been brought to the club the previous season as cover for the injured Morley but coming under attack before a UEFA Cup game wasn't written into any contract he'd signed.

LIAM KELLY: *"It was an incredible sight. My uncle, Robbie, used to come and watch us all the time. He was in his seventies. There were lads older than him holding these scarves up with 'no surrender' written on them and firing bottles of beer at the bus. One of the bottles missed the bus, went across the road and hit a Rangers fan in the head and split him open. We were absolutely gob-smacked at how vicious it was. It wasn't kids or people that you'd expect or who you might say, 'They don't understand'. It was actually grown men. We got up to the ground and the bus reversed up to within inches of the door. We had to run in with our bags over our heads in case anything was thrown over the top of the bus. We got into the dressing room and we're sitting there, twenty or so of us in the squad and all the staff. This guy that had been hit with the bottle was brought in on a stretcher to get first aid. He actually tried to get off the stretcher and get into the dressing room. His head was wide open, there were twenty-five of us in the dressing room and he's trying to get in at us. It was incredible stuff."*

If the scene hadn't been set for a battle out on the field, it was now.

PAT SCULLY: "It was an experience to be in those hostile situations. They're all great tests for a player and a team, how you're going to react. I thoroughly enjoyed that."

Fenlon fancied the occasion too. He'd taken his fair share of abuse from the terraces and stands in the League of Ireland ever since he returned from three years at Linfield. So, he was ready for anything Rangers could throw at him, verbally as well as physically.

PAT FENLON: "When Linfield made an approach it was a difficult decision for me, there's no point in saying anything different. I grew up as a staunch Celtic fan, a lot of my friends would have been the same. I had to think about it. It was around a time that I needed a bit of a change. My dad had just died and I'd sort of lost a bit of belief in the game here and wanted a new challenge. Probably, the challenge for me was to go and prove people wrong on both sides of the border. In the end, I'd still say it was the best club I've played for. It was run as a professional football club and was totally different to anything I'd experienced in the League of Ireland."

When Fenlon ran out onto Tranmere's pitch, a crowd of Linfield supporters who'd travelled to watch Rangers called him over and wished him well. He needed it. Chairman David Murray had given new Rangers boss Dick Advocaat an open cheque book after being beaten to a historic ten-in-a-row of League titles by Celtic. Like Byrne at Shelbourne, the Rangers supremo craved League titles, then European domination. Advocaat responded by flooding Ibrox with international talent. Two weeks after being beaten by Brazil in the World Cup semi-finals Dutch duo Giovanni van Bronckhorst and Artur Numan were signed. Goalkeeper Lionel Charbonnier, the sub goalkeeper with World Cup winners, France, was brought in to put pressure on Antti Niemi. Striker Gabriel Amato and former Manchester United hero Andrei Kanchelskis were next in. Rod Wallace came on a free transfer from Leeds. In all, Rangers' summer spending clocked in at Stg£21 million. The top pay band at Shelbourne was just over IR£200 a week.

MARK RUTHERFORD: "Van Bronckhorst, Kanchelskis – their big toes were worth more than our whole team."

PAT MORLEY: "They had Jorg Albertz as well and Amato the Argentinean, Jonas Thern and Gordon Durie, who'd played for Scotland in the World Cup, and Jonathan Johansson. That amount of talent is frightening. That's what we played against."

The sight of Advocaat taking his place in the Rangers dug-out for his first game in charge focused the Shelbourne players on the task in hand as kick-off loomed.

LIAM KELLY: "He (Advocaat) had done an article, I think, a few days before the first game. He was asked what his thoughts were and said, 'We're playing a bunch of plumbers and carpenters. I'd be expecting the score to be 9 or 10-0'. That was all we needed to hear. If we weren't built up for it enough that was all that was needed."

In his first game as boss, Keely started ten of the eleven players that lined out against Cork in the Cup final. The only change was an enforced one as striker, Stephen Geoghegan, missed out with a groin injury. A newly-fit Morley was the obvious replacement, despite missing the previous season, and slotted in beside Kelly up front.

LIAM KELLY: "Dermot had gone to watch Rangers the previous week in some game and they had Jonas Thern, the Swedish International, playing. Dermot decided that I was going to man mark him and if he moved I was to kick him. I said, 'Right, no problem'. Every time he came near the ball for the first five minutes I absolutely assassinated him. I left him then and broke forward, the ball was crossed by Dessie

Baker and I had a tap-in only for Porrini, the Italian lad, slid in in front of me and headed it in for an own goal. I was jogging back, delighted, and all I could hear was Dermot roaring at me that if I left your man's side again he was taking me off. I was going, 'We've just scored, I made a great run'. He says, 'I'm telling you now, if you leave his side once more you're coming off'. So that was it, then. Neither of us kicked the ball until they took him off in the second half."

Shels were in dreamland when they made it 2-0 just before half time. Big defender, Scully, headed a corner kick back across goal, Morley missed it with a despairing lunge of his leg but Rutherford was behind him to hammer home into the roof of the net before whirling away in delirious celebration. He'd scored against Kilmarnock and SK Brann in previous European ties but this one eclipsed the lot.

MARK RUTHERFORD: "I was right in front of the Rangers supporters as well. I've actually got a photograph of the moment I struck the ball and all you can see is the faces of the Rangers supporters behind the goal. They were looking at me in disgust as the ball hit the back of the net."

The travelling Rangers fans had anticipated a routine win over the "plumbers and carpenters", but became increasingly agitated as the goals flew into their own net.

PAT MORLEY: "There was an incident late in the first half where Gattuso knocked the ball out and I went to take a quick throw-in. As I went to pick up the ball there was this sound behind me, it's hard to describe it, like a low growling or coughing. I wasn't sure what it was. Afterwards, I looked at my shirt and I was covered in spit."

A missile was hurled at Shelbourne 'keeper, Alan Gough, from the crowd. Closer inspection revealed it was a bottle of red sauce. Gough's nonplussed reaction demonstrated how tuned in he and the Shelbourne players were to the game itself. The dressing room at half-time had an eerie feel to it. No rollickings were needed, everything was going to plan. They were beating Rangers 2-0.

PAT FENLON: "When Dermot came in at half time I mean, as a manager, what do you say? It was pretty much like, 'Okay, keep doing the same thing'."

They didn't listen to him. Instead, they scored another and increased their lead to a three goal advantage. Fenlon picked the ball up in the middle after fifty-eight minutes and slid it forward to Morley. He was pushed wide by Thern towards the left of the penalty area but instinctively waited for Niemi to go down for the ball and expertly chipped it over him into the net. What happened next almost made the Rangers fans choke on their spit. Celebrating in front of the raging crowd Morley raised his hands to his head and slowly blessed himself. The previous January, Paul Gascoigne had pretended to play a flute in front of Celtic fans, a loyalist gesture that made him a hate figure among the green half of Glasgow. Morley insists his admittedly provocative act wasn't rooted in any religious bigotry but represented an outpouring of joy after returning from the brink of retirement with his knee problem to fulfil a life's ambition.

PAT MORLEY: "I'm not a religious person in any way or form. It's just something that when Gascoigne played the flute there was murder over it. I'd always said if I ever played with Celtic and scored against Rangers I'd bless myself and I wouldn't care what the consequences were. It's not that I was sectarian or anything like that. It's just if you do something that you've always wanted to do in your life then you'll want to do something to remember it by. I just turned around and put my hand up to my head and blessed myself and, just as I finished it, I was mobbed. It's one of those moments. It was great winning Leagues and Cups and I've got all the personal awards, but that was it for me. Do you know what it's like? It's like Harrington winning his first major. You have the incident where his young fella runs out and says, 'Will we put ladybirds in the cup?' It's something in sport that you can only dream about. I'd done it at the highest level, scoring in a UEFA Cup match against a serious team with a manager who had serious talent. I never got an Irish cap. I was close but, even if I got an Irish cap, this would outweigh it, by a mile."

LIAM KELLY: *"I think he blessed himself about a hundred times, just in case we didn't see him! I was thinking, 'Man! He's going to get killed!' He had it planned. In fairness to him, there was no way he wasn't going to go through with it. He was true to his word and did it."*

PAT FENLON: *"Sometimes the supporters are willing to dish out the stick so the players should be able to have a bit of banter back with them."*

LIAM KELLY: *"It was a fantastic finish for the goal but it didn't surprise me. When you looked at Pat Morley in training, I mean, people talk about all the goals 'Geogho' got but Morley in training was outstanding. 'Geogho' could take it or leave it in training, he'd turn it on more so for matches. If you needed a goal in a game you knew 'Geogho' was going to get it. In training, Morley rarely missed. His finishing was frightening. He was only coming back from his injury then. He hadn't even had many games or much training or anything. I just remember thinking, 'He must have been some player'."*

With three goals in the bag, Keely took the opportunity on the sideline to pass a comment or two to his opposite number Advocaat about the "plumbers and carpenters" jibe. Struck dumb by events on the pitch Advocaat stood silent.

LIAM KELLY: *"Amoruso, this big huge defender, was crying on the pitch when Morley scored, actually physically crying. I was looking at him saying to myself, 'These boys are gone'."*

DAMIEN RICHARDSON: "I think that just completed my sort of belief that we had something good at Shelbourne. I was delighted for Pat Morley because he'd been to Celtic as a young player. He always was and still is a Celtic fan. For him to do that at Rangers was particularly momentous for him."

A famous photo still hangs in Tolka Park. It's a picture of the scoreboard at Prenton Park after fifty-eight minutes – Shelbourne 3 Rangers 0. Morley got copies of the snap, framed and signed them and sent them off to everyone who'd pitched in through the lean times of his cruciate recovery. The O'Herlihy family who looked after him in Dublin, Alan Byrne, Alan Kinsella, Kieran Corcoran, they all got one. It's just as well the photographer didn't wait another minute to take the picture otherwise it would have been lost for all time. Almost immediately after scoring, Shelbourne committed football's cardinal sin, they conceded one. Albertz swung over a corner kick from the left that McCarthy handled and Albertz drilled home the penalty. It was a critical concession by Shelbourne that completely changed the game.

PAT SCULLY: "I have to say, as a defender, my first thought at 3-0 was to keep it tight for the next ten minutes – really keep it tight and concentrate – but we gave away a goal straightaway."

Keely admitted he froze on the sideline when his side went three ahead.

PAT FENLON: "I thought maybe Mick Neville might have come on when we conceded the first to get a bit of experience into the back four. But we all make mistakes. I know we made more mistakes as players than Dermot did as the manager."

Whatever about the soft goal, the final twenty minutes were always going to test Shelbourne's resolve. They were a part-time team playing their first game of the season against a side expected to press hard to win the competition. The introduction of Jonathan Johansson for David

Graham was key to Rangers' revival. The Swede offered fresh legs down the left and tore Shelbourne asunder on the flank. Soon after Albertz's goal, Advocaat bit the bullet and hauled off Thern whom Kelly had kept under his thumb.

LIAM KELLY: "When Thern went off, they swapped him for Ian Ferguson. Now, I'm sure Ferguson had been watching how things were going between me and Thern. Ferguson ran on and came straight at me. He stuck his elbow up to give me one. I seen it and gave him one back. It ended up the two of us elbowing each other straight in the face as he ran onto the pitch. The next ball between us I nicked it around him and he absolutely flew into me and got booked. Greg Costello (former Shels player) always slags me when I see him, saying, 'You retired Jonas Thern, he was never seen after that game in Prenton Park!'"

JONAS THERN: "I can remember that, at that time, I had big problems with injuries. I remember playing with Gattuso in midfield against Shelbourne. He was still a youngster coming from Italy and working hard. I felt that my physical status was not at the top level. I had knee injuries and operations and hoped to come back to play at a decent level. That's the big memory I have from that game, physically, big problems. I never actually got back to the quality and shape that I expected at that level. I expected more from myself and for my career to finish better than the way it did."

Down on their luck, starved of possession and, by now, battling fatigue, Shelbourne leaked a second in the seventy-second minute. Again, it was a scrappy goal as Amato seized on a rebound and struck a deflected shot from the left of the box to beat Gough at his near post. Then, two minutes later, van Bronckhorst played a brilliant one-two down the left and struck a low shot to the left corner past Gough: 3-3. Shelbourne hearts sank. Morley now realised his race was run and Tony Sheridan, the hero of their 1996 FAI Cup success, replaced him.

PAT MORLEY: "Dermot took me off. I was gone at that stage. He brought 'Shero' on. It was all over for me once I scored."

Almost inevitably, Rangers scored a fourth goal eight minutes from time, moving ominously ahead in the tie for the first time. The damage was all done down the left again, where Johansson got free to curl in a perfect cross for the unmarked Amato to nod home. Basic errors were killing Shelbourne as the players fought cramp and struggled to maintain their composure in the face of exhaustion. One of the most bizarre 5-3 victories ever witnessed in the UEFA Cup was sealed for Rangers five minutes from time. Just as their goal siege began, with an Albertz penalty conversion following a McCarthy handball, so it ended with the big centre-half inexplicably repeating exactly the same handball offence. A bad night at the office for McCarthy.

PAT SCULLY: "I kind of said to Tony, 'What the fuck are you doing?' But he was just knackered, physically absolutely knackered. It was unfortunate for Tony but, when you're physically that tired, you make mistakes."

LIAM KELLY: "To this day I don't know, I just can't understand what happened. The ball was going over his head for the first one and I think he thought his man was going to get it but, to me, it looked like it was going to beat everyone. He just put his hand up. Like, he's six foot three or four, Tony, he had the hand full length up in the air and he was jumping so he was right up there. I don't know what height your man behind him would have had to be to head it! We just couldn't believe it and then to do it a second time. His head was gone, obviously."

PAT SCULLY: "Tony is a great lad and was a really good player. Obviously, he was disappointed but we were all devastated. We could have got one of the best results that any Irish team has ever got in Europe. We let it slip through our fingers."

MARK RUTHERFORD: "It would have been totally different at Tolka Park. Imagine if we went 3-0 up at Tolka Park and to have the crowd behind us. It might have been the difference."

PAT FENLON: "Just devastation at the end of the game, to be honest. It was very, very disappointing because we had Rangers by the throat, 3-0 in a European match and you're saying, 'This could go down in history as a major thing. This could be the biggest result ever by a League of Ireland team if we get 3-2 or 3-1'. I think most of the lads were disappointed, devastated, because they were there for the taking. If we'd held on for another bit, we might have beat a team they paid millions and millions to put together."

PAT MORLEY: "'Scullyer' and the lads will say, 'Yeah, the result, giving away five goals ...' but, for me, from a personal satisfaction side of things, nothing will ever, ever top that night. Even if I got a hole-in-one in golf – that won't happen – but it wouldn't top it anyway. Maybe if my young fella goes and plays in the Masters and I caddy for him, then maybe. It's one of those moments in sport. Andy Warhol says people have fifteen minutes of fame. They were mine. Four and a half million people on Eurosport watching. I got messages on my phone from fellas in Majorca, Marbella and Tenerife coming out of the ground saying, 'You're a legend, we're locked in Tenerife!'"

Insult was, literally, added to injury for the rest of the Shelbourne players when they togged in and headed for tea and sandwiches as planned.

LIAM KELLY: "They kept a function room for us with food and stuff but, seemingly, fans had broken into it and ransacked it. So, we got no food or anything after the game which had been laid on. When they were three down they went ballistic. Unfortunately for us, they turned the score around but the food was still gone."

Later, the Shelbourne players were scheduled to link up with the charter flight taking the St Patrick's Athletic team back from their Champions League qualifier with Glasgow Celtic. Shelbourne were late getting out of Prenton Park so the plane was forced to wait on the runway for them to arrive. It was a fitting end to a crazy night. After shipping five away goals, the tie was effectively over. It was technically only half time, but Shelbourne now needed to win by three goals at Ibrox to progress. It was a lot to ask for, particularly as Rangers' new big name signings planned on giving a good account of themselves in front of their new supporters. The 'Gers also felt they'd let themselves down for an hour at Prenton Park.

JONAS THERN: "We had a good team but maybe the preparation for the first Shelbourne game could have been better, physically. I think sometimes when you go out and play in the qualifying games in Europe, if you haven't been preparing as well as you should, you're going to fail. It's a small difference between teams and, if you're not prepared, you're going to fail. We didn't lose against Shelbourne but we did the previous season in very similar circumstances against Gothenburg, here in Sweden. We were 3-0 down during that game also, and never managed to come back. Maybe Gothenburg were a little bit better than Shelbourne but it's always a difficulty for teams that are favourites. If you're not prepared mentally, ready for hard work over ninety minutes then the skill difference between the players isn't so big."

Following a UEFA investigation, Rangers were fined 25,000 Swiss Francs (IR£10,000) for the behaviour of their fans at Prenton Park, eleven of whom were arrested, cautioned and later released. Shelbourne expected to run a similar gauntlet of abuse during their stay in Glasgow but the early signs were positive. Rangers officially apologised for events in and around Prenton Park and proved to be good hosts in Glasgow laying on limos, drivers and guides to bring the visitors wherever they needed to go.

PAT MORLEY: *"We were brought up to Parkhead as guests of honour one of the days. We went out onto the pitch and sat in the dug-outs. I remember a couple of people coming out wanting to take photographs with the guy who'd blessed himself!"*

Rangers never lost their competitive streak, though.

LIAM KELLY: *"The night before the game they had done their session on the full of the Ibrox pitch and we only got part of it for ours. They had people watching us, also, so Keely announced that we were going to play Gaelic. The boys were up there with their notes looking at our set pieces and we're lamping balls all over Ibrox. They might have come away with some info about our high fielding full-forwards but not much more than that!"*

PAT MORLEY: *"Your man, the groundsman, was being an arsehole. He just wouldn't leave us to play the length of the pitch. We said, 'Right, fuck you' and we had a game of GAA and we dug divots up through the pitch. They went ballistic! It was the first game of GAA there. And the last."*

The following day the bus arrived to pick Shelbourne up for the game. The tension onboard was palpable as the players privately pondered what lay in store for them at the ground.

LIAM KELLY: *"We were thinking, 'Here we go, we're going to get pummelled with bottles again'. 'Nutsy' Fenlon is blaring out all his republican music out the top of the bus and we're all thinking, 'We're going to get murdered here'. We pulled up at Ibrox. I just remember looking at the path, a big wide path about twenty feet from the door. I thought, 'Here it is now'. There's barriers either side but there's people everywhere, 'We're going to get pounded'. We jumped off the bus expecting the worst but they were asking for our autographs. When we got in we were asking, 'What's the difference?' We were told that all the scumbags who travel to away games with them are banned from within a couple of miles of the ground. Only proper fans actually come in to the home games. The only trouble they get, really, is when they go away from home and they can't monitor who gets near the ground. They were an absolute joy up there."*

In the tunnel before the match a couple of Shelbourne players took the opportunity to make a timely fashion statement – revealing T-shirts beneath their jerseys with, 'Celtic, Champions' printed on them. Heated words were exchanged. It may not have been the wisest ploy by the Irish because Rangers scored after just four minutes to end any hopes of an upset. Shelbourne's tormentor at Tranmere, Johansson, scored the first and added a second in the eighty-ninth minute to complete a 2-0 home win. Again, Shelbourne's efforts weren't adequately reflected on the scoreboard as they held the hosts scoreless for eighty-five minutes and were competitive throughout.

PAT SCULLY: "You'll always look at the second leg and, although we played well, it was pretty much game over when they got the first goal so early on. They maybe didn't go through the second game at full pelt, compared to what they would have done if they needed to win it. That's the frustrating thing about the first leg. If we'd been able to hold it with a win, or even a draw, we could have went to Ibrox with something to hang on to."

Rangers underlined their vast budget by handing debuts to right-winger Kanchelskis, their Stg£5.5million signing from Fiorentina, and World Cup semi-finalist Numan, for whom they paid PSV Eindhoven Stg£4.5million. Long before the full-time whistle sounded, the Shelbourne players had accepted their fate and were quietly considering who they'd swap jerseys with. Rangers proved impregnable in that regard, too.

LIAM KELLY: "I had asked Amoruso for his jersey but they wouldn't swap. Then, out of nowhere afterwards, Amoruso came out with a towel around him. He pointed at me and said, 'My shirt'. He brought me into the Rangers dressing room and they're all sitting there eating bowls of fruit and yoghurt. He had the shirt there and gave it to me and I swapped with him. I walked back in and here's our lads with cans of McEwans lager in their hands! The Rangers lads were going for the bowls of fruit with natural yoghurt, sitting around almost religiously contemplating the game. Back in our dressing room 'Shero' is throwing out tins of McEwans lager. The cans were free. I remember one of the lads heading out of Ibrox with the gear bag full of cans."

After the greatest escape of their careers, Rangers went on to beat PAOK Salonika, Beitar Jerusalem and Bayer Leverkusen in the UEFA Cup. They were only denied a place in the quarter finals by Parma who, with Fabio Cannavaro, Juan Veron and Hernan Crespo in their side won the competition outright. Normal service was resumed in Scotland as Rangers reclaimed the League title. Shelbourne finished the League of Ireland campaign in third position but captured the title Byrne demanded in 2000. By that stage, Morley was back in Cork playing for his hometown club. The Prenton Park heroics had smoothed out previously strained relations with fans and allowed him to return to Leeside in October 1998, where he retired a legend.

PAT MORLEY: "When I first left Cork, people didn't really appreciate me for leaving and I was called everything under the sun. I'll always remember, when I did leave Cork, I was ushered out of the town one day when I was inside buying some CDs for the car journey up to Shelbourne. Five or six months later, after I scored against Rangers, I did exactly the same thing and people applauded me after coming out of the shop. So, it obviously doesn't take much to win over the Cork fans!"

UEFA CUP

First round, first leg
July 22, 1998
Prenton Park, Birkenhead
Attendance: 6,000

Shelbourne: 3
(Porrini og 7, Rutherford 42, Morley 58)

Rangers: 5
(Albertz 59 and 85 pens, Amato 72 and 82, van Bronckhorst 74)

Shelbourne: Gough; Smith, McCarthy, Scully, D. Geoghegan; D. Baker, Fenlon, Fitzgerald, Rutherford; Morley (Sheridan 78), Kelly.

Rangers: Niemi; Porrini, Amoruso, Petric, Albertz; Van Bronckhorst, Gattuso (Amato 46), B. Ferguson, Thern (I. Ferguson 63); Graham (Johansson 46), Durie.

Referee: V. Anghelinei (Romania).

First round, second leg
July 29, 1998
Ibrox Park, Glasgow
Attendance: 46,906

Rangers: 2
(Johansson 4, 89)

Shelbourne: 0

Rangers: Niemi; Porrini, Moore, Amoruso, Numan; Kanchelskis (Amato h/t), B. Ferguson, van Bronckhorst (I. Ferguson 74), Albertz; Durie (Gattuso 63), Johansson.

Shelbourne: Gough; Smith, McCarthy, Scully, D. Geoghegan; D. Baker, Fenlon, Fitzgerald, Rutherford; Morley (Sheridan 67), Kelly.

Referee: M. Milewski (Poland).

CHAPTER 10

SHELBOURNE VS KR REYKJAVIK
First qualifying round, July 14 and 21, 2004

SHELBOURNE VS HADJUK SPLIT
Second qualifying round, July 28 and August 4, 2004

SHELBOURNE VS DEPORTIVO LA CORUÑA
Third qualifying round, August 11 and 24, 2004

SHELBOURNE VS LILLE
First round, September 16 and 30, 2004

"We had tried to get some DVDs of Deportivo and the only two I could get were of them playing in the semi-final of the Champions League the previous season against Porto, the two matches. I sat the lads down and said, 'Just watch these videos and we'll go through a few things'. I think it was about halfway through and someone said, 'Well, what game is this anyway?' I said, 'They're actually the semi-finals from last year'. So there was a little bit of panic in the room at that stage." PAT FENLON.

It was during a press conference on the Dublin quays to mark his second coming as Shelbourne chairman in September 2001 that Finbarr Flood dared to consider the impossible dream; qualification for the group stages of the Champions League – within three years. Having risen from the ranks of messenger boy at Guinness in the early 1950s to Managing Director of the St James' Gate brewery by the 1990s nobody was in any doubt about Flood's ability to reach out and grab the stars if he so desired. 'Our aim is to emulate clubs like Rosenborg and Brondby and become regular participants in the Champions League group stages', he said. 'We've formulated a three-year plan and during that time we aim to prove that that is a feasible proposition. We see no reason why it shouldn't happen'. Flood's first spell as Shelbourne chairman lasted four years in the late 1990s. It was in this period and while working alongside ambitious Chief Executive Ollie Byrne that the seed was sewn about the rich financial harvest available beyond our international borders. After the barren spells of the 1970s and 1980s, businessman Tony Donnelly came on board as chairman and benefactor of the club and Shels prospered, qualifying six times in the 1990s for European competition. In 14 games, they won just once, a 3-1 victory over Ukrainians Karpaty Lvov which took them through to the first round proper of the 1993/94 European Cup winners' Cup. But with a stronger team, solid investment in the right areas and a level of strategic planning the European market was a niche the club could happily explore.

FINBARR FLOOD: "In the beginning it wasn't even about the money. I know that sounds strange to say. The money thing became the key thing because we were eventually spending so much of it but in the beginning it was the honour of being able to do what a club like Rosenborg did. It was the dream that we could make it in Europe and we could get to where other teams all wanted to go. In the beginning you'd only a quarter believe it was possible. But over time you began to think, 'With a little bit of luck we could get there'."

Byrne, the son of a former Shelbourne chairman, stood at the helm of day-to-day operations at the club and was sold on the European project from a long way out. He'd seen with his own eyes how Rosenborg, a club of modest means from the fishing town of Trondheim in the western reaches of Norway, had been utterly transformed by the revenue streams from regular Champions League group stage qualification throughout the 1990s. In 2000, Shels became the first Irish team to advance beyond the first qualifying round of the competition and were paired off with Rosenborg. After a 3-1 home defeat, Shels pulled off a creditable 1-1 draw in Trondheim. The Norwegian champions went on to reach the group stages of the Champions League for the sixth straight season, guaranteeing themselves millions in TV money, endorsements and UEFA prize money. Shels got another thought provoking glimpse of how a club from an unfashionable league could profit in Europe the following season when they were beaten 5-0 on aggregate by Danish side Brondby in the UEFA Cup. A year after Flood had spoken of Shelbourne's burning passion for a European breakthrough, they lost 3-2 on aggregate to Hibernians of Malta and crashed out of qualifying for the 2002/03 Champions League at the first hurdle. Pat Fenlon's first European tie as manager unhappily coincided with the first time a Maltese side had advanced at the expense of Irish opposition. Flood's three-year plan now seemed more pathetic than prophetic. It would be the summer of 2004 before Shels would get another shot at the Champions League and if the three-year dream was to come to fruition it was now or never. Bankrolled by the money Byrne was making available – by literally begging and borrowing – Fenlon had gathered a strong squad capable of raising the club's pulse in Europe again. He'd prised Jason Byrne away from Bray Wanderers for an unreleased fee, believed to be a new League record, and the striker's twenty one goals secured the club's eleventh league title win in late 2003. Byrne's form continued throughout 2004, allowing him to emulate his cousin, Robbie Keane, by playing for Ireland in April. It was considered only a matter of time before team-mate Owen Heary, the finest full-back in the league, also gained international recognition, along with U-21 cap Wes Hoolahan, the driving force behind all of Shels' midfield invention. In the weeks approaching their Champions League first qualifying round tie against KR Reykjavik another International, Alan Moore, was recruited. The midfielder had spent ten years at Middlesbrough before moving to Burnley and at twenty-nine still had several good seasons ahead of him. The big signing reflected Shelbourne's ambitions.

PAT FENLON: *"The thing with 'Mooresy' is, you bring him in and people expect that he's earning a fortune. In fairness to him he wasn't.*

216

I went to meet Alan in a Manchester airport. He was playing with Burnley at the time and earning a fair bit of money. I made him an offer and he agreed to sign. I was back on the next plane home. Job done."

When Fenlon next arrived at Dublin Airport he had the best set of players in Irish club soccer with him, the League of Ireland champions destined for Reykjavik. The omens were good. They would play KR Reykjavik at the same Laugardals Stadium where in 1986 Jack Charlton steered Ireland to a triangular tournament success with wins over Iceland and Czechoslovakia.

PAT FENLON: "That to me was always going to be the hardest game because we were expected to get through. We'd obviously assembled a very, very good squad and people expected us to make some sort of in-road and at the very least go through that first round. So there was that pressure there. I remember us going two down out there and panicking a little."

STUART BYRNE: "We conceded two silly goals from set pieces. But I remember when we conceded the second goal there seemed to be this immediate response, a positive response. Normally when you look at those situations in times gone by in European games, the head would just go down with Irish teams playing in Europe. But we responded really well, really positively and straightaway. Alan Moore, straight from the tip off, went on this solo run and all of a sudden it got us on the front foot again. We went on to get two goals. We drew 2-2."

Moore's impact at the club was instant as he latched onto Hoolahan's clever 84th minute through ball and slotted home. The draw was secured when a Reykjavik defender turned winger Ollie Cahill's searching cross into his own net. After toying with serious trouble the Shels players were more than happy to get out of Dodge with a 2-2 draw. A scoreless stalemate at Tolka Park would now be enough to secure

Shels' place in the second-round. A pre determined draw had paired the winners with Croatian champions Hadjuk Split.

STUART BYRNE: *"In the end we got through on the 0-0 we needed. In fairness to Reykjavik they were better in the second leg. They were a good side. They had some Icelandic Internationals and full-time players."*

PAT FENLON: *"You could see it in the players' faces. It was, 'Well, that's done. Anything now is a bonus for us'. The draw hadn't been kind to us in relation to who we got, Hadjuk Split."*

Split would host the first leg at one of European football's most hostile arenas, the Poljud Stadium. The 35,000 capacity venue was also home to the *Torcida*, Hadjuk's support group named in recognition of Brazil's passionate followers at the 1950 World Cup. Stumble across graffiti of a man with a mask covering his face and bearing the letter 'H', for Hadjuk, and you knew you were in *Torcida* territory. On big game days flares, emitting coloured smoke clouded the hisses and boos that rained down on rival teams. Their intimidation tactics were legendary. When Tottenham Hotspur visited for the first leg of a UEFA Cup semi-final tie in early 1984 they were greeted by the sight of a cockerel being slaughtered on the pitch. The cockerel, of course, is featured on Tottenham's emblem. In purely footballing terms, Shels had their work cut out to progress past a strong and storied club who'd reached the Champions League quarter-finals not so long earlier in 1995 and were currently in the midst of winning back-to-back Croatian league titles. Over the previous twenty years or so the club had began the careers of International stars like Robert Jarni, Slaven Bilic, Aljosa Asanovic, Alen Boksic and Igor Stimac, now Hadjuk's Sporting Director. They signed future Portsmouth FA Cup winner and current Tottenham midfielder Niko Kranjcar after the Shels games and with a technically impressive side, were ultra confident of going through to the final qualifying round to face Deportivo La Coruña in another pre-determined draw.

PAT FENLON: "We had a fair bit of work done on Hadjuk. We'd gone through the whole lot, myself and Eamonn Collins. Dave Henderson had watched them a bit and we knew they were a decent side. I think our worry going there having done that bit of homework was in relation to the atmosphere in the ground. It was frightening on the night. They were there for three or four hours before the match."

STUART BYRNE: "It was hysteria. You couldn't hear yourself shouting at someone or you wouldn't know if someone was shouting at you. You just couldn't hear anything, the line, the bench, nothing. It was that real eastern European hostile atmosphere, that Galatasaray, Turkish type of scene. It was a gorgeous stadium and there were 20,000 or 25,000 at it but it was a really hostile atmosphere, very difficult to play in."

Fenlon's cautious approach to the first leg was buttressed by a 4-1-4-1 formation which placed Stuart Byrne in a holding role between the defence and midfield. Given Jason Byrne's scoring form it was impossible to drop him but Fenlon favoured a lone forward more adept at holding the ball up and retaining possession. So, Glen Fitzpatrick started up front on his own, displacing Irish International striker Byrne to the right wing, a tactic that would be a feature of their campaign. A small pocket of around 100 travelling supporters were embedded in the 22,000-strong crowd and braced themselves for a long night of watching their team mount a rearguard offensive. They were even more astounded than the *Torcida* to see Fitzpatrick put Shels ahead with a virtuoso opening goal after only five minutes. Hoolahan held up the ball in midfield before finding Moore. He, in turn, spotted Fitzpatrick's run off the shoulder of his marker on the left of the penalty area and after gaining possession Fitzpatrick drilled an early left footed shot across the 'keeper to the far corner of the net.

STUART BYRNE: "If you look at the goal there was a real air of quality about it. Glen at the time was flying. He was quick, strong, he was able to hold off people and the finish was unbelievable. In fairness to him he buried it right in the corner."

The fuming Croats whistled in derision and launched flares down at the pitch.

GLEN FITZPATRICK: "The place went bananas. There'd been a lot of reports, media stuff for the first few days that they didn't rate us at all. They were sort of over confident and they'd apparently booked their flights already to Deportivo for the next round. They definitely took a bit of arrogance into the games."

As galling as the goal concession was to Hadjuk manager Ivan Katalinic it had at least come against the general run of play. He sensed that if his side continued to dominate as they had from the start they would undoubtedly get their chance to level. Croatian International Mario Carevic was a constant threat on the left flank and when he combined high up the field with striker Dragan Blatnjak they purred menacingly. Shels goalkeeper Steve Williams denied a procession of attacks before Blatnjak almost inevitably levelled the game in the 18th minute. Stuart Byrne missed a great chance to put Shels back ahead with a header from Moore's corner late in the half but the lead would have flattered them.

STUART BYRNE: "We were delighted to be going in 1-1 at half-time. You could see they were a really quality side."

That quality told again within minutes of the restart when Petar Suto put the hosts ahead for the first time, 2-1. Save for a couple of half chances Shels were forced to defend in the second-half as if their lives depended on not conceding a third. Things got worse before getting a whole lot better in an intriguing final half hour or so. Split finally got their third goal after eighty-five minutes to open up a vital two goal advantage in the tie when Blatnjak rose up between the two defenders and headed powerfully past Williams. But, content that their evening's work had all but secured their passage to the inviting coastal town of La Coruňa, they made the fatal mistake of sitting back and admiring their handy work. A minute of normal time remained when Moore repeated his Iceland heroics with a valuable Shels goal that swung the course of the tie violently back towards an equal footing. Left full Crawley put in a hopeful diagonal ball to the right of the Hadjuk penalty area which broke kindly off Ger McCarthy for Moore. He was surrounded by bodies but cleverly nodded the ball ahead into space before deftly clipping a right footed shot across the 'keeper. The strike turned the tie on its head. Shels still trailed but they now possessed two crucial away goals. The realisation that a 1-0 home win in Dublin would be enough to see Shels through hit the Split players like a bolt between the eyes. Tensions spilled over as the final whistle sounded, erupting into all out war. Bodies came from different directions, swelling a melee that saw both sets of players trade punches, shoves, shoulders and swear words in their native tongues.

PAT FENLON: "Jamie Harris caught one of their lads very late in the face and that kind of started things but the goal late on had added to it. They were just frustrated and there was a bit of aggro."

STUART BYRNE: "Them conceding the second goal kind of frustrated them a little. They knew they were up against it then. The difference between 3-1 and 3-2 is huge. It's absolutely massive. It's the difference between two away goals and just one. So, there was a bit of frustration from them there I'd imagine. I just remember there being a big mêlée and running over to try to calm everything down."

JASON BYRNE: "It kicked off and there were a few digs thrown but that's part and parcel of it when you go to countries like that. They try to intimidate you. The lads stood tall and we stood toe-to-toe with them and we put it up to them."

OWEN HEARY: "It started on the pitch and went on down the tunnel.

Luckily enough we had a big fella who also did the FAI security. He sort of stepped in and pushed a few of them away and sorted it out."

When the red mist cleared and the smoke from the umpteenth flare had dispersed into the warm evening air above Croatia's second largest city, the sense of a job well done far from home was strong among the Shels squad. A 3-2 defeat never tasted so sweet.

PAT FENLON: "I knew after the game in Split, and I think everyone knew, that there was a major fear on their behalf. We knew coming in that night they were rattled a little bit and we had the upper hand because we knew they wouldn't fancy coming to Tolka, to be honest, once they seen it."

Tolka certainly wasn't what the *Torcida* and Hadjuk's glut of International talent were used to. The compact old ground could squeeze in a little over 10,000 at a push. Unlike the majestic bowl shaped Poljud Stadium which dominated the Split skyline, Shelbourne's all-seater ground nestled unobtrusively between houses in Drumcondra's residential heartland. From the bridge that crosses the Tolka River only a few hundred yards away, the new stand behind the goals is all that diverts the eye from rows of rooftops that rise up to form the skyline. Its location, just off the north road in and out of Dublin, made it a prime target for builders and speculators who saw in the several acres of land unlimited potential for development close to the city centre to feed the ravenous hunger of the Celtic Tiger property boom. Approaching the height of the building explosion in late-2003, Ollie Byrne sold the option to buy Tolka Park to developers who would take control of the ground and level it once Shels found a new home. In the meantime, Byrne was able to draw down on payments against the future sale price of the ground, widely reported to be between €20m and €25m, to help with the day-to-day running of the club. It was a risky business plan dependant on some form of future windfall to offset the devaluation of their primary asset, the stadium. The club also had to hope that the value of the ground was held up by a strong property market. In early August 2004, Hadjuk arrived at Tolka Park to find, on the face of things, a strong club and a thriving team that had won the backing of a nation. If financial concerns about keeping the whole show on the road gnawed away at Byrne it wasn't visibly apparent as he, Flood and everyone associated with the club savoured the occasion. In front of a capacity crowd, history was close at hand. If Shels could unlock Hadjuk's defence just once and escape with a 1-0 victory they'd become the first Irish side to make the final qualification stage of the Champions League. Then Flood could proudly stand over his three-year plan. Aside from the aggregate deficit, Shels also sought to overcome a losing streak in home European games that stretched back to 1993 when they beat Karpaty Lvov. Fenlon responded to that much-debated stat by claiming that history didn't matter because most of his current players weren't involved in the '90s. He added Joseph Ndo, the Cameroonian International and veteran of two World Cup finals tournaments, to his squad before the Split rematch. The midfielder started all three of Cameroon's games at France '98 and four years later was on the bench when they drew 1-1 with Mick McCarthy's Ireland in Niigata at the 2002 finals. At twenty-seven he also possessed two African Cup of Nations winners' medals. Hadjuk greeted the Tolka Park tie with a remarkably carefree attitude. Boss Katalanic only arrived in Dublin with his team at 2am on the Tuesday morning, the day before the game. 'They showed us that sort of disrespect when we were out there but it doesn't bother me,' said Fenlon to reporters. 'It's their choice'.

GLEN FITZPATRICK: "They didn't fancy it over here. They were making complaints about the ground and they were complaining about the dugouts, petty stuff. They didn't really rate us at all. They thought it was going to be a stroll."

Wes Hoolahan overcame a calf injury so Fenlon named the same side that had started in Split. The visitors made several changes following a shaky run of form that included a loss the previous weekend to NK

Zagreb but were certain nonetheless that victory was theirs. Sporting Director Stimac lit the touch paper before the game by stating, 'I don't think Shelbourne have the quality to organise for the ninty minutes against a good side – and I would consider Hadjuk to be a good side'.

JASON BYRNE: "Pat said, 'Right lads, I'm not going to send you out to go hell for leather. We'll get a chance and when we do it's important to take it'. So we stuck to the 4-5-1 formation that had done us well."

GLEN FITZPATRICK: "Pat always seemed to get the tactics spot on in fairness to him. The second leg at Tolka Park against Hadjuk was the epitome of it really. We had talked about our game plan for days beforehand. We knew we were only losing 3-2 and that just one goal would do it. Pat said, 'Look, if we're drawing 0-0 with fifteen or twenty minutes to go we'll gladly take that because we can then push on and throw everything at them'."

Stuart Byrne was detailed again as the midfield spoiler though with more of a licence to link up with the midfield during attacking movements, allowing Hoolahan to weave his artistry further up the pitch. Shels retained priceless creativity in other positions around the field too with Ollie Cahill supplying darting crosses from the left wing and Jason Byrne putting in the hard yards on the opposite flank. Moore got to the pace of the game early on and had two great chances to give the big crowd reason for applause. Firstly, he flicked Jason Byrne's cross just over the bar, then he won back possession in midfield and launched a thunderbolt that was tipped out for a corner by goalkeeper Tvrtko Kale. It was the first of a series of great stops on the night from Kale who was one of the personnel changes from the first leg. Blatnjak had tortured Shels in Split but was a peripheral figure up front this time, mirroring Hadjuk's general inability to impose themselves on the game.

STUART BYRNE: "They never turned up to be honest with you. The momentum was all with us. That second goal out there in the first leg

*had swung the momentum in our favour. We knew it and we were
excellent."*

A scoreless draw was still useless, though, and would amount to nothing
more than another moral victory for an Irish club if Shels exited the
competition. They found it difficult also to maintain the verve and
ferocity of their attacking play after the break. What they did direct
goalwards was met with a flamboyant save by the increasingly extrovert
Kale. Fenlon was unruffled. As far as he was concerned, the game plan
was intact. The first significant move from the sideline came with
around twenty minutes to go, when Jason Byrne came in from the right
wing and joined Fitzpatrick up front in a more attacking 4-4-2
formation. Fitzpatrick had been the target of rough-house treatment
throughout as the Split players who'd been part of the first leg mêlée
dished out some heavy hits. Fenlon eventually called the big man ashore
with seventeen minutes to go leaving Ger McCarthy and Byrne up front.
What Fenlon couldn't possibly have planned for was that, just as hope
was fading, just when the League's naysayers seemed to have a point, a
central defender who'd barely set foot out of his own half over the two
legs would make the breakthrough with a wonder strike. In his wildest
dreams Fenlon couldn't have conjured up the image of Dave Rogers
turning his body perfectly into a seventy-eighth minute loose ball, just
outside the left side of the penalty box, and rifling a left footed volley to
the top corner of the Ballybough End goal. The day before the game,
Rogers did a couple of media interviews. He retraced the steps through
his early childhood in Liverpool, to playing professional football in
England, Scotland and Holland, to arriving at Tolka Park in 2003. A
lifelong Everton fan and youth team player up to 16, he reflected on the
Toffees' European Cup winners' Cup success of 1985 as the focal point
of his football education. Watching Trevor Steven loft the ball over the
Bayern Munich goalkeeper at Goodison Park to seal their place in the
final was a special moment. He said he'd thought his heart may burst
with pride. Those same emotions surged through the crowd at Tolka
Park as Moore's ball across the penalty area was only half headed clear,

fell kindly in front of Rogers and exploded off his boot past the fingertips of a full length Kale. 'What a goal! What a fabulous goal!' whooped George Hamilton in the RTÉ TV commentary box at the other end of the ground. Jamie Harris and Stuart Byrne were first on the scene to embrace their colleague. They couldn't lay a hand on him. He was floating on air.

DAVE ROGERS: *"I just couldn't believe it. Part of me probably never will. Their goalkeeper was playing fantastic. He was coming out for every cross. His shot stopping was fantastic and when it got to the last few minutes I thought we had no chance of getting past him. I was thinking to myself it would take something special to beat him but not for a minute expecting I would be the one to do it. As soon as I hit it I could see where it was going, straight into the top corner. Looking back on it now, it was the highlight of my career. I mean I played at Rangers in front of 50,000 and in front of 60,000 at Celtic but this was unbelievable. It was something very special for all of us."*

OWEN HEARY: *"It was unbelievable because of the fact that we were absolutely peppering their goal and their 'keeper had saved everything. I remember he was jumping up and giving it loads because he was pulling off all these saves. You're looking at that thinking, 'It's not going to happen here'. Then all of a sudden Rogers, from nowhere ... I mean, he can try that another fifteen times and he won't hit the target. He'll tell you he would but there's no chance."*

PAT FENLON: *"We'd said to them, 'With ten or fifteen minutes to go we'll give you the signal and you can throw the kitchen sink at it then'. That's pretty much when 'Rodgy' came up with that goal. It was a fantastic goal."*

STUART BYRNE: *"In fairness to Dave he's technically very good with his left foot. I never saw him do anything like that before, of course, but to be fair to him he'd have it in him all right. He has a good left foot on him. He didn't whack it, he didn't drill it. If you look at it again he gave it enough pace, but not too much, that it dipped in at just the right time. It was perfectly placed. It's a fantastic memory for him to have for the rest of his life."*

The goal levelled the tie on aggregate, 3-3. Shels were now in the driving seat thanks to their two away goals and played out the final few minutes with roars of approval from a spellbound crowd ringing in their ears. If ever a goal was worthy of deciding such an occasion it was Rogers' screamer. But on a night when one club single-handedly elevated the League of Ireland's reputation to an unprecedented standing, Shels secured their greatest victory with a second goal three minutes into injury time. Fenlon brought Ndo on with normal time nearly up. He told the midfielder to get on the ball and run down the clock. It smacked of using a Porsche to do the job of a family four door but Fenlon wasn't about to apologise given the circumstances. Deep into injury-time Ndo picked up possession on the right of the penalty area. With his back to goal the smart move was to head for the corner flag. Instead, he dropped his left shoulder, turned his man with an injection of pace and pulled the ball across for the unmarked Moore whose third goal in four European games was nothing short of gift wrapped.

OWEN HEARY: "We were screaming at Joseph, 'Keep it in the corner, keep it in the corner'. Then he turned his man and I was saying, 'I'm going to kill him now for not going into that corner'. But, all of a sudden, he puts the ball across and the man that pops up again is Alan Moore, two Internationals combining."

STUART BYRNE: "It was unbelievable from Joe, a fantastic bit of skill. Of course, you're right, anybody else would have wellied it into the corner and been happy with a throw in maybe but he just made it look so easy, he was so casual. It looked so easy, like the defence had totally been deserted but it was actually the quality of the move that opened up the whole space. After that it was a tap in."

The sound of the full-time whistle confirming a 2-0 victory was drowned out by a chorus of 'We are Shels, we are Shels' that shook the birds from their perched positions on the Croke Park stands nearby.

STUART BYRNE: "God, I mean will you ever have it again? I really don't know. You see the pictures the next day of Ollie (Byrne) and ... I mean, even when you're thinking back on it, it's not that you pinch yourself but you'd be very proud of it. It's a very proud moment for the players that were involved and for the management and for anyone that was there that night. It's a great memory to have."

PAT FENLON: "That was probably the best night I've had in football so far. As a player you're a bit selfish and you look at yourself after a game and you say, 'I did all right. We won. Grand'. As a manager you sit down at the end and there's so much more to it. I remember myself and Eamonn Collins sitting down an hour and a half, probably two hours after the game, drained, and saying, 'Did you see the amount of people that were ecstatic, happy, fulfilled?' It was from the players right through to the people involved with the club and the supporters. I loved that night, not because I had made that many people so happy but because we had and you were part of it. It was fantastic."

It wasn't long before the win and Rogers' famous strike, made it into prose on a soccer website;

Art critics state without a doubt
that it's their solemn duty,
to tell the great unwashed about
great works of lucent beauty.
But nothing of artistic fame
in my opinion qualifies for
more worldwide acclaim
than Davy Rogers' volley.

Ollie Byrne caught Fenlon's gaze in the celebrations and they embraced among the hoards of joyous pitch invaders. Rogers did a lap of the ground and clapped the supporters on all four sides, anything to stay out on the pitch a minute longer for when he set foot back in the dressing-room it would all become a memory. Rogers thought of Roddy Collins, his former manager at Carlisle United, whom he'd sounded out about Shels when Fenlon expressed an interest. 'They're a good club. Go for it', advised Collins. The next morning Rogers' mobile phone buzzed into life with an incoming text message. It was from Celtic and Scotland goalkeeper Rab Douglas, his former team mate at Dundee. Rogers had sent him a message telling him to keep an eye out for his screamer on Sky News. 'So you've scored a two-yard tap-in then?' came the reply. Ollie Byrne was making good use of his own phone, successfully negotiating a deal to play the first leg of the Deportivo La Coruña game at Lansdowne Road instead of Spain, as originally drawn. He'd put Lansdowne on standby for Wednesday, August 11, the date of the first leg, in case Shels beat Hadjuk. Deportivo readily agreed to the change, boss Javier Irureta only too happy to bring his team to Dublin first and play the crucial second leg at home. Byrne's move made sound financial sense as it virtually guaranteed a full house at Lansdowne Road and God knows Shels needed the estimated €400,000 that the game would generate. Their wage bill vastly exceeded what they were pulling in at the gates. Yet the implication of his actions was that Shelbourne would suffer a significant defeat in Spain, hardly a morale booster for Fenlon and his team. If Byrne had simply done nothing, and overlooked both Lansdowne Road and the short-term financial gain from switching the legs around, Shelbourne would have been looking forward to the decisive second leg at Tolka Park, their fortress. Even if they had been beaten 1-0 or even 2-0 out in La Coruña they'd already proven against Hadjuk that they were capable of turning that type of margin around. And, of course, if they beat Deportivo and qualified for the Champions League group stage the €400,000 would be a mere pittance. They could hope to make twenty times that.

FINBARR FLOOD: "Ollie's view, and I asked Ollie this, 'How much is this (Champions League group stage qualification) worth and how soon will we get it?' And it was €10m for qualifying for the group stages. That was what he told me. You'd get the money fairly quickly, according to him. But, of course, he reminded me that we'd then be in the group stages and we'd have to, you know, in order to have a good run at it we'd have to sign some European players. I said, 'How much is that going to cost?' 'About twenty-five million', he said. 'Jesus', I said, 'That's great. We qualify for ten and we spend twenty-five'."

Unless the Shelbourne players themselves could pull it off, it would all be just 'ifs' and numbers on a sheet of paper. After beating Hadjuk they were feted as heroes. Both their professional and private lives were greeted with new levels of interest. The *Irish Daily Mirror* newspaper did an 'at home with the Hearys' style colour feature piece that was flagged on the front page. It wasn't so long previously that Heary's full-time job was as a material handler at Hickeys in the city centre. Wes Hoolahan had considered working as a plumber for a while, too. It was new and uncharted ground for League of Ireland players to be on but if Shels beat Deportivo then heightened media scrutiny was something they would have to get used to and quickly. The affable Shels players had no problem with that. They were on the cusp of transforming their lives, of securing improved contracts and pay terms the like of which had never been seen before in Irish football and it was full steam ahead.

JASON BYRNE: "Those were the things that were mentioned a couple of times. I know you didn't want to get distracted by it but it was a massive, massive incentive for the club and the players themselves."

OWEN HEARY: "I don't think it's even the money thing you were thinking about. It's more the publicity for the league, for the team. You're going to be in the Champions League. Hopefully, the League will take off on the back of that. That's the sort of stuff you were thinking about."

STUART BYRNE: "We were thinking, 'We could get into the group stages'. That was the way we were thinking. Nobody was thinking about money. Obviously, once you're through to the group stages the money takes care of itself. We were genuinely just thinking about the opportunity of getting through to the group stages of the Champions League and to play in it as players at that level, to play against superstars."

Shels quickly realised that there were superstars in the qualifying stages of the Champions League also – and many of them played for Deportivo. Javier Irureta had assembled a crack team in the North West corner of Spain valued by one Irish newspaper in the build up to the first leg at €120m. A €400,000 price tag was put on the entire Shelbourne team. The disparity was immense. Deportivo defenders Manuel Pablo and Euro 2004 finalist Jorge Andrade had reported €96m and €60m buy out clauses in their respective contracts. Newcastle United bought their International winger Albert Luque for €15m the following year while midfielder Mauro Silva was an ever present in Brazil's World Cup 1994 success. At the more recent 2002 finals, Juan Valeron, Enrique Romero, Luque and Sergio were all part of the Spanish squad that beat Ireland. All that talent came together for Deportivo in spectacular fashion to give one of the greatest Champions League displays ever witnessed in April 2004, just months before they travelled to Ireland. Deportivo had hosted Champions League holders AC Milan in the second leg of the 2003/04 quarter-finals. Milan held a slightly flattering 4-1 advantage from the first leg at the San Siro when Deportivo had fared well but leaked four goals in nine second-half minutes. At their Riazor base in Spain, they beat Milan 4-0. European football expert and Sky Sports analyst Graham Hunter, who lives in Spain, attended that game.

GRAHAM HUNTER: "Milan were reigning champions and they were just thrashed. They had their pants taken down and they were spanked. They were run off the pitch. It should have been more. I will never forget how they just went for it and Milan, well, they had no answer. I thought the stadium was going to fall with the noise. They absolutely tore the legs off Milan. A 3-0 win would have put them through but when they got to 3-0 they didn't let up. It was glorious to watch and that is the context of what Shelbourne faced a few months later."

Deportivo lost to Jose Mourinho's Porto, the eventual tournament winners, by a single goal, from a penalty, in the semi-finals. UEFA rules decreed that Lansdowne's terracing was shut off but 24,000 seating tickets were snapped up within days.

FINBARR FLOOD: "We could have sold another 24,000 tickets."

Just about every class of Irish soccer supporter was represented in that 24,000; from hardcore League of Ireland fans to fair-weather friends and, of course, Drumcondra's most famous son, An Taoiseach Bertie Ahern, who cut short a holiday in Kerry to attend. For true Shelbourne fans that held the history of the old club close to their hearts it was a sort of homecoming. The club was officially born in Ringsend in 1895, just up the road. The crowd were slightly further away from the action than normal as the pitch dimensions were narrowed, under Fenlon's orders, in an attempt to clip Deportivo's wings. They couldn't get behind their team either, not technically at least, as both ends of the ground were shut. But those in the packed east and west stands made their presence felt all the same. The PA man played Bagatelle's 'Summer in Dublin' and the tones jostled in the evening air with the chants of supporters. St Patrick's Athletic manager Johnny McDonnell summed it all up as best he could when he declared; "This is big time. It's like Madonna coming to Slane". In the Shelbourne dressing room, players were taking their final instructions. Most of it was defensively minded. Fenlon, for instance, had noticed that when Luque whipped in his crosses from the left they tended to fall at the near post. Jamie Harris and Dave Rogers were told to file mental notes of this. Depor also liked to play with a link man between the midfield and lone attacker Walter Pandiani. The technically gifted Juan Valeron was identified as the key man in this position. His vision and range of passing allowed him to pull all of those around him into play. He was Deportivo's heart beat. Stuart Byrne was detailed to man mark him and to rip the life out of their team.

STUART BYRNE: *"It would be the equivalent of marking Kaka these days. This guy was the main man, he was the playmaker for the Spanish international side. Everything revolved around him and in fairness he had serious quality about him. What surprised me about him was his height. He was about six foot two and he had these great feet."*

Autumn rain left the Lansdowne surface wet and slick. The sod seemed heavier than normal. That suited Shelbourne as tentative Depor had already expressed reservations about playing at the 'cathedral of rugby'. Fenlon resisted the temptation to start Ndo and instead selected the same side that played against Hadjuk at Tolka Park. In another defensive 4-1-4-1 formation, twenty-two year old Hoolahan was their creative spark and turned in a brilliant performance. Sergio tracked Moore with the hugely experienced Mauro Silva, fourteen years Hoolahan's senior and the club captain, giving the Dubliner some latitude by rarely straying too far from a position in front of the back four. Legendary clubman Fran was left out over a contract dispute, Moroccan defender Nourredine Naybet was suspended while striker Diego Tristan was injured. Even allowing for their absences, the visitors lined up with eleven current or former Internationals. Jason Byrne rifled an early free kick at the defensive wall and there were vain appeals for a penalty minutes later when Stuart Byrne's vicious shot struck Jorge Andrade's arm. Both teams probed cautiously though they failed to create any clear cut opportunities. Shels' most positive play was either started by or flowed through Hoolahan. Sergio struggled to get to grips with him and got a yellow card for a jersey tug. Hoolahan produced a stunning thirty-eighth minute pass to pick out Fitzpatrick. From it came two separate moments of panic for Depor with Andrade averting the danger on both occasions. In esteemed company Shels were more than holding their own. Owen Heary was relishing his dual with Luque.

OWEN HEARY: "I remember a few days before the game and Pat saying, 'I don't think Luque's travelling over. I think Barcelona are buying him for €18m or something'. I went, 'Ah grand'. Then when the game got close, Pat says, 'He's after travelling. He's on the list but I don't think he's going to play'. Then, on the day of the game, 'He's playing'. I'm like, 'Cheers Pat, thanks for telling me!'"

PAT FENLON: "Owen was well able for him. Our run that year probably put Owen up on the level that he deserves to be on because probably, in my time, he was the best player to play League of Ireland football. Pat Byrne would probably be the best player I ever seen in the game, from a supporter's point of view, but I think Owen would be on a par with Pat. As a captain of a club and as a player, and as an individual, he's a fantastic guy."

Heary capitalised on Enrique Romero's injury-time slip and took off on an overlapping move down the right wing which was fed by the alert Hoolahan. Heary whipped the ball in across the box to Jason Byrne who had space to shoot and the net at his mercy. It was the game's first real opening and, from a Shels perspective, it couldn't have fallen to a better player, the League's top scorer between 2003 and 2006.

JASON BYRNE: "I knew that I wouldn't get many chances being stuck out on the right wing. Normally if a chance does come you'd hope to at least hit the target. I was disappointed because while it came fast at me and was on my left foot I should have put it towards goal even. But I shanked it. I miskicked it altogether. It's one of those things I suppose. That's one of those things in Europe – if you get chances you have to take them because down the other end you'll usually get punished if you don't take them."

Bookmaker Paddy Power released a sigh of relief. As part of his company's sponsorship of the game they'd given Shelbourne a free €10,000 bet at odds of 10/1 to qualify for the Champions League group stages. It was a nice gesture yet ominous given the old adage that you rarely see a poor bookmaker. Steve Williams wasn't tested in the Shels goal until around the same time as Jason Byrne's chance when Victor slammed a shot straight at him. Depor doubled their 'shots on target' tally to two straight after the restart. Sergio found Luque with a clever pass that released him for a shot but he took it on the turn and dragged it wide. Shels had been let off the hook but instead of tightening up they gave away another gift. Harris committed the cardinal sin for a defender by letting a long ball bounce in front him. It bounded over his head, setting Pandiani clear but as he attempted to round Williams, Heary cleared the danger with a wonderful sliding challenge. Fenlon made an important switch after an hour, bringing on midfielder Ndo for Fitzpatrick which freed Jason Byrne to return to his best position up front. The formation didn't change but Ndo's clever, often unorthodox play, gave Depor more to think about around the middle. Pandiani was booked for dissent as the tempo of the game increased. Cahill passed to Jason Byrne who fired a thirty-yard shot over before Moore, with just twelve minutes to go, came so close to scoring. A blocked cross fell to Hoolahan and the little wizard provided a perfect chip to Moore who headed goalwards from the edge of the box. Goalkeeper Gustavo Munua flung himself desperately at the ball and touched it around the left upright for a corner. Aldo Duscher, the Argentinean who became public enemy number one in Britain ahead of the 2002 World Cup finals when he broke David Beckham's metatarsal bone in a Champions League tie, almost endured the wrath of Shels fans in the dying minutes. He dribbled through a forest of bodies before setting Pandiani loose for a shot that whistled by Williams' right post. In the end they finished as they'd begun, scoreless. The Shels players were clapped off the field, twice, after returning for an encore. They'd given an extraordinarily competent performance against a team that, only months earlier, had finished among Europe's top four. Hoolahan had been the best player on the pitch and the likes of Heary, who years earlier pulled out of a move to Dutch club Willem II, partly to save uprooting a young family, proved to himself he could hack it at this level. Still, they'd failed to score and they now had to go to the Riazor, where AC Milan had been crushed 4-0 the previous April, and get at least a score draw to qualify.

STUART BYRNE: *"Not scoring in Lansdowne was the real killer for us. We knew we'd be up against it after that."*

Shels may have narrowed the pitch dimensions to make Lansdowne feel more like home. But, as the billboards advertising League of Ireland games around Drumcondra used to claim, 'There's only one Tolka Park'.

OWEN HEARY: *"I think we'd have beaten them at Tolka. Because at Tolka the crowd is in on top of you and they wouldn't have been used to that, to such a small tight ground. I think the reason why they moved it to Lansdowne, and the players were disappointed with this, was because they knew they'd fill it and make money. We wanted Tolka because we knew if you got anyone in Tolka at that time we could have beaten them. None of us had played at Lansdowne apart from, I think, Alan Moore and that was a big thing."*

Nobody was losing hope just yet, though, least of all Finbarr Flood whose three-year plan looked more and more visionary with each passing game. Razing Deportivo's Champions League ambitions to rubble at the Riazor now became the sole purpose of everyone associated with Shelbourne. A thousand or so travelling supporters descended on La Coruña in the North Westerly tip of Spain for the decisive second leg.

PAT FENLON: *"There was a fantastic set up out there. The stadium was right next to the beach. Family and all were out there. It was a fantastic occasion, it really was."*

Heary's son trotted out with the Shels team as their mascot. Ndo was among the starters for the first time in the campaign with Fitzpatrick making way. Jason Byrne flew solo up front. Depor went with an unchanged side. Both teams dreamed of where ninty minutes could take them. Penalties were a possibility. Shelbourne surprisingly played a higher line than in Dublin with the midfield offering more in terms of support to Jason Byrne. For his part, he felt at home again in attack. Stuart Byrne found Valeron tougher to track this time though as the playmaker took his lead from 25,000 encouraging Galicians. There were only two minutes on the clock when Valeron struck a warning shot into Williams' midriff. Williams had been a bystander for much of the first leg but now found himself a central figure. Luque's free skimmed the woodwork and, soon after, the winger drove in a corner that Williams allowed to float onto the bar and behind. Defence was Shels' instinct in these testing times but when in possession they looked more of a threat than they had done a fortnight earlier. They even created the clearest chance of the half after twenty-five minutes. Crawley played a one-two with Cahill before curling in an inch perfect cross for Jason Byrne who beat defender Cesar Martin to get his head on the ball. 'An Briogaid Dearg' rose to their feet in anticipation behind a banner proclaiming their support for Shels.

JASON BYRNE: *"The ball came across and I had a header and I tried to head it down. From listening to people they'd always say, 'Head the ball down in the box' but I probably should have put it back across. The 'keeper saved it handy enough."*

STUART BYRNE: *"I thought they were tentative out there in the first-half. It was cat and mouse stuff. They didn't throw all guns at us."*

At half time, phase one of Fenlon's master plan was complete: Deportivo were scoreless. Immortality beckoned. One goal was still all that was needed. But the €10m goal never arrived. Instead, the team labelled 'Super Depor' on the back of their breakthrough La Liga title success in

2000, summoned three moments of inspiration that resulted in three cracking goals which settled the tie. Right midfielder Victor provided the initial stimulus with the first goal after 149 minutes of action. Hoolahan and Rogers got in a mix up 50 yards from goal allowing Sergio to play Victor into space. Victor capitalised, sprinting away uncontested all the way into the right side of the penalty area before planting a low shot into the bottom right hand corner of the net. It was a terrific strike only outdone by his second seven minutes later. Again, the Spanish International found room to race from the centre circle to around 40 yards out without a challenge being laid upon him. Crawley and Stuart Byrne attended to the danger when they came galloping in from either side to close him down but the man with the golden right foot got an unmerciful shot away that flew straight into the top corner of the net. Put against Rogers' strike at Tolka Park there's nothing to separate the two in terms of skill and execution. They were both one-offs which effectively settled crucial games. Jason Byrne was gifted an unlikely opportunity to pull one back when he chased down Sergio's under hit back pass in the eighty-first minute but with Molina off his line the lobbed shot sailed over the bar. Deportivo's third came with just two minutes to go, Pandiani curling a right footed free to the far corner of the net from just outside the penalty area. 3-0. A brilliant solo goal, a wonder goal from 40 yards and a cracking free-kick. That's what it had taken to undo perhaps the greatest Irish club side ever assembled.

PAT FENLON: "'Stuey' Byrne was devastated coming off because he'd put so much effort into it, like the rest of the lads, but 'Stuey' stormed off the pitch at the end. We had to get him back out to clap the fans. He was so disappointed. To me that was a great thing because in years gone by we'd have been happy just to swap a jersey, salute the fans and take our 3-0 or 4-0 beating. To see a player so disappointed because he thought they had a great chance of going through, that said to me, 'Well, we've made a fair bit of progress in the years we've been at the club'."

STUART BYRNE: "Ah I was gutted. I was sick. I was really sick after that game, I have to say. Because I knew, that was it now. We weren't going to qualify. It was just the level of expectation was so high that it was a massive kick in the nuts when you do go out."

OWEN HEARY: "I think if we had got another team other than Deportivo, we would have qualified."

JASON BYRNE: "Yeah, without a doubt. I think that was probably the hardest draw we could have got which was good for the country and football here but it probably wasn't good for us because you obviously wanted to get through. That said, we gave it a good go and we had our chances. If it was a lesser team we probably would have beaten them."

Afterwards, Depor manager Irureta maintained that, 'Shelbourne are not far away from Champions League group level'. Kind words, even if the Holy Grail felt as far away as ever. Progressing to the final qualifying round meant that Shels would at least transfer to the UEFA Cup and the final qualifying round of that competition. It was the first time that the UEFA Cup would also incorporate a group stage.

FINBARR FLOOD: "The money wouldn't have been the same at all. You were going for the group stages as well but it was the UEFA Cup and you wouldn't have got the same type of money out of it. The big money was in qualifying for the Champions League."

The following Friday morning, Shels went into the hat along with nine other teams – Bodo/Glimt (Norway), Besiktas (Turkey), Grazer AK (Austria), Litex Lovech (Bulgaria), Hearts (Scotland), FC Braga (Portugal), Lazio (Italy), Metalurh Donetsk (Ukraine) and Lille (France) – in a complex, open draw system for the UEFA Cup. They drew Lille. At first glance it seemed a middle of the road draw, not quite the intimidating spectre of travelling to face Lazio in Rome yet not as enticing as a clash with a very beatable Hearts team. Lille plotted a successful path through the competition's feeder tournament, the Intertoto Cup, with wins over Dinamo Minsk, NK Slaven Koprivnica and Portuguese side UD Leiria. They would finish the French season in second place and were no strangers to Europe. Based close to the Belgian border in the north of France, they'd competed alongside Deportivo, Manchester United and Olympiakos in the group stages of the Champions League three years earlier and finished third. That earned them a passport to the UEFA Cup where they beat Fiorentina before going out in the last sixteen on the away goals rule to tournament runners-up Borussia Dortmund. Claude Puel's side had been weakened by the departure of leading scorer Vladimir Manchev to Levante in a €2.5m deal. French full-back Eric Abidal, a World Cup finalist two years later, also left for home town club Lyon for €6.6m. But they still had more than enough brawn, in the shape of former Arsenal centre-half Efstathios Tavlaridis, and brains in ex Tottenham playmaker Milenko Acimovic to seriously trouble Shels.

JASON BYRNE: "It was hard to pick yourself up because the whole buzz throughout the country was about the Champions League. So it was hard to motivate yourself again against Lille."

Shels were drawn at home first and, again, opted to play the game at Lansdowne Road in anticipation of another sell out. UEFA's decree that Tolka Park's lights weren't up to scratch and that any game there would have to be played in daylight, influenced the move as did the lack of media and corporate facilities. But the primary motivation was money. On a cold, dark, wet and windy evening just 7,463 – around 5,000 less than the reported break even figure – turned out at Lansdowne.

FINBARR FLOOD: "It was disastrous. But then the Lille game was played on a day when it had rained solid from the night before right through the day and it was a disaster. On the other hand we had done so well at Lansdowne Road the match before, so it was very hard to turn around and say to supporters, 'We're going back to Tolka', when they couldn't all get in. We made a decision we were going to do it. But it was a disaster."

Even without the injured Acimovic, Lille tore into Shels and required just twenty minutes to do what KR Reykjavik, Hadjuk Split and Deportivo La Coruña had all failed to do – score in Dublin. Matthieu Bodmer was gifted too much space and from 20 yards out seized the chance to get a low shot away that skidded off the wet surface past Williams. A minute before half-time Lille's second arrived courtesy of Christophe Landrin. A 2-0 advantage didn't flatter them. Between the two strikes they'd put together seven efforts on goal. A big beating was a possibility though to Shels' credit they didn't concede any more. In fact, in the 80th minute the seemingly unthinkable happened as they pulled back one goal, then another three minutes later. Both were wonderfully angled headers across goal from Fitzpatrick who'd come on for Thomas Morgan. Those who'd written Shels off as a jaded, spent force after the Riazor experience should have known better – all but one of the eight goals they scored in the entire European run came inside the last twelve minutes of games. As Neil O'Riordan pointed out the following morning in *The Irish Sun*, 'Whatever Shels are they are not Lille-livered'. More portentously however, we were informed that, '80 per cent of sides who claim a 2-2 draw away from home in the first-leg progress to the next round'. The stats didn't lie. Another lion-hearted Shels performance a fortnight later at Lille's Stade Metropole couldn't prevent their UEFA Cup end game from occurring. Acimovic was back after a knee problem and oozed class, putting the home team 1-0 ahead with a shot from distance after just eighteen minutes. Shortly after, Crawford threw himself into a thunderous tackle on Acimovic and the ball spun out to Matt Moussilou. Confidence wasn't a problem after scoring five times in their Intertoto Cup run and the former French U-21 international striker's shot deflected in off Harris. As at Lansdowne, Lille's early heroics indicated a rout but, again, they were held scoreless for the rest of the game. Crucially, so were Shels and the dream was officially over.

PAT FENLON: "The Lille games were, to me, and I think if you ask most of the players they'll say this, Lille were probably the best team we played. They were a fantastic side. They had it all, physically, athletically, touch wise, movement, they were a very, very good side."

JASON BYRNE: "They were a top, top quality football team and they gave us a little bit of a lesson because I don't think we touched the ball for 90 minutes over there. I know we probably were flattered to get a 2-2 draw at Lansdowne after being 2-0 down. From a football perspective they were absolutely fantastic. Probably, at the time, I think they were as good as Deportivo all right. They were a brilliant team and kept the ball well. I don't know whether it was the whole hype of Deportivo and knowing that we'd given everything we had in those games and were knocked out, all that disappointment, probably that was one of the main factors, but in fairness to Lille they were a class team, first class."

STUART BYRNE: "Considering what Lille went on to achieve, qualifying for the group stages of the Champions League in two consecutive years, beating Manchester United in their group a year after we played them, they were a serious team, a serious side."

Back at base, Ollie Byrne totted up the takings from the European campaign. The papers speculated it could have been worth anything up to €1m.

FINBARR FLOOD: "No, we didn't make anything like that. I genuinely can't remember what it was. I think it was a couple of hundred grand we made. That was about it. The big prize was in qualifying and we didn't do that. We made money that year on the Deportivo game in Lansdowne Road. But then when you have to travel away it's very expensive. Like, we were travelling away at times when it was the peak for holidays, August, so you were paying through the nose for a plane if you were hiring it. If you weren't you were paying through the nose for seats because it was the peak holiday season. So it was very expensive to cover yourself in the matches away."

To borrow an Ollie Byrne phrase, 'It would be fair to say' the only man who knew exactly how much money passed in, but mostly out, of Shelbourne Football Club in this period was Byrne himself. He passed away in August 2007, having been diagnosed with a brain tumour. He left behind him a club in crisis that, three years after coming within half an hour of the Champions League group stage, wasn't deemed in a fit enough state to take its place in the 2007 League of Ireland top flight. Shels had retained the League title in November 2004 after the European marathon, a feat of monumental endurance considering the strains and demands placed on the players throughout a remarkable season. Despite mounting debts Shels continued to play a deadly game of Russian roulette by gambling heavily on future Champions League group stage qualification. They assembled the most costly League of Ireland team up to that point when, in 2005, Irish International striker Glen Crowe, ex Coventry City centre-half Colin Hawkins and winger Bobby Ryan were all signed from Bohemians in a grandiose transfer coup. The League's 1999 Young Player of the Year, Richie Baker, also returned from a stint in America while Gary O'Neill's arrival from Dublin City ensured a near embarrassment of attacking riches. Their next effort at making the Champions League group stages in August 2005 fell miserably short with a 4-1 aggregate defeat to Steaua Bucharest in the second qualifying round and, slowly but surely, a castle that was built on quicksand began to crumble. The 2005 season ended with Shels in third position and while they won the title for the thirteenth time in 2006 it was a deeply hollow success. The title had been bought with money the club didn't really possess. For stretches of that season the players went unpaid due to crippling debts. On one occasion, close to the end of the 2006 season, the takings at the gate were gathered straight after the game and dished out to pay the players. Whatever money was amassed from the 2004 European campaign clearly hadn't lasted long.

OWEN HEARY: "It wasn't even the players they signed, it was more the way they threw away money on stupid things. The money should have been there but we still went on and won the League in 2006. I don't think many teams would go on and win the League without getting paid. We managed to do it. I think we went eight weeks without getting paid and we still won the League. Pat never let us lose our focus. He could have said, 'Feck it, you're not getting paid, don't worry about it'. But, no, it was, 'Right we're all going to break up at the end of the year. Do you want to break up with a winners' medal in your pocket or do you just want to walk away and say, what if, for the rest of your life?'"

Only two months after collecting the 2006 title, Shels were refused their premier division licence for 2007 because of severe financial irregularities. They received permission to play on in the first division and were grateful for that much. In February 2007, *The Irish Times* revealed that Shels' and, more specifically, Byrne's business dealings had left the club with debts of between €4m and €5m to 'various creditors'. Those creditors included individuals and associates of Byrne's who had, apparently, 'advanced low, six-figure sums over a period of years often on the basis that Byrne would provide access to tickets for International and big Premiership games while the money was outstanding'. Meanwhile, Byrne had also reportedly drawn down over €6m from the developers who'd bought the lease to Tolka Park several years earlier. To suggest that at least €10m was blown on chasing Europe would appear to be conservative. Flood had left as Chairman due to ill health but returned in a caretaker capacity to deal with the crisis.

FINBARR FLOOD: "No, it didn't surprise me (learning the full extent of the debts) because the ground was sold. Ollie had sold the ground and the money that we were over-spending was being supplied by the developers. Every year there was about a million extra being given and that was keeping the club going. But the problem is it (Tolka Park's sale for development) hasn't been completed now. There's obviously a difficulty with the way building went. The need, the excitement and the urgency about doing it disappeared."

Shels played their 2010 first division games at Tolka Park. What the future holds having agreed to vacate the stadium when the bulldozers move in, whenever that may be, is unclear. Talk of a new stadium at various venues around Dublin including Finglas and Donabate was mooted during Byrne's reign but has long since petered out. Like Champions League qualification, a new stadium, or one bought by Shelbourne at least, is a non-runner for the foreseeable future. Shelbourne aren't the only club that flew too close to the sun in the 2000s only to come crashing down to earth with scalded wings. Cork City and Derry City both invested heavily and made significant progress in Europe. They enjoyed famous nights at the Brandywell and at Turner's Cross, hosting glamorous clubs like Gothenburg, Paris Saint Germain and Malmo. Remarkably, all three Irish clubs – or an incarnation of the old club in Cork's case – were reduced to the purgatory of first division football in 2010 as they collectively atoned for their sins. Drogheda United too have been forced to radically strip back on their spending after the high of pushing Dynamo Kiev so close in the second qualifying phase of the 2008/09 Champions League campaign. Like society at large, the next generation may ultimately be the ones that put the harsh lessons of the last ten years to best use going forward. For those of us who witnessed the great European nights, the memories at least are ours to keep.

UEFA CHAMPIONS LEAGUE

First qualifying round, first leg
July 14, 2004
Laugardals Stadium, Reykjavik
Attendance: 1,200

KR Reykjavik: 2
(Sigurgeirsson 47, Olafsson 54)

Shelbourne: 2
(Moore 84, Sigurdsson og 86)

KR Reykjavik: Kristjan Finnbogason; Elisabetarson, Einarsson, Sigurdsson, Podzemsky; Thorsteinsson, Olafsson, Gylfason, Sidurgeirsson; Gunnlaugsson (Bjarnason 70), Kristjansson (Kjartan Finnbogason 46).

Shelbourne: Williams; Heary, Harris, Rogers, Crawley; Hoolahan, S. Byrne, Moore (Morgan 85), Cahill; J. Byrne, McCarthy (Cawley 76).

Referee: P. Vervecken (Belgium).

First qualifying round, second leg
July 21, 2004
Tolka Park, Dublin
Attendance: 3,500

Shelbourne: 0

KR Reykjavik: 0

Shelbourne: Williams; Heary, Harris, Rogers, Crawley; Hoolahan (Cawley 88), Morgan, S. Byrne, Cahill; J. Byrne (Rowe 94), Moore (McCarthy 83).

KR Reykjavik: Kristjan Finnbogason; Elisabetarson, Einarsson (Magnusson 68), Sigurdsson, Podzemsky; Davidsson, Olafsson, Gylfason, Kristjansson (Bjarnason 74); A. Gunnlaugsson (Benediktsson 74), Kjartan Finnbogason.

Referee: M. Svendsen (Sweden).

UEFA CHAMPIONS LEAGUE

Second qualifying round, first leg
July 28, 2004
Poljud Stadium, Split
Attendance: 22,000

Hadjuk Split: 3
(Blatnjak 18 and 85; Suto 48)

Shelbourne: 2
(Fitzpatrick 5, Moore 89)

Hadjuk Split: Balic; Rukavina, Vejic, Neretljak; Suto, Cacic, Turkovic (Munhoz 61), Pralija, Carevic; Racki (Mesic 70), Blatnjak.

Shelbourne: Williams; Heary, Harris, Rogers, Crawley; S. Byrne; J. Byrne (Crawford 78), Hoolahan (McCarthy 87), Moore, Cahill; Fitzpatrick.

Referee: V. Kassai (Hungary).

Second qualifying round, second leg
August 4, 2004
Tolka Park, Dublin
Attendance: 11,000

Shelbourne: 2
(Rogers 78, Moore 90+2)

Hadjuk Split: 0

Shelbourne: Williams; Heary, Harris, Rogers, Crawley; S. Byrne; J. Byrne (Ndo 89), Hoolahan (Crawford 86), Moore, Cahill; Fitzpatrick (McCarthy 7).

Hadjuk Split: Kale; Rukavina (Mesic 82), Zilic, Neretljak; Suto (Damjanovic 82), Vejic, Filekovic, Pralija, Carevic; Racki (Dragicevic 56), Blatnjak.

Referee: S. Sukhina (Russia).

UEFA CHAMPIONS LEAGUE

Third qualifying round, first leg
August 11, 2004
Lansdowne Road, Dublin
Attendance: 24,000

Shelbourne: 0

Deportivo La Coruña: 0

Shelbourne: Williams; Heary, Harris, Rogers, Crawley; S. Byrne; J. Byrne, Hoolahan, Moore, Cahill; Fitzpatrick (Ndo 61)

Deportivo La Coruña: Molina (Munua 41); Manuel Pablo, Cesar Martin, Andrade, Romero; Victor, Sergio (Duscher 66), Mauro Silva, Luque (Munitis 78); Valeron; Pandiani.

Referee: M. Benes (Czech Republic).

Third qualifying round, second leg
August 24, 2004
Riazor, La Coruña
Attendance: 25,000

Deportivo La Coruña: 3
(Victor 59 and 66; Pandiani 88)

Shelbourne: 0

Deportivo La Coruña: Molina; Manuel Pablo (Scaloni 69), Cesar Martin, Andrade, Romero; Victor, Sergio, Mauro Silva (Duscher h/t), Luque (Munitis 77); Valeron; Pandiani.

Shelbourne: Williams; Heary, Harris, Rogers, Crawley; S. Byrne; Ndo, Hoolahan (Crawford 69), Moore, Cahill; J. Byrne.

Referee: A. Hamer (Luxemburg).

UEFA CUP

First round, first leg
September 16, 2004
Lansdowne Road, Dublin
Attendance: 7,463

Shelbourne: 2
(Fitzpatrick 80 and 83)

Lille: 2
(Bodmer 20, Landrin 44)

Shelbourne: Williams; Heary, Harris, Rogers, Crawley; Crawford; Hoolahan (McCarthy 81), Morgan (Fitzpatrick 67), Ndo (Cawley 46), Cahill; J. Byrne.

Lille: Sylva; Angbwa, Tavlaridis, Vitakic, Tafforeau; Dumont, Makoun; Landrin, Bodmer (Audel 70), Brunel (Chalme 81); Moussilou (Raynier 76).

Referee: C. Kapitanas (Cyprus).

First round, second leg
September 30, 2004
Stade Metropole, Lille
Attendance: 10,787

Lille: 2
(Acimovic 18, Moussilou 26)

Shelbourne: 0

Lille: Sylva; Angbwa, Tavlaridis, Schmitz, Tafforeau; Bodmer, Makoun; Landrin, Acimovic (Chalme 84), Audel (Miralas 90); Moussilou (Brunel 67).

Shelbourne: Williams; Heary, Harris, Rogers, Crawley; Crawford; Hoolahan (McCarthy 80), Moore (Fitzpatrick 65), S. Byrne (Cawley 88), Cahill; J. Byrne.

Referee: E. Bozinovski (Macedonia).